Red Book and Cotton

Journey to True-Freedom

I0039058

JOHN SOLOMON SANDRIDGE

NATUROPATHIC SPIRITUAL INTUITIVE CTCMHS
(CERTIFIED TEACHER COACH MINISTER
OF HEALTH AND SELF-HEALING)

Free the Mind
PRODUCTIONS, INC.
BIRMINGHAM, AL

Published by:

Free the Mind Productions, Inc.
3100 Lorna Road, Ste. 310
Hoover, Al 35216
www.freethemindproductions.com

Visit John Solomon Sandridge online at:
www.johnsolomonsandridge.com

Set in Adobe Garamond Pro

ISBN: 978-0-9667336-4-8

Printed in the United States of America

INTRODUCTION

I HAVE TWO QUESTIONS: WHAT IF AMERICA'S black and white children's unconscious beliefs and present experiences are influenced by the history of her deceased children's past experiences? And, is there a difference in "believing in" something or someone, and "knowing" that something or someone?

When I was a baby I did not believe in God.

When I was a child, my family and church taught me to believe in God.

I became a teenager and forgot to believe in God.

As a young man, my unfavorable circumstances moved me to renew my belief in God.

When I approached middle age, fear, loneliness, confusion, and desperation forced me to search for God.

Today, I realize God is superlative to my believing in a mean, angry, vicious, cruel, revengeful image I called god. I see God as Something/Someone More: beyond my perception and comprehension; exceedingly unknowable and far greater than my fear-based beliefs. My "believing in" implies that I do not *know*. For instance, I do not believe I am a man. I know I am a man. Consequently, I once believed in what I was *unsure of*.

On the other hand, *knowing* implies there is personal *interaction*—(1832 *noun*) mutual or reciprocal action or influence; synergy.

Today, I feel free to say . . . I am coming to *know* God.

What I know—adverb (pre 12th century): after the past, immediately before the present and future, which is void of time, space, and distance—about God is what I perceive through personal cognition of visual, audible, tactile, physical, and spiritual experiences.

Me seeking to know God has led to the most important quest—The Journey of Life. This quest, which began soon after birth, was to know and consciously connect with God (Something/Someone More), and is my way of seeking enlightenment—Spiritual Freedom.

At every stage of my quest, I have had "so-called" unnatural, weird, bizarre, harebrained, far-out, strange, and crazy experiences. Throughout human existence, similar experiences have happened to everyone. Fortunately, the benefits I have gained from the experiences were spiritual growth, self-awareness, greater consciousness, self-love, love for others, and freedom from fear-based-beliefs about God.

My first conscious recall of having an unnatural, weird, bizarre, harebrained, far-out, strange, and crazy experience happened when I was two years old. This was the beginning of my gathering knowledge of that Something/Someone More. Sitting on the living room floor, I watched a green creature slither from beneath the wood-burning heater. It came toward me, and I crawled toward it. I reached out and picked it up. It wrapped itself around my clenched hand and outstretched arm. I heard a loud scream and released it. It fell to the floor and quickly disappeared beneath the heater. My eighteen-year-old momma grabbed me up and demanded that I never pickup another snake.

When I was three years old, my momma routinely spread a quilt next to the bed and placed me on it for a nap. When she left the room, I heard audible (and at times inaudible) voices. The walls, ceiling, and floor vanished. Visible shapes and forms appeared, grew large, shrank, and blended into each other. I experienced those happenings until age four. I told my momma what was happening, but I obviously did not explain things in a way she could understand. She told me my experiences were crazy. I did not understand her.

When I was five and six, my two brothers, my sister, and I routinely saw transparent people enter and leave our bedroom at night.

From age seven to nine, I interacted with visible inanimate objects and had both audible and inaudible conversations with the invisible spirit-beings I played games with. By that time, I was smart enough not to tell anyone what I saw, not even my brothers and sister.

From age ten to fourteen, I felt and heard mysterious things. I could not explain how or why they happened.

From age fifteen to seventeen, I watched inanimate objects move. I was constantly aware of the presence of invisible spirit-beings and deceased people.

From age eighteen to twenty-one, I was spared death several times in serious automobile accidents. In one, while en route to perform at a nightclub, I would have been decapitated had I not sat down three seconds earlier. When purchasing drugs, I was spared being struck and killed by the bullets of six gunmen as I heard and felt the hail of lead that whistled past my head and passed through the fringes of my shirt and pants.

At age twenty-two, I saw inanimate objects move without observable outside force. I also felt the bed I lay on levitating. That same year I wanted to kill a buddy who I had taught Tae Kwon Do (a Korean martial art) after he had deliberately kicked me with a bone-crushing roundhouse kick to the rib cage. As I dropped to the floor, I thought of ways in which I could kill him. My plan was averted when I heard an inaudible voice that came from a corner ceiling telling me not to kill him, but to leave immediately and go home. I gathered my things and left.

From age twenty-three to twenty-nine, I began an all-out search for God. One night, an angelic being—an eight-foot-tall ovoid of blinding light—appeared in my bedroom and told me in an inaudible voice that I had been chosen to participate in bringing good to the lives of others. During those six years, I was baptized in water and spirit by five different Christian ministers into five different denominations, and was also anointed with oil by six ministers. Each believed that God had given him and his organization "the truth." It was during that period when I realized that Something/Someone More was greater than my belief in the god I had invented with my mind.

From age thirty to thirty-eight, I had a near-death experience and could not leave my bedroom or house without becoming deathly sick for months. A well-meaning friend who had had five major surgeries and healed herself of cancer told me, "You'll never get better." But I did. That experience forced me to go within and search for something more than what I believed in. It was then that I came to realize that my prior, so-called unnatural, weird, bizarre, harebrained, far-out, strange, and crazy experiences were a validation that the Something/Someone More had been with me since birth. I began to practice waking meditation, walking meditation, conscious meditation, and deep meditation. As a result, I learned to intentionally leave my body and astral travel, which was verified in conversations with friends and clients I visited day or night.

At age thirty-nine, I rented a cabin at Alabama Cheaha State Park. After I had arrived and was settled in, a fly flew in front of me and hovered. I sensed it wanted to communicate with me. I heard the word *Flodusa*. Wherever I was in the cabin and held out my hand and called aloud, "Flodusa," the fly came and alighted in my hand, facing me. One day after a late lunch, I went for a walk in the woods. As I passed a large rock behind the cabin, an inaudible voice told me I would sit on it at three o'clock the next morning. The next morning, at 2:45 a.m., I was awakened from a deep sleep and immediately sat up in bed. I got dressed in the dark and went to the rock, where I sat in a meditative position. I closed my eyes and waited. During the meditation, I left my body and a spirit person and I traveled in and out of countless universes and galaxies. About fifteen minutes later, which seemed like an eternity to me, I came back into my body. I opened my eyes and saw, a short distance away, three glowing spheres of light hovering just above the ground. They came toward me and paused about thirty feet from me. My heart was pounding. They repeated this action (my heart pounded), and their action was repeated several times. When about fifteen feet away they stopped, paused, and then vanished. From that experience until now I *know* my every unnatural, weird, bizarre, harebrained, far-out, strange, and crazy experience is *my truth*. It is my way of experiencing life as a human being who is consciously connected to that Something/Someone More, which I now humbly refer to as . . . *The Creator Of Life*.

At age forty, I was working as a Naturopathic Spiritual Intuitive in Miami, Florida, for a well known singer. An associate and I poured fresh fruit juice from a pitcher into eight ounce glasses and drank it. To our astonishment, the volume of juice in the pitcher was not reduced as we drank two glasses each. That experience was so unreal, we stared at the pitcher and each other in amazement.

The most significant experience I have had, however, came through ancestors that visibly appeared and at times audibly, and other times inaudibly, dictated the book you are holding in your hands, *Red Book and Cotton*.

When I saw my ancestors, they appeared as celestial beings: transparent and glowing. They appeared and disappeared at random, day or night, early or late. They dictated their personal experiences in the dialects that were common for people who lived decades ago in the rural south. I wrote or typed what they said, and I heard, smelt, felt, saw, and tasted what they had experienced.

Before my ancestors appeared, the atmosphere in my work area (an extra bedroom) transformed from a matter-heavy feeling to an ethereal-light feeling. This was accompanied by deep silence. The silence flushed out all noises: sounds coming from neighboring apartments, children playing outside, automobile traffic, and airplanes. I knew they were coming, as the clues were the smell of perfumed powder, stale cigarette smoke on clothing, pungent cigar smoke on the skin, liquor mixed with foul breath, the aroma of cooked food, and the body odor that comes from hard work.

On March 28, 2001, Wednesday, 3:00 a.m., in my home-town of Gadsden, Alabama, I completed the transcription of my ancestor's life-story: *Red Book and Cotton*. Seven years later, Saturday, March 15, at 6:37 a.m., in Dallas, Texas, I sat at the computer to do a final edit of the manuscript. The loft studio where I worked gradually changed from an earthy-busyness to a heavenly-serenity. The early morning light that poured in the window changed to a moonlight-blue, and the room and its furnishings became surreal. Peace beyond description filled my heart, and a stream of memories of my ancestors' previous visitations flashed through my mind. I knew someone was about to make his or her appearance. I continued to work and wait.

He first appeared below the balcony as a faint figure, and then walked up the stairs along the wall. The one individual who did not appear when I had transcribed *Red Book and Cotton* was finally making an appearance. He came over, sat down beside me, to my left, and crossed his tiny short legs. His metallic blue-black skin glowed. I felt honored, privileged, and grateful to sit in his presence. I heard him say these words without opening his mouth, "*I am . . . Papa-horse*".

What my deceased great-great-grandfather, whose name was Nimrod, sought more than a century past, I seek today. Transcribing his memorandum gave me the opportunity to have an intimate experience with him as he traveled The Journey of Life. His and my other ancestors' belief in God and spent lives inspired me to upgrade my believing in God to knowing The Creator Of Life.

I presently live and work at two facets of my purpose: the first is the work I have done as Naturopathic Spiritual Intuitive for the past thirty-four years, in which I train others to self-heal themselves through natural methods and techniques that prompt the body-mind's natural ability to self-heal itself of sickness and disease. The second is to leave something of lasting value for the love I received from family, friends, neighbors, and others, for the time I have lived on earth, the space I took up during my earthly journey, and the water, air, and food I consumed to sustain my physical body while on earth.

Read Nimrod's memorandum. I know the part of you that is ready to live beyond fear-based beliefs will be inspired to embrace your own so-called unnatural, weird, bizarre, harebrained, far-out, strange, and crazy experiences. Doing so will certainly give you the self-confidence to embrace your spirit-self, which is needed while traveling The Journey of Life. Know "your truth", and you will find your path and keep it, which will lead you to uncover and live "your purpose". Never deny your physical or spiritual experiences, and you will make a significant difference in your life and in the world.

I, John Solomon Sandridge, Naturopathic Spiritual Intuitive and CTCSMH (Certified Teacher Coach Student Minister of Health), present Nimrod's memorandum as he and others dictated their story, his history (his-story) in their words. I recorded what I vicariously lived and heard as their words and their lives the . . . *Red Book and Cotton*.

*A world without dreams and stories
is a world without flowers and trees.*

*Man can't invent stories or dreams,
But dreams and stories can create the man:
Dreams invoke the visionary with visions,
And stories rouse the dreamer with dreams.*

*Dreams and stories bloom in the soul:
Dreams shed light on the unknown,
Enlightening the dreamer.
Stories give hope.
Causing the listener to build a better tomorrow
Today.*

*Dreams and stories have life—
Their own.*

*Dreams and stories
Free the mind.
The mind frees
The man.*

I AM NIMROD.
I was a slave.
Today, I am a free man.
The opening words of this memorandum were spoken to me by the wise old man, Papa-horse. The first time I heard them, I was a boy standing at the foot of a mountain, which is life. Today I stand on the mountaintop of life, which is old age. Tomorrow I will descend below the horizon into death, then rise like the phoenix and soar up into heaven. Papa-horse, my experiences, and God taught me that dreams and stories breathe meaning and purpose into a man's life.

My long life and my countless experiences give me much to be thankful for, yet when I look down on the valley of my past I do not see my mother and father. Papa-horse was the only mother and father figure I had ever known. Papa-horse filled my days with stories, God filled my nights with dreams, and both led me to the path and journey that leads to freedom.

Papa-horse taught me that a man will spend hours, days, and years preparing for a trade, his chosen career, his marriage, and his family. But the part of life that needs his greatest preparatory work and deserves special attention before he leaves this world is death. He said, "Death brings the greatest rewards. In death, a man finds the wonderful things he spent a lifetime searching for: unhindered love, the Fountain of Youth, eternal life, milk and honey, and streets of gold. Freedom." I am forever grateful for Papa-horse's wisdom and love.

Many years ago, Papa-horse took me into the woods of Lonesome Bend, our favorite praying place. He sat me on his knee and told me story after story. That summer we sat at the edge of Dancing Pond with our toes skimming the surface of its cool water. He said, "Son, one man's hateful and cruel deeds are fed to him by dead dreams. After he dies the world will despise him. Another man's kind and loving acts are inspired by living stories and dreams. His name is recorded in heaven.

"Although you were born a slave, you have a purpose. And if you're to live as a free man, you must find that purpose. There're four things that can help you. Two give purpose to life, and two give freedom. They are dreams and stories and reading and writing. Dreams and stories will give purpose to your life, your reason for being. Reading and writing are the great liberators. They will set your mind and heart free to pursue your purpose.

"No matter what your situation is, dreams and stories and reading and writing will challenge you to live with dignity. Be loving when dealing with others, all people."

I, Nimrod, have spent a great deal of time searching for keys that will open doors that lead to freedom. Freedom was my right, as it was of all men, and I was determined to have it. My journey to freedom has been tiresome and rewarding, painful and pleasurable. I have sought the keys to freedom not only for myself, but also for all people. Especially you.

You, the reader of my words, up to now do not know me. Yet I know you, and I want you to know me. If this is to happen, it must be soon, as I am old and will be leaving this world, passing from mortality into immortality. Time is no longer a free gift. It has become a commodity that I purchase each day by making right decisions. Though most of my life has been filled with mountainous difficulties, it has also been landscaped with meadows of good. I must share the good and the bad with you.

What I am sharing, I share solely with you. If you will but listen, so as to receive the significance of my message and adapt that significance to your actions, I promise you that you will harvest a bounty of wisdom, wisdom gleaned from my suffering. You will live a life of freedom. You will not have to get all your wisdom from personal pain and suffering. Nor will you have to wait to experience the countless good rewards of heaven, rewards that come from having and using wisdom. Happiness, peace, and freedom will be yours for a lifetime. I beg you, please, listen to me and learn from my long life, from my numerous mistakes, pain, and suffering.

What you are going to read is about me, about my life as a slave and a free man. My words will reveal a man you have not known, but you should know me and uncover a way of life and world that must never return. Expose a past way of life that I pray you will never experience. Expose the place to find freedom at its source.

Why share your experiences with me, you may ask.

And I answer: My reasons are special, very special. But I warn you, reader, beware.

The message of this: My memorandum is going to awaken in you an awareness of the twin beasts that lurk below the surface of consciousness of all men. This information will lure the twins up from their dark abyss of ignorance to the banks of understanding. They will stir you with emotions you have not been in touch with, making themselves known, heard, and felt. As they are exposed to the light of understanding, you will be moved by an uneasiness that heals men of certain ills. So I warn you, be prepared for your odyssey.

The twins are these: prejudice and racism. If you are like me and other men, your mind is now saying, 'I may be many things, but I'm not a prejudiced or racist person.'

Papa-horse said, "Racism, like all Isms, separates men. And all men are tainted with racism. Discriminating acts based on the belief that one's race, and family, is naturally superior to other races, is racism. Men who form opinions about something or someone without first obtaining knowledge or an honest examination are prejudging. To presuppose that a thing is such and such or this or that is, prejudice."

As always, he was right.

When Papa-horse told me, "You sleep with the twins," I looked him square in the eyes and declared that his words were untrue. I refused to accept that I, Nimrod, an ex-slave, a black man, could be prejudiced and a racist.

Though that part of me was obvious to Papa-horse, he who knew me best, I did not see myself as a racist. For years I swore I was not. He said, "Nimrod, it is natural for you and all men to feel that your race is better than the other man's race. It springs from that part of man that tells him that he is different from all others, an individual. Who is the man among men that can say, 'I've never felt that my family, culture, country, or race was better than others?' Show me that man, and I will quickly tell him, 'You're the lucky one among men, and all other men are infernally lost.'" Thus racism becomes unnaturally dangerous when one allows it to be the prevailing feeling that moves him to enslave and kill others unjustly.

Then one day, my disavowed attitude and acts of prejudice and racism were revealed to my full view. I plainly saw that my attitude and actions had been contradicting my words. It was then that I was ready to admit the twin beasts had been a part of my life.

So once more I say to you, my dear reader, be prepared for this journey. It will lead you into the unknown regions of your undiscovered self, to the understanding of all men. The unimaginable and shocking truths about slavery and freedom are going to leap from the past and lay hard against your chest.

The bleakest period of my life has passed, yet the memories of that past are the constant companions that have dutifully inspired me to act at this time. For urgings that I could not bring myself to obey in the past, what I am now doing, contacting you, is what I have wanted to do for more than thirty years. We can never reclaim the years that have slipped past. The few that lie ahead of us, me in particular, we can seize if we will grab them. But we must hold them as if tomorrow will never come.

As Papa-horse's stories were the sun, and my dreams were the raindrops, and reading was the soil, what I write to you at this time is the Christmas rose that has sprung forth. Please pluck it during your youth from the vine of life and enjoy its fragrance of inspiration before you are as I am, old.

Yes, it is I who bear the blame for not contacting you before now. If you are incensed, as I imagine you are, with my seeming neglectfulness, I understand. Yet I ask your forgiveness. If you will permit me, I wish to take this opportunity to give you an explanation. So I come to you in spirit, on paper, with this, my humble request: Please, I beg of you, please place your hand in mine and walk with me through the arduous years of my past. Mind you, this will not be a Sunday excursion, for it is the life of an African American slave. But I am of the opinion that my painful past will inspire you. It will enlighten your future and fill your days with the healing power of hope.

For the reason that you and I have not walked together down the lane of intimate love, it is with trepidation I ask for your indulgence. Time, change, and different circumstances have delivered into my hands this new and foreboding opportunity. Finally, as decided by destiny, I am moved to share with you that part of me that is more precious than life. A story.

I shall not share just any story, but the one story that you need to hear. Its contents are of great value, and I want you to have it before I leave this world. You, especially you, need to know this story. Yet, I feel it is better that I refrain from sharing the specifics at this time. I shall share those details towards the end of this writing.

The early years of my life were speckled with constant dread, pain, sorrow, and suffering. I would have you know that America's history (his-story) was written by a handful of her white children. The white men who penned her darkened history on the snowy pages of schoolbooks have not been wholly honest. A fleeting glance of their books tells one, we who survived slavery, that they were less than honorable with their writings.

If you are to have a more completed picture of who you are, how you are to live in this world, and especially what you are, it is high time for you to hear America's history—his-story—from the black experience. America's past, as it flows from the pen of an ex-slave, my pen, my past, and my-story will forthright open your heart and mind to a more complete and truer story.

My-story, which is your past, is based on my opinions, my experiences as a slave, a freed man, and my experiments and experiences with whites. As you read my-story you shall see that I have taken liberty to write freely about my life and the lives of people I knew, holding back nothing. We, blacks and whites, were happy and sad; we loved and hated each other and ourselves. There were times when we were right and times when we were wrong both free and bound. These experiences caused both races to live in both slavery and freedom.

I shall show through my-story that I, the man named Nimrod (who was once a slave who lived in abject poverty and became the free man he had dreamed of being, who came to possess all the material goods he had desired, and was a black man who had always been forever free inside without knowing it), was healed from generational pain and hurt by understanding the unseen causes of the experiences of being a slave who was free and the free man who was a slave.

Thus, I am of the opinion that it is possible for all men, both black and white, to be healed of the ancestral pain and hurt that resides in their broken hearts and damaged souls. And some day, all people will love each other as members of one family, God's family. But as things are today, this will not occur at the present time because of certain written laws, nor will it occur within my generation or yours. Time, the great healer, is in control of this matter, and we must leave this matter to her fixing.

As Papa-horse would say, "A man without a written story is the man who did not exist." These words were spoken when I was a slave and mere boy, a child who did not understand the weightiness of such words. Now that I am an old man, I not only understand his words, but I have also acquired a measure of the freedom that comes with understanding. I can truthfully say that it was his many sayings, stories, and my God-given dreams that delivered me from the stranglehold of personal anger that was great enough to set the world aflame. Stories and dreams have kept me from hating all of my white brothers and sisters. Had I known then what I know today, and had I understood in the past what I understand now, my attitude would have been different. I would have dealt with the obstacles of life with a greater wisdom. I would have reduced the intensity of my anger sooner and saved myself a great deal of unnecessary suffering, the suffering that pours out from the womb of youthful ignorance.

If you will but meet my request with an open mind and a receptive heart your future may not be as painful as my past.

Thus, I write this, THE MEMORANDUM OF A SLAVE, specifically for you.

MY ANGER

IF YOU ARE TO BENEFIT FROM my story, it is necessary that you not be alarmed by my anger. It is natural for me, one who was a slave for the greater portion of his life, to be angry. I ask you, please, look beyond the anger, and you will see the hope. Hope is the complete assurance and certitude regarding God's purpose for man, and man's God-given ability and strength to carry out that purpose. It is God's appraisal of godly work. Hope has kept this country afloat. It keeps the world spinning on its axis, forcing men to wake up by way of evolutionary change. The hope that gave the black race the strength to endure slavery was expressed when Papa-horse said, "As the sun is to the flower; without it, the flower dies. So it is with men without hope; their souls wither in pain and die." And my story is about hope.

When I was a child, there was always someone about who told me what to do and when to do it. But as I grew in size and strength, no man could tell me to "Come and do this," or "Go and do that," lest he became the violator who instantly experienced my manliness. I felt I was a free man who should speak freely about whatever was on his mind and whatever came from his heart, most of which was fueled by anger. Now I try to speak as the need presents itself and only say what is required.

Though I believe a man should bridle his anger with compassion, I am also of the opinion that all blacks have the right to feel and vent their inbred anger—as it is a residue of slavery. We are the people who were stolen from our families and native homes in Africa and sold to evil taskmasters in a strange and foreboding land.

Though my outer raiment is as black as the night and my heart pumps the blood of an African ancestry through darkened veins, I have had no personal experience with my dear Africa. Though my mind was filled with many wonderful stories about her, I knew her not. All these years my heart has longed for her warm soil to embrace my tired feet, yet I do not know her touch. My mouth and tongue have desired to taste her foods. My lungs have longed for her steamy air. When I am still and quiet, my body can remember her. What I know about Africa is in my head, and that knowledge came from my wise old teacher, Papa-horse.

Sometimes, to admit that America is my home causes my heart to be filled with dismal dread. Yet she is the only mother home I have personally known, and it is in timidity that I have come to love her. Should I look at her, America, as the evil stepmother, and Africa as the biological-mother? Maybe so, but then again, America is all I know. And I love my America.

I do not blame America for the wrongs her white children brought against me and my race during slavery. But I do hold the slave owners and those whites who hated blacks in contempt. And if it is healthy for me to blame my mother, America, for the wrong of her white children, then I must confess to the fearful hate and anger that I carry in my chest for my mother, Africa. It was Africa's black children who delivered my ancestors into the hands of the slave-trading English, Dutch, Portuguese, French, and Spanish in exchange for trinkets of little value. My black ancestors are guilty of treachery. They will pay. The souls of millions of trusting African children, young men, and young women cry out from their watery graves in the ocean and under the foreign soil of strange lands, asking that their deaths be avenged. As Esau sold his birthright to Jacob for a bowl of soup, so it was with Africa's black children: they sold their brothers and sisters to Europe's white children. Which of the two am I to hate the most—America's white children or Africa's black children?

America's enslaving white children robbed me of my God-given right to live my entire life in freedom. Holding me as chattel, they used me and other blacks to gain their gold and silver. And Africa's greedy black children robbed me of my God-given right to live my entire life in freedom because of their direful desire to possess Europe's nonessential garnishes! Both are guilty, as they have sinned against the blacks who were enslaved in the Americas!

And though what I say is true about my American and African mothers, their children are kin. Blacks and whites are part of a greater whole that has a purpose of its own. It extends beyond the needs, desires, and wants of the individual's reason for being. When we are in the first half of life, we think we are born for ourselves. We run here and we run there, doing as we please. In the second half of life, we discover that we are being led. We are moved from this to that, doing as the greater whole would have us do. When one has reached my age, one comes to realize that the function of all men is to serve the purpose of the greater whole, which is just one of the many purposes of God. I will show through my story that slavery was one of those greater purposes, a purpose with a God-given intent.

Once, a long time ago, Papa-horse said, "One day the black race and the white race, and all races, will become one race, the human race." His words have not come true, but as I am older and wiser, I can see that his prediction will be fulfilled in generations to come. In spite of my moments of doubt, his words have always come true.

First, I shall present to you, as you follow the weaving of my story, a fuller view of the soiled tapestry of my American mother's shawl, the other side of her incomplete his-story. As I do, you will have a more complete picture of her founding history. You will know what it was like to be one of her black children in those years. Then I shall reveal Africa's dirty sheets, as her black children slept with odd bedfellows by selling their black brothers and sisters into slavery to the whites. Then you will see that all men are both free and enslaved.

From America's beginning, the four strands of her his-story— slavery, spirit, morals, and law—moved forward in an unsteady pattern, swaying from side to side to create the dank rugs that now hang in the doorway of her halls of justice and churches. Yet it was the strange turnabout of her wealthy white children, those who made the laws and wrote the moral decrees about human life being equal and just for all who live in the land of sleeping justice, who acted contrary to three of the most sacred decrees ever written by men. They were the few individuals who created the institution of slavery for an entire nation, setting an example for the world to witness.

As I sit here and dip the quill's tip into the blackness of the inkwell, I am well aware of the fact that my story does not constitute the whole of African-American slave history. Yet, I also know that you, and all blacks and whites, need to know what I once felt and why I feel as I do now.

As you look at the past through my eyes, you will come to see the source of your hurt. That way, you will better understand why you may have certain feelings and urges that rise from an unknown source, the unspoken pain that you cannot pinpoint. And maybe whites will understand why blacks deal with them as they do, and blacks will understand why whites deal with them as they do.

Besides, if I fail to record my-story, it will be but another part of America's darkened history that was not told by one of her black sons, one who had a story and a history to tell. It will fade into the falsified annals—white history books that were written by those few devious whites who would not have their beliefs and actions known by their progeny and the world. Mind you, their children are the same posterity the Constitution of the United States refers to in its opening statement, the white sons and daughters of those who wrote their Constitution.

I say that America's white children of this era need to know and understand that their forefathers have not truthfully documented the crimes they committed against blacks—Innocent human beings. If these white children do not become fully familiar with those ghastly crimes, they are apt to adopt the same old attitude and create a similar fate for you and your sons and daughters. Thus, the proverb that history repeats itself may be fulfilled.

As I write to you, concerning the matter of my story, I am reminded of two questions that were cast at my feet. They were as poisonous darts from a blowpipe. The first query came from a burly redheaded gentleman who attended a freedom rally where I spoke as the keynote speaker. He stood and said, "Ol' negra man, by what authority do you trounce these things, matters that should be left to others to censure, those who are dutifully qualified?"

I moved, taking slow and short steps, from behind the lectern and walked to the edge of the platform. I stood still. I looked down at him, square in the eyes, and addressed his question directly.

I said, "Sir, Mr. White Man, I am Nimrod, an ex-slave. I speak from personal experience, and the competence that I've gained from many years of pain and suffering as a slave. Suffering that has inspired me with a will to live beyond a lashing tongue and inept insults such as yours.

"Pain has gotten my attention when nothing or no one else could. Pain, that great teacher, has brought me to this very moment.

"Look about you, sir, and you will see from this one gathering that times have changed and will continue to change. As I now stand before you and the gentle people of this gathering, I speak what I please. I know what I know from personal experience.

"Sir, it's obvious that you remember the yesterdays, the days when your kind would have lashed me for speaking as I do now. But it's also obvious that you must yet be reminded that today, if you so much as think of disrespectfully touching me with words or deeds, I am free to fell you like a rotten tree.

"And, kind sir, since you're the expert that you are, you're qualified to ask such a question. And since I am the ex-slave that I am, I am thus qualified to speak as an expert on the matter of slavery. It is my most recent past."

My words drew clapping and cheers from the audience. The man sat down quietly and listened to the remainder of my lecture.

The second pungent question came from a certain gray-haired, wealthy white woman who was a prominent patron of a church where I was speaking.

"Uncle, why are you talking about slavery? You people are free now. You should spend your time doing more productive things, like farming or something of that nature, helping this country to recover its losses. Let it die. That matter is dead."

"Auntie," I said ironically, "first of all, for you to address me as 'uncle,' which means you recognize me as your father's or mother's brother, you are acknowledging me as a blood kinsman, your male relative.

"You may want to rethink that.

"Secondly, to answer your question, why do I still talk about slavery? It's simple.

"Throughout the world there's a shortage of freedom and an abundance of slavery. Men have enslaved each other from the beginning of time. Every nation and every race has been enslaved by or has enslaved others. That means man knows more about slavery than he does about freedom.

"One man's desire to enslave another springs from his need to control himself. And since he does not, and is not in control of himself, he seeks to control others. And slavery is only one way of controlling another.

"And since man has not learned that his need is to control himself, life has chosen this country, this time period, and your race to demonstrate to all men that enslaving other men is the one sign that freedom is lacking in all the world, that freedom is needed by all.

"This generation, mine and yours, has experienced slavery in its most devastating form, the effects of which have touched the entire world and will continue to do so for generations to come.

"I believe the day is coming when mankind, all men, will benefit from the painful lesson of America's form of slavery. And I only regret that my race got the short end of the stick.

"Nonetheless, that day is coming. Blacks and whites, generations and years down the road, ahead of you and me, will benefit from the pain that blacks and whites suffered during slavery. Our pain, suffering, and hate for one another are going to lead both races, yours and mine, to freedom.

"But today, during this time, we'll individually become free when we understand what slavery has done to this country and all of its people. And it is today that we, you and I, must understand that the man who enslaves another is the one who is seeking personal freedom. Freedom will only come to the world when all men have discovered that personal freedom comes from inside.

"I believe we all can, and must, become free if there is to be a free world where all people are free and at peace with one another.

"When we study and know slavery as it was, we discover that freedom is missing the world over. We discover that all men are enslaved, in one way or another, to something. We come to understand what freedom is and what it is not.

"Thus, we discover the freedom that's within us.

"Even if we all bury our heads in sand and pretend that slavery didn't take place, the effects of slavery won't just go away. My message brings hope.

"And, Miss Lady, I've done all the farming I intend to do. Nowadays, like you, I prefer to garden when I have the time."

For this reply, I received a standing ovation from the blacks in the balcony and quiet disconcerted clapping from the few poor whites who sat in the back of the church. The eyes of the wealthy whites who sat in the front of the church bore holes in my soul. Their faces were cast in stone, and their stiff arms were draped over their motionless chests. What that white man and that white woman felt and said about my lecturing on the matter of slavery was common for their kind. And what they did not know was that I had learned to read and write when I was a child. In 1900, at the age of seventy-seven, I spent a year at Berea College in Berea, Kentucky. (I will share the details of how I learned to read and write, and my stay at Berea, later.)

The whites that had been slave owners, or were in favor of slavery, were not capable of being sympathetic with blacks, as they did not see them as human. This inability permitted them to treat us with less compassion than they did their pets. They believed what I was revealing about slavery would promote racial problems. But what they really feared was that blacks would learn to think for themselves and stand up for their rights. They feared that our black children would marry their white sons and daughters.

In years past, some whites have feared the thought of your hearing what my story reveals, which is the real history of the blacks and whites that were the founders of the United States. Today there are still whites that fear that individuals like you will discover the source of real freedom, as that source will be plainly revealed in my story. I believe that you and all men are to discover this freedom and become the enlightened creations you are meant to be. Thus their edifice of the quaint notion that white supremacy comes from God crumbles like a building without foundation or internal framework. They become the fragile creatures they are, mere human beings.

I argue that race relations are going to get worse as long as blacks and whites are ignorant of slavery and don't know what it meant to be black and a slave in America, don't know how the wealthy whites looked at the poor whites, and don't understand the depth of the physical, mental, and emotional scars that slavery caused for all, both black and white.

If the people of this country, both black and white, continue their ineffective attempt to bury the ill effects of slavery in the soil of the past, those very same effects are going to sprout as the symptomatic social ills our country presently suffers. As Papa-horse said, "Refusing to face guilt is like burying arsenic in the garden. Not only does it poison the soil, but it also poisons the plants and those who eat them. In the end, everything dies."

Accurate knowledge of slavery, on the other hand, will allow race relations to move into a position of healing and hopefully keep this country from collapsing from within. Blacks and whites, especially whites, cannot understand racial problems for what they were until slavery is revealed for what it truly was and how it molded the thinking of both races.

When most whites are asked about slavery, all they can say is, "Well, I didn't live then, so I don't know. All I know is it was good for whites and bad for blacks."

Attitudes like this reveal that it is common for whites not to know slavery for what it was—black people suffering and dying because their skin color was different from the slave owners'. They refuse to see slavery in all its brutal significance. Slavery is the painful part of America's history that still inspires the white race with a haunting guilt. Slavery is that part of America's history that chains the past to the present, and to the future, too. The past lives in the hearts and minds of both races as inbred feelings and beliefs based on hate. It will infect the future with a greater guilt and hate. I am convinced that when one gains a sound knowledge of slavery, freedom becomes a natural discovery and leads to the peace and happiness that all men seek.

There have been times, and there still are, when such men and women as mentioned above are able to stop me from speaking in public places, but they can not prevent me from writing my story and sharing it with you. Their death-dealing deeds can no longer be hidden behind paper lies and false words about their god, who is a bearded white man, seated on a throne in some far-away heaven. I say their injustices will haunt them, their children, and their grandchildren for generations to come. When light is cast upon darkness, it flees. Their dark deeds are being thrust into the light of truth. If I can lend but a sliver of insight on the issues of slavery and freedom, some of their descendants (and ours) may have a promising chance to walk hand-in-hand toward the horizon of a brighter and better tomorrow. If not, may God be with us all.

Who can know the life of a slave?

No one but the slave.

Who should know of the damage that slavery caused in the lives of the slaves and the slave owners?

Everyone.

Given my past and the history of the blacks that lived in America during slavery, I have every reason on earth to be angry. It is my right! The anger I speak of is not the natural anger that men are created with. It is the inbred anger that arises from not being free to live as a man, from not being free to marry and have a family, not being free to eat a decent meal when we are hungry, not being free to worship God as his creator. My anger came by way of slavery.

Am I angry about the suffering I experienced during slavery?

Yes. Most certainly, I am angry. But I am not blinded by rage. Slavery gave me, as it did all blacks, the right to be angry.

How can I not be angry when my body and mind are scarred with physical and emotional wounds that were created by cruel slave masters? The senseless and brutal acts that the white slave owners inflicted upon me and my people were acts that would give anyone reason to be angry and scarred. These scars ... I will have to wear them for the rest of my days. Thus, my anger is well-earned and well-deserved.

Do I hate all whites for their callous lack of human sympathy that slave owners brought against me and my people?

No. Not all whites.

In fact, today I feel pity for the slave owners. They were men and women who lived with bodies but without souls. They could no more feel the warmth of compassion flow through their veins for blacks any more than people who died a hundred years before the birth of Christ.

Who am I angry at?

Everyone who had a share in my ancestors becoming slaves, thus enslaving me: Africans and Americans.

As you read my-story, you will come to understand how and why the wealthy whites, the slave owners and lawmakers thought and acted as they did, not only toward blacks, but also toward each other, especially poor whites. You will see that there was a force at work, a force that was stronger than their lies and schemes. It did not allow them to control their actions, for they were mere clay in the hands of greater masters. They were the pawns on the board of time, and the evolutionary force of life called their every move. All people suffer from the process we humans call life.

THE EVOLUTIONARY PHASE OF LIFE:
SLAVERY AND THE ENTITY CALLED TIME

THE INFORMATION I AM GOING to share with you about the Evolutionary Phase of Life and Time may lead you to consider me rabid. Yes, though it is true that I am filled with uncontrollable emotions, I would have you know that I do not suffer from fanaticism. As I reflect back to the time Papa-horse first presented these matters to me, my legs trembled and my stomach fluttered. I was weakened by awe.

As I have indicated, blacks and whites had no choice in deciding whether they were going to be a part of America's slave history. The life I have lived, the books I have read, Papa-horse's teachings, and God have all led me to understand this fact about life: there are portions of life (apportionments) that are beyond the control of man. For instance, when a child is entering the adolescent phase of life, that child is not in control of what is happening in his body, nor is he in control of his actions. The same is true of women when they are in their monthly-cycle phase of life and passing through the menopausal phase of life. This is equally true of men when they are passing through the middle-age phase of life.

Papa-horse said that children, women, and men are all rendered helpless when they're passing through the phases of being human. Any and all attempts to control those phases are as futile as spitting into the wind. I say that Papa-horse was right.

I want to make this clear to you, so I am stating it again: it is my opinion, and I am thoroughly convinced of this, that man had no control over the Evolutionary Phase of Life that led blacks and whites into the slave-master relationship in which they found themselves. For some four hundred years they were under its control. When I began to study slavery with an open mind and a loving heart, I understood that the Evolutionary Phase of Life had a different purpose for blacks and whites, which was altogether different from the purpose they had when they set sail for the New World.

When those individuals arrived here in North America, human life had already begun to move into its new phase. Men were being forced into new ways of thinking, believing, and relating to each other and God. And they had no clue what was going on, no clue at all.

While experiencing life during that most difficult time of slavery, blacks and whites were being led into the realization that neither had a clue about the true meaning of love. As man does not choose life; it chooses him. It also leads him wherever it is going, and man has no choice but to be led by it. All in all, the Evolutionary Phase of Life chose the black race and the white race to participate in the epoch of change that was being ushered in on men around the world through the earmarked Institution of Slavery.

The Institution of Slavery was a public charter that proved, once and for all and to all men, that mankind needs to be and will be freed from the human illusion that man is less than what God created him to be.

The day is coming when men will experience life as free beings, loving each other and God from their hearts. Though I believe this to be true, I will not dilute the cruel acts of the wealthy whites, the slave owners, the lawmakers, and black slaves by writing a story that is less than truthful. I will be forthright in presenting the harsh realities of slavery as I experienced it at the hands of both my black and white brothers and sisters. I will show the good and the bad.

There are books that tell us about the future, the Bible foremost among them. Throughout the ages, men have written and preached about the time when all men will live as a free world society and love each other. The same have even made claims of knowing when this time will come. But not one of them has told us how the Evolutionary Phase of Life plans to get us from where we are to that time. It is here that I voice my opinion again and say that slavery was part and parcel of those plans. What the Evolutionary Phase of Life has destined to happen, in the full range of human existence, has been happening and is still happening. What is to be, is to be, and humans are in for a long, bumpy, challenging ride that will be most auspicious in its end.

In spite of the fact that all men have a unique purpose for being, the Evolutionary Phase of Life's purpose presupposes men's needs, plans, and purpose. Men's lives, like all human affairs, are under the control of its imminent purpose, which is to move man into change and lead him into his rightful place with God.

If a man, a race, a culture, a country, or mankind in general does not change and move into the next phase of life willingly, the Evolutionary Phase of Life will force the change even if it means death for man or race that refuses to change.

The Evolutionary Phase of Life specifically chose the black race and the white race to carry out its irrefutable purpose. As far as slavery goes, both races were chosen because of certain specific-qualities. It recognized dominant qualities of both races and saw that it could use those qualities to further its plans and purpose of keeping man moving forward. The qualities were objective extraversion and subjective introversion, polar temperamental opposites.

Though there are always exceptions to the rule, the white race was chosen by the Evolutionary Phase of Life because of its objective extraversion, which describes individuals who characteristically experience life outside of personal thoughts and feelings when dealing with situations and other individuals. This is an impersonal approach. During slavery, whites were possessed by the Evolutionary Phase of Life to carry out its purpose of demonstrating man's inability to love other men who appear to be different from them.

On the other hand, the black race was chosen by the Evolutionary Phase of Life, because of its subjective introversion, which is described as individuals who characteristically experience life from inner thoughts and feelings when dealing with situations and other individuals. This is a personal approach. During slavery, blacks were possessed by the Evolutionary Phase of Life to carry out its purpose of demonstrating what happens to men when they are not loved by other men because they appear to be different.

If man deliberately seeks Life's purpose, consciously follows that purpose, and is willing to make necessary changes, all men will live in the New Heavens and on the New Earth. All will gain freedom from the self-imposed limits under which humans live.

Thus did the Evolutionary Phase of Life demonstrate the fact that men are not in control of their lives, history, or Time itself.

TIME: THE MOTHER OF CHANGE

NOW, I SHALL TELL YOU ABOUT THE great mystical being called Time, the Mother of Change. Time is an altogether different matter. Or should I say substance, which is not what man has believed her to be. Throughout the ages Time, that mysterious truth, has baffled great minds the world over. Not one of them has been able to figure her out or know her for who and what she truly is. I say what man refers to as Time is one of the most salient phenomena that man's understanding has been blinded to. But I am confident that you will come to understand Time as I have come to understand her. She is the reigning queen of the Evolutionary Phases of Life.

In my opinion, if man is to become free, he must first study himself and thus discover who and what God is. The Apostle Paul plainly spoke of this process when he said that God is in Man. In no uncertain terms he tells us: "Know ye not that ye are the temple of God, and that the Spirit of God dwelleth in you" (1 Corinthians 3:16)? When Paul wrote this, he was no doubt referring to what he had read in what many call the Old Testament of the Bible. In Genesis 1:26-27, we read, "Let us make man in our image, after our likeness." The results of that command are confirmed by the next verse: "So God created man in his own image, in the image of God created he him: male and female created he them."

The point of those words is as clear to me as a glass of cool water taken from a stream. So clear, they need no filtering, no interpretation.

When I first read the words and works of alchemist, Gerhard Dorn, I plainly saw that he and all the great alchemists approached their work from the basics of Paul's words (beliefs that were similar to those of the Ishermans). What I mean is this: The alchemists believed that man was one with God and that it was better to get the information they needed from the source, God in them, rather than an outside source. Instead of treating God's creations, calcium, iron, iodine, magnesium, zinc, selenium, copper, manganese, chromium, potassium, gold, as if they were dead objects to experiment on by heating them in a vessel, they asked the minerals specific questions. After spending hours praying and meditating, they asked these questions: What are you? What kind of life do you have? What is your purpose? How does it feel to be melted? And since the minerals were within man, the alchemists expected the answers to be forthcoming from God, who was also in them.

Now I come to the particular point where I shall present Time as being who She is. Time, that unrecognized entity, is a living being. Regardless of how man perceives Time, whether referring to her as material, matter, stuff, a thing, a being, or a substance, she is very much alive.

Everything that God created has God's Spirit dwelling in it, God's life. As bacteria are alive, so are minerals, plants, insects, and animals. So is man alive, so is Time alive.

Man's first step in coming to understand Time was to divide her into mathematical increments and units of measure: seconds, minutes, hours, days, weeks, months, seasons, years, decades, centuries, eons and eternity.

Therefore, man idolized Time as another of his dead objects, presenting his view of her lucid presence to the world on the lifeless faces of his clocks, watches, and calendars. I say it is high time that man comes to see Time in all her glory. It is time to stop his ineffective struggling of being less than he was created to be, to accept her godly wisdom concerning how to do all things, and to experience all the supernatural things he dreams of doing, including communicating without words and the aid of talking apparatuses, flying without the aid of machines, traveling without the aid of animals or machines. The evidence of these and other possibilities can be heard in the words of Paul: "I knew a man in Christ above fourteen years ago, whether in the body, I cannot tell; or whether out of the body, I cannot tell: God knoweth; such a one caught up to the third heaven. And I knew such a man, whether in the body, or out of the body, I cannot tell: God knoweth; how that he was caught into paradise, and heard unspeakable words, which is not lawful for a man to utter" (2 Corinthians 12:204).

Although Paul is not sure whether his travel to the third heaven was in or out of the body, he nonetheless tells of his experience of travel without the use of animal or machine. The time is coming when man will work with Time and live as the supernatural being he is.

I will share my particular experience with Time, what Papa-horse shared with me about Time, and what God has taught me about Time. I believe her appearance will become clearer to you. You will but "look through a glass clearly" and see her divine beauty as it is seen by God.

Time, that substance part of God, only permits man to control some of the choices he makes, but none of the periods of his life and definitely none of the things that mankind has, is, and will experience during the course of human existence. That includes blacks selling their brothers and sisters and whites purchasing those brothers and sisters as slaves.

ISSUES OF FREEDOM AND THE DAMAGES OF SLAVERY

THERE ARE TWO VERY SIMPLE, but powerful, things a man should know and have if he is to live as a human being. First, a man should know where he originated, the country he came from. He should know his parents and grandparents and where they came from. Second, he should have the freedoms listed in the Declaration of Independence: the right to live with the "unalienable Rights" the Creator endowed the human race with life and liberty, and the right to the pursuit of happiness that belongs to all men.

During slavery, most whites, by the most part, knew their parents and grandparents and often had paintings of them, plus their hand-written records. The freedom whites had was an invented kind, which they invented for themselves and found ways to experience. But we blacks had neither the privilege of inventing anything that resembled freedom nor permission, and certainly would not have been allowed to experience such. Take me as an example. I lived the better part of my life as a slave on the Sandridge farm in Decherd, Tennessee. I knew nothing about my parents and grandparents. I can only imagine them as being free people who once lived in the lush jungles of Africa. One day they were free. The next day they were stolen from their homes and brought to the untamed shores of the New World, where they died as slaves. Thus I was born a slave. And the same was true for most black people.

Regarding the matter of blacks being free, well, there is nothing to say, except to say that what is written in the Declaration of Independence did not apply to us. And though this is true, I want you to know from the beginning that I believe all men are brothers under the skin, with the most noticeable difference being skin color.

I do not wish to be associated in thought or in deed with the blacks that believe all whites are soulless "white-devils" who have no conscience. At the same time, I am of the opinion that the white slave owners suffered from a severe guilt complex that created their psychotic and neurotic conditions. They were thus enabled to kill blacks and Indians without an active faculty of discriminating thought. There were two qualities those men and women did not seem to have: love and fear. Their ability to love anyone, including their families and themselves, was impaired by their act of enslaving their black brothers and sisters. They seemed to have been possessed by a certain evilness that did not permit them to fear the consequences of the merciless act of enslaving others. My story shall reveal these indictments to be the facts they are.

The white slave owners did not, and could not comprehend the impact their thoughtless and dehumanizing actions would have on blacks. And why not? They themselves were in desperate need of help. Their mental and emotional states prohibited such understanding. Nor did they think about the retribution that was to come to their children and grandchildren, those who would pay for their ancestors' wrongs.

The atrocities slave owners inflicted upon blacks created in us physical, mental, and emotional damage that extends beyond the human ability to repair. Those atrocities damaged all of America's children, and only Time, the great healer, can bring about the healing we all need. The whites I refer to were the unstable personalities who established the great and tragic American institution of tragedy called slavery. I write this to say that if you are to be free, it is important that you know that the calamitous results of slavery, which is their signature of disaster is a disaster that will affect both blacks and whites for generations to come. This includes you, the reader.

The disastrous effects of slavery cannot be resolved without severe punishment. The law of sowing and reaping shall bring the slave owners, their blood stained hands bound behind their backs, to the table of justice. Justice alone can cleanse the hands of those who have wantonly shed the blood of millions of innocent black men, women, and children.

Those whites who say, "Slavery is a thing of the past, let it die. You people are not slaves today," are unaware of their own pain. This unawareness makes them capable of creating pain for others. They are to be feared the most.

It is true that not all blacks have personally experienced the pains of slavery. Yet no matter who they are, or where they live, black people have been affected by slavery, and all blacks suffer from its persistent consequences. This is a case history of a race suffering from what its individual members have suffered. I make it plain that I do not say all whites are guilty of the savage act of enslaving blacks. But, I do say that the white race is paying, and will pay in full, for those atrocities, even in ways that may seem unrelated to the acts that were committed by their forefathers. This is a case history of a race paying for the gross wrongs that individual members of the race committed.

My story is about my life as it was lived in the closing chapters of the 1800s. Although I lived the greater portion of that life on the Sandridge farm as a slave, my story has more to do with the issues of the human struggle to be free than it does with blacks being enslaved by whites.

To keep us blacks subservient, slave owners invented insidious methods of manipulation to control our mind and emotions. The most common were associated with fear, food, and sex. For instance, often times the babies of slaves were sold from farm to farm without documents, which caused us to be a people without a name or inheritance. The surnames that were placed on us came from slave masters who found it necessary to label their property. They called us by whatever name they wished, even when the names were intended to break our spirits. When they separated children from their mothers and fathers, husbands from wives, and families from families, they created a void in our lives that could not be filled. We lived in a constant fear that would be passed from generation to generation.

Fear was the playmate of slave children, who were punished by slave owners for the simplest wrongs, or what they considered wrong. A child that fell asleep, for example, after having been up all night caring for the mistress's baby was lashed with the whip or beaten with a stick of firewood. If a child took food, whether a biscuit from the slave owner's table or fruit from a tree, he was beaten. The food that house slaves stole from the master's kitchen to feed to their children was not for the pleasure of having extra, but to keep their children alive. If this food had not been stolen, more of our children would have died.

Once, there was a slave who stole a piece of cheese from his master's kitchen. The master asked who had taken the cheese, but no one spoke up. To discover who had taken the cheese, the master called all the slaves together and told them that the cheese had been poisoned and he was the only one who had an antidote. The guilty slave confessed and was beaten. If a slave was fortunate enough to eat before going to work in the field, he would have eaten a breakfast of lard, cornmeal, and sometimes molasses before sunrise.

The matter of sex for slaves, as far as slave owners were concerned, was not a matter of love, but breeding. It was a common practice for slave masters to match big slave men with the large slave women. The slave owners wanted slave children who could work in the hot and cold all day, nonstop, even if it meant falling dead from the work. Some slave owners believed that it was better to have new slaves shipped into the country rather than take care of the ones they had, which was another of their many insidious method for keeping slaves from learning, and underfoot. Slave owners had the black women sexually anytime they wanted them. Even when a black woman had a husband and children, the owners would go to the shack, order the husband and children to leave, and have their way with the woman, thus satisfying their lust.

Wealthy whites who held blacks as slaves either had no understanding of the bedraggled future they were creating for the black race and the country, or it was not, as has been suggested, within their capacity to love and care for others. My opinion and feelings are, their personal pain blinded them to the emotional damage they were creating for all people, including themselves. When they stripped the black race of its right and need to experience family life, they robbed an entire race of its identity. They took the fate of blacks into their hands and shaped America into what she is today, a damaged replica of what God intended for her to be.

The act of snatching a child from the hands of his father certainly creates emotional damage for the child. But the act of stealing a child from his mother's bosom is an entirely different matter. Both acts rob a child of the nourishment that provides him with the capacity to be gentle and the ability to display humaneness. The first act creates a human being who will have difficulty in dealing with men and women. The second, forcing a child to grow up without a mother's brand of love, creates a man or woman who will have serious difficulty relating to other men and women, himself, and God.

Papa-horse said, "The child that has been deprived of the warm milk of its mother's breast, that liquid love, and the calming sound of her heartbeat, is the child who will bring a blizzard of pain to the world. Children come into the world through a mother's womb. Only a mother's love can empower a child to love God, others, and self." The truthfulness of Papa-horse's words is evident in the lives of children today. Who can know what the future will bring?

To keep us blacks under their control, whites needed to destroy our ability to love others and believe in the God of justice. And if the God of justice does exist, and I believe there is such a God, wealthy whites and slave owners will pay dearly for their dastardly deeds.

What can I say about the white children of wealthy whites and slave owners and the damage that slavery caused them? No, sir, they were not immune to the havoc their parents were creating. It was common for white children to eyewitness the atrocities their parents inflicted on innocent blacks. It was also common for them to witness the wrongs their parents brought against the poor whites, and it was just as common for them to personally experience emotional scarring, as those parents were cruel to them, too. Slavery damaged all of us— blacks, poor whites, wealthy whites, and slave owners and their wives and children. No one escaped. No one will escape.

Emotions move me to ask: Why didn't someone among the slave owners foresee the horrific damage their actions would cause for future generations?

Hindsight makes me answer: That was impossible. Slave owners were victims of a purpose that was far greater and wiser than they themselves were.

What do I mean by a purpose? I shall explain, but first I ask that you give special effort and attention to understanding what I am about to share. As I have never attempted this before, I admit I am walking on shaky ground. Nonetheless, I feel that my opinion will be as valuable to you as it has been to me.

The great storyteller, Papa-horse, once said, "Freedom is the goal all humans are striving for, and love is that journeying process that can lead them there."

THE INVENTION OF CHRISTIAN, AMERICAN INSTITUTION OF SLAVERY ON BRITISH AMERICAN SOIL

THE PRECARIOUS RELATIONSHIP THAT blacks, wealthy whites, and poor whites find themselves in today in America was contrived in the white motherland, Europe.

Some of Europe's white children became tired of their oppressive rulers and decided to find a new world, which would become their promised land. In the beginning, the blacks and whites who settled in the New World struggled together, and worked the land as equals. Those naive English settlers came to America seeking freedom, thinking that they could settle their families in this new and strange land without much struggle. They believed they had a God-given right to drive the Indians out and tame the land at will. Being ill-prepared for what could happen, they did not foresee the future. And the worst caught them by surprise. The harsh realities of a new beginning in a new land and living in unfamiliar conditions were merciless. Most English settlers died within a year of their arrival. In 1609, five hundred settlers set up camp in Jamestown, Virginia. In 1610, only sixty were still alive. In 1622, three thousand new settlers arrived in Virginia. In 1624, William Tucker, the first black child was born. In 1650 there were nineteen thousand whites and four hundred blacks living in British America. There were twenty free blacks, of whom thirteen owned their own homes.

The early years of America's history found blacks and whites as landowners, and both had servants. In 1650, in Hampton County, Virginia, Anthony Johnson, a black man, owned two hundred fifty acres of land and had five workers, some of whom were white. At that time, there were no laws that dealt with race slavery, only that pertained to servitude and indentured servants. As things were at that time the wealthy white men were in control of government and land distribution.

Poor whites who were eighteen to twenty-five years old when they arrived from Europe were indentured servants, as were blacks. For the first fifty years in the colonies, most of the indentured servants were white. As servants under British law, blacks and whites were under obligation to work out their time on the farms of wealthy whites. They had no say in the matter of lawmaking.

Soon the wealthy white men, in their need to dominate others (which seems to be an inbred trait of all humans), began to exert their power of control over the blacks and poor whites. They knew the notion of brotherly love because they had suffered from the horrors of European oppression at home in Europe, but they became the tyrants they ran from and repeated what they had escaped from. They brought to bear the sins of their European heritage with them and heaped them on the shoulders of blacks and poor whites.

After the blacks and poor whites had completed their terms of indentured servitude, they were, by British law, supposed to receive a bushel of corn, a change of clothes, and a hundred acres of land to give them a new start. In the beginning, things went as planned, and blacks and poor whites were freed after they had served their required time. But when some began to prosper alongside the wealthy men, these men became fearful. Although the markings of class distinction were present, the signs became clearer as wealthy whites found ways to limit the progress of the emerging class of wealth-gaining blacks and poor whites.

Among the many unjust practices wealthy whites committed against the new middle class, there was one, in my opinion, that was the seed that grew into slavery. This was keeping blacks and poor whites in servitude for more years than agreed upon—a repeating of Africa and Europe's deadly mistake of brothers enslaving brothers. Circumventing the laws pertaining to indentured servitude was the wealthy white man's route march into the stream of endless lies that led to broken treaties and amended and nullified laws. The wealthy white lawmakers' proclivity to lie on paper without sound reasons and their fear of accepting others as equals led them to invent the greatest institution that has ever existed on American soil: slavery.

The Institution of Slavery caused the Americas to become a breading ground for uprisings and wars between abolitionists and slavers. Blacks and poor whites began to rebel against the tyranny of the wealthy white men. They struck out with acts of violence. The rebels were caught and punished. Though their crimes were equal, some were punished more unjustly than others, which planted the seeds of class distinction that sprouted into the young tree of slavery.

In 1640, the wealthy whites' retaliation against rebels became progressively violent. Three men, one black and two whites, broke their servitude contracts and ran away, only to be recaptured. The black man, John Punch, was brutally punished. But the courts were tolerant of the two poor white men, James Gregory and Victor.

The courts sentenced Victor and James to be whipped thirty lashes each, and gave them both an additional three years of service to the British Colony. But John was sentenced to a lifetime of service. He was the first recorded black man to be dealt with in such a harsh and unforgiving manner. There are no records that show that a white man was ever dealt with likewise.

I say, Virginia, the birthplace of institutionalized slavery, committed that one act of punishing John Punch unjustly, and in doing so discharged the semen of racial discrimination that impregnated British America with racism. Soon afterwards, the colonies gave birth to the wanton hate that produced laws that gave whites the power to lash out against blacks at will, forcing them into abject slavery. In 1641, Massachusetts became the first colony to recognize slavery as a legal institution. In 1650, Connecticut became the second. In 1663, Maryland became the third. In 1664, New York and New Jersey were fourth, and in 1750, Georgia threw in her hat and became the fifth.

When the slavers brought the first boatload of blacks from Africa, twenty Africans were sold by a Captain Job to the governor of Jamestown, Virginia. America's unborn history was tarnished like fine silver stored in a damp cave. In 1661, Virginia's law courts declared all children to be free or slave according to their mother's race, which meant only blacks could be slaves. In the same year, rebellion broke out and caused America's white colonists to take up arms and go to war—their first Civil War of 1676. As a result, Jamestown, America's womb of slavery, was burned to the ground, but that did not mean that she became sterile. By 1672, selling blacks into slavery had become a thriving business that was owned by the king of England, the governor of Jamestown, John Locke the philosopher of liberty, and others. The Civil War of 1676 was not about to have an adverse affect on slave trade. In fact, it forced the increase that wealth whites had desired.

The tremendous wealth of the New World did not come from the work of those who dreamed up and wrote the laws of the land. It came from the blood, sweat, tears, and lives of blacks and poor whites. Those men, women, and children were the steps upon which the wealthy white men, slave owners, and the government mounted to touch the sky. The English slave trade became the most profitable enterprise in England. By commonwealth law, all freeborn Englishmen could sell blacks into slavery. Within sixteen years, they sold over ninety thousand blacks. Money-hungry, slave-trading whites were responsible for kidnapping more than twenty million Africans from their homes, with fewer than ten million arriving alive on the west coast of the continent, and a quarter million ending up in North America—"The Home of the Free and the Brave."

The more slave traders brought Africans into America, the more the laws were changed.

In June of 1680, white lawmakers passed laws that stated that members of the black population in North America could be killed without such an act being a felony. By 1691, it was illegal to free a black man unless he was leaving the colony. (Where could he go?) In 1765, the Stamp Act was concocted, and it was against the law for a free Negro to invite a slave or Indian into his home.

As I stated earlier, I do not intend to portray my white brothers and sisters as devils without a conscience, as some of my black brothers and sisters believe them to be. Nor will I represent my black brothers and sisters as people who are in need of pity because they lack intelligence, as some of my white brothers and sisters have propagated. But I will clearly demonstrate that white slave owners, even though they controlled the wherewithal of blacks and poor whites, they themselves were not wholly free from a form of slavery. And though blacks were America's children who became the cogs and wheels of The Institution of Slavery, they were not wholly innocent of wrongdoing themselves.

Slavery is not a matter that should be taken lightly. Not only did blacks suffer at the hands of their white owners and taskmasters, but all Americans, including whites, the rich and poor, living today, suffer from the ill effects of slavery.

THE STRUGGLE THAT CONTINUES

I COMPILE THIS INFORMATION IN the hope that I may assist you to escape the avoidable suffering that comes from ignorance and making improper choices when dealing with things not understood.

I am not saying that I can protect you from the pain that comes with being human. I am saying that I believe your future will be much better, with less of the suffering that is due to simple ignorance, if you are aware of the past, mine and this country's, than if you are not. And though pain is a natural part of life, it may not be necessary for you to suffer from every obstacle that life lay in your path, especially the suffering that comes from not recognizing the residual effects of slavery and the harm that comes from not knowing what it means to be truly free.

TWO FREEDOMS

FREEDOM IS NOT A SOMETHING THAT one can experience through ownership of money, land, a house, or material goods. Possessing material goods does not make a man free. This was clearly demonstrated by the lives of the wealthy whites and the slave owners. Nor was America's government able to give this freedom to her black and white children—for it is more than material goods and laws. I believe there are some blacks and poor whites that must come to understand that material wealth cannot give them freedom, nor can it be legislated by government. When you and I, and every individual, find true freedom, the world of mankind will become free.

What I share is not only for you, but for the blacks, the poor whites, and even the whites who are born to wealthy and loving parents, for they soon learn that freedom does not come with a birth certificate, nor from wealth, nor from having white skin. As human creations of God, if we do not have freedom, we are leaves falling from the tree, caught by the wind, driven where it wills, and landing in some unfamiliar place to decay.

One man's notion of freedom is as unique to him as beliefs about God are to men of different religious ideologies. It will become apparent to you that what I say about freedom has to do with the greater freedom, the freedom that we humans are capable of experiencing. This is the freedom that is of God.

During slavery time it did not matter what a person's position was. Slave or master, rich or poor, we all were struggling for the same thing: to be free. Blacks wanted freedom from oppressive and cruel masters, and wealthy whites and slave owners needed to be freed from guilt and hatred. Both needed to be freed from the slavery that caused men to act and live in ways that were less than the way God created them to live. Each man must find the keys that open the doors on the journey to freedom. My desire is to be helpful.

When wealthy whites arrived in America from Europe, their old emotional scars from being mistreated by a harsh ruling class festered into uncontrollable hot boils of hatred. Then came the Civil War of 1676, the American Revolutionary War of 1786, and the Civil War of 1861. There was no room left in their hearts to love anything that resembled themselves. I am moved to say that the man who is fast asleep in his fecal matter cannot be sensitive to the pain that others suffer. He is not able to concern himself with future events and the consequences of personal and race-related actions.

When I was a boy, Papa-horse began to teach me about the two freedoms. I wanted both of them. The first freedom is paper freedom: privileges we slaves were supposed to receive in 1863, when President Lincoln signed the Emancipation Proclamation papers. Based on the tenors of this country's founding fathers words of the Constitution, the president was attempting to give us the privileges that were rightfully ours. And when we had received them, at best, those privileges were supposed to have a minimum affect on our outer lives: the kinds of food we would eat, what we would wear, and where we could live. All of those things depended on the money we could earn, if we found paying work.

Papa-horse said, "The Emancipation Proclamation is paper freedom. It can only bring temporary changes that fade fast. And that kind of freedom is a privilege that is given by men and taken back by the same men. The second freedom is true freedom. This is the freedom that comes from within the secret chambers of a man's soul. This freedom frees a man from the inside. Then it stretches to the outside, where it can be shared with others. Man does not give true freedom, nor can man take it away.

"Each individual," he said, "has to work hard at conquering himself if he is to experience true freedom. After years of grappling with personal demons, a man may be rewarded with a taste of true freedom. And if by chance he is successful at retaining a portion of that freedom, it becomes possible for him to experience it for the remainder of his life, even forever."

For years, men and women have fought and died for the first freedom—paper freedom. And I believe many of those individuals had an inner knowledge of the second freedom—true freedom—even if they did not understand what it was. In my opinion, it was true freedom that supplied many slaves with the courage to endure the unbelievable crimes that white slave owners brought against them. Not only did those blacks want freedom for themselves, but they also wanted it for their future generations, and for poor whites, too.

If a man gains the first freedom only, he will enjoy the fruits of earthly privileges and possibly own material goods. If he only gains the second freedom, he opens himself up to the spiritual world and will live with the spiritual qualities that God endowed him with, a measure of peace and love. But if he gains both freedoms, he gains the best of both worlds, earthly and heavenly. This is the freedom that was created by God.

When Papa-horse talked to me about freedom, he spoke more about the second freedom. At the beginning of my journey, I thought I wanted true freedom more than paper freedom, but time and Papa-horse's teachings showed me that I wanted paper freedom most. Yet, because of my drive to be free, nothing slaked my thirst for understanding freedom more than good conversation. And nothing squared my hunger for knowledge of freedom more than a good book. Understanding and knowledge caused me to be open to God's reach, to the keys to true freedom.

PAPER FREEDOM

IN 1868 IT HAD BEEN FIVE YEARS SINCE President Lincoln signed the Emancipation Proclamation, and we blacks and poor whites still did not have the freedom that paper promised.

One morning I woke up before sunrise, while the land was still hidden from plain view. I walked through the tall grass in Red Lice Field, a tract of land on the Sandridge farm. Spring hung heavy in the air. The cool morning dew ran down my bare ankles and soothed my aching feet. I stood in the center of the field. With my arms stretched out to the sides, my head back, my eyes closed, and soaked up the warmth of the sun. I inhaled the air, and the delicate scents of spring rushed into my nostrils, and flowed deep into the crevices of my lungs. I became intoxicated by the aroma of the honeysuckles, the wildflowers, the pines. My mind spun with thoughts about freedom. It was then, in that moment, that I realized that I was alive in America for reasons other than being a slave. I immediately kneeled down and thanked God. I remained on my knees for more than an hour.

When I stood again and looked around, I saw that a new day was truly dawning. I felt different, as if change were about to carry me deep into the heart of life's process of changing men and races for the better. Things seemed clearer and more meaningful. Through his signs, God revealed the mysteries of my life that day. I looked about. The dark, damp trunks of the tall pines that bordered the adjoining cornfield were hidden by a pale gray mist. I took this as a sign that I was to stand in the midst of the unknown and meet it face to face. I watched a red fox chase a rabbit across the opened field and took this as a warning that I needed to be careful and not let my animal feelings (my flaming anger) get the best of me. I saw bright green leaves at the tops of the hardwood trees and took that as a sign that I would need to look at the experiences of that day from a loftier perspective, from God's perspective.

I watched the clouds drift across the sky. A new era was riding on the tail of the wind. The present, as the wealthy whites knew it, was a fading reality. The future, as blacks and poor whites wished it to be, was an approaching illusion. And both would clash in the unconsciousness of all men.

Like most people of that period, I believed a man's word was as good as gold. I wanted to believe that the president's signature on that document was meant to be good for blacks and poor whites, but I also knew that a man's signature on paper, any man's, could not give us what we wanted, nor what we deserved. I knew for certain the president's signature would not do any favors for blacks and poor whites. Because the wealthy whites were not free themselves, our impeding freedom would only force them to find other ways to make life difficult for us. I believed they despised us for reasons they themselves did not know. That made matters worse for all of us.

As far back as 1865, there were blacks that believed that President Lincoln signed the Emancipation Proclamation and freed the slaves because of his good heartedness, but I tell you in no uncertain terms that was not so.

President Lincoln did not free the slaves because of his noble stand against slavery, nor because he loved his black brothers, as he and his wife owned slaves. His position on the issue of slavery was made clear when he said:

"My paramount objective in this struggle is to save the Union and is not either to save or destroy slavery. If I could save the Union without freeing any slave I would do it. If I could save it by freeing all the slaves I would do it. And if I could save it by freeing some and leaving others alone I would also do that."

Frederick Douglass, the runaway slave and abolitionist, and others had encouraged President Lincoln to emancipate the slaves, as the Civil War had become a solvent issue that involved slavery. In fact the paramount issue and reason for blacks and whites to fight in the Civil War was because of slavery: the immoral act of whites retaining blacks as livestock, the freedom of whites to do what they would with blacks versus blacks being free to live as human beings. The Declaration and the Constitution that had been drawn up by wealthy whites who were less than honorable; what they wrote, their thinking and feelings, were not favorable where blacks were concerned.

However, President Lincoln was slow to accept the good advice of Douglass and others. After thousands of Union soldiers had been slaughtered, including his son, his pride was brought under submission. It was then that he was able to express a measure of humanness by drawing up the Emancipation Proclamation and signing it.

After I had prayed in the field that morning, my mind was filled with volumes of thoughts that had to do with the meaning of freedom and its source. I also wondered how and why wealthy whites and slave owners could do the cruel things they were doing to blacks and poor whites. Most important were the things Papa-horse was teaching me time and time again through object lessons. As I plowed forward on my journey to freedom, he was by my side for years. He taught me how to live in freedom and to love all people.

I looked up and watched the sun as it crept toward the heavens. Its warm rays laid about my face and bare arms. I breathed deeply and asked myself these questions: How can we expect the wealthy whites and lawmakers to give us freedom when the Declaration of Independence, the Constitution of the United States, and the Emancipation Proclamation were all concocted by white men who were only concerned with their own well-being and the welfare of the wealthy? Where are the reason and logic of it all?

Blacks fought and died in their wars because they hoped to gain freedom, but the most any of us ever received was a semblance of freedom. And the thing that was dubious was that poor whites had no real interest in fighting, especially in the Revolutionary War. Besides, wealthy whites were not giving us freedom, as they needed us to do the work they weren't willing to do.

WAR AND FREEDOM

IN RECENT TIMES, YOUNG blacks have asked me, "If things were so bad and slaves wanted freedom, why didn't they wage war against the whites?"

I would have those young blacks, and all people, to know that the war between blacks and the wealthy whites, slave owners, and lawmakers began when black indentured servants were more severely punished than the white indentured servants. I must admit that there was a time when I expressed the same sentiment as those young blacks. I wanted to kill the wealthy whites, the slave owners, and the lawmakers for causing my life to be a living hell.

On several occasions I made plans to do that very thing, wage war against the white race, but each time Papa-horse reminded me of what had happened to men like Nat Turner, John Brown and his sons (who were whites), and other blacks who had intended to war with the whites. They had all failed. He helped me realize that blacks could not successfully fight the wealthy whites in warfare and gain freedom. They outnumbered us. We had neither the weapons nor the military skills to stage a full-blown war against an enemy that was in control of everything that had to do with war, and our lives.

From personal observation, I came to the conclusion that wealthy whites and slave owners were a breed of a different sort, not at all like other men. They seemed to have no fear, none whatsoever, of dying. Their will to live was couched in matters that pertained to death, like stealing other men from their homeland, taking land that was not theirs, and warring with each other and anyone else who resisted their demands to be in control. They were willing to walk into any situation that held the promise of a thrill, even when death was an imminent probability. For instance, when they landed on the coast of Mother Africa to rob her of gold and her black children, if they stayed longer than three years, they died from her searing heat. But they were so filled with greed that many took that chance, and died. After the first boatload of whites arrived from England in Jamestown, Virginia, white men and women died like poisoned maggots. In 1609, there were five hundred colonists, but this number had dwindled to sixty within a year. After the Indians realized that whites were less than honorable when it came to keeping their promises, they warred against them and tried to drive them back into the sea. But whites continued to come by the boatloads, all prepared to die in a strange and forebodingly hostile land.

Many times, when blacks made plans to revolt against their white slave owners, their plans were known beforehand by the owners. This was a far too common occurrence. How did they know? Well, their plans to revolt were revealed by other blacks. It seemed as if the black race was predestined to lose at every turn, and the white race had a copy of that blueprint and knew what to do before blacks made their move. Therefore, many blacks waited and prayed for better days while others were relentless in their efforts to gain freedom and continued to rebel.

But I would have you know, however, that not all blacks subscribed to the notion that they were to succumb to the efforts of the wealthy whites, slave owners, and lawmaker's efforts to keep them in slavery. Among all of God's children, the black race has certainly had the strongest will to live and survive under the most devastating conditions. And slavery has proven this to be the fact.

THE BLACK SECRET SOCIETY

I SHALL NOW PRESENT TO YOU some of those men who had an indomitable will to live and protect the black race from its would-be annihilators: wealthy whites, slave owners, and lawmakers.

What I am revealing about The Twelve I have never before shared with anyone else. I seriously doubt whether anyone among them ever done so, either. They were the original members who made up one of America's most obscure organizations. In all her history America has never had an organization that has been as secret as The Twelve, the black secret society.

Whether or not President Lincoln and the lawmakers could have ever admitted that the Civil War was fought over the issue of slavery does not matter. That is why it was fought. Since that war opened the way for blacks to gain their pseudo-constitutional freedom, Southern whites became infuriated. As blacks had finally won the struggle for control over their own lives, the whites were the losers. Following the turbulent years of the Civil War, white men who were members of the Masons and the Protestant Church formed the Ku Klux Klan (KKK) to avenge their damaged pride and protect and preserve the doubtful purity of the white race. One of their goals was to keep their white women from black men. But I shall demonstrate later that they were trying to do the impossible in attempting to keep grown women from deciding who they would bed with. The KKK organization was founded in 1865 in Pulaski, Tennessee (my home state), by six confederate officers. Those white men knew the adult slaves told their children "hant stories" (stories about ghosts) to frighten them so they would not venture outside after sundown. Adult slaves did that because it was common for poor whites to kidnap black children and sell them to other slave owners. Armed with that knowledge, the founding members of the KKK dressed in white sheets and pointed hoods and pretended to be the dead soldiers who fought in the Civil War. They roamed the South and tried to sabotage the government's reconstruction efforts. For more than three years, they terrorized blacks by burning their homes and churches and whipping, mutilating and hanging men and women (after raping the women), and killing children. In 1867, Confederate general and Freemason, Nathan Bedford Forrest, became the KKK's first Imperial Wizard. A year later, he traveled throughout the South, establishing new chapters and advising new members.

It is common knowledge that the KKK was established to keep the white race pure so that it could continue as the so-called superior race. But the impetus that moved those white men to form that organization is not as well known. And I shall now reveal their real reason. That ominous order of the fraternal organization of The KKK was founded because The Twelve (twelve black men) had already established the America's soil. Though The Twelve never came to the public's awareness, America's white Founding Fathers had an internal sense that such a black organization would, or did, exist.

From the KKK's inception, the sole purpose of this clan of angry white men has been to thaw the mission of that secret society of black men. As I reveal that mission and the strategy of The Twelve for warring against whites, you will come to know of blacks who did not intend to, and did not, sit idly by and allow whites to lead them into slaughter like dumb livestock. The war of The Twelve was like no other war that had ever been devised by a group of dedicated men, black or white.

If this information were to reach certain white men, it would strike them sharply about the heart with awe, their knees would give way, and their bodies would crumble to the ground. Their entire being would be filled with fear and dread of the black man's power.

The Twelve organized themselves not simply because they feared for their lives, but they also feared that the black race and its cultural heritage would be brought to an end by those whites who were in fear of the black race's God-given power to change the face of all races forever.

Have you ever wondered why white men were so adamant and uncompromisingly cruel to black men? Why they were quick to castrate the black man for the slightest infraction? So eager to cut off the black man's penis even after he had been beaten or burned to death?

I will answer those questions and the others as I present the organizational handbook of the black ministers who called themselves The Twelve Talons of God. The Twelve established the most invisible secret society that has ever been established on American soil.

The Sacred Secret Society
for the Preservation of Black Heritage
and Its Cultural Birthright
(The Lord's children's war against the white genocide brought against them.)

First I shall provide you with a bit of background information about the members of The Sacred Secret Society for the Preservation of Black Heritage and Its Cultural Birthright (SSSPBHCB), especially the youngest and eldest members. Then I will share information that pertains to the organization and its function. But I will never reveal the names of any of the members. That act would be a profanation of the sacred custom of the Isherman, who believed and lived the tenet that to share the name of a Holy Man with the uninitiated is to pour the soul of that Holy Man into the flames of hell (quote from page 80 of their handbook).

From the beginning, there have always been twelve members of the SSSPBHCB, men who were descendants of the Ishermans. The eldest member was born in a cave on January 1, 1707, and died December 31, 1842, in the same cave. He never saw the light of day. His mother was a slave girl who was a direct descendant of the Isherman. She gave birth to her only child at the age of sixteen. After the child was born, the mother lived the remainder of her life in the cave, caring for his every need. Like all Isherman women, she was considered unclean for the seven days of the month while she had a monthly discharge. During that period, she had to leave the cave, and she returned after her flow had stopped. She died in 1725 at the age of thirty-five. As she had learned to read and write, having been taught by her white mistress, she taught her son to read and write. He was a virgin all his life, he never saw white skin, and he lived to be one hundred thirty-five years old. He was the SSSPBHCB's first and last scribe. During his lifetime he transcribed three of America's most important documents into what The Twelve called The Black Man's Heavenly Decrees.

The youngest member of the SSSPBHCB was the runner. He was responsible for gathering all information from and delivering it to the members. Because, except for two, the eldest and the youngest, they lived on different farms, it was difficult for members to communicate with each other. At times, months and years would pass before they could make contact with each other. Sometimes they used music, drumming, and smoke signals, but for the most part, the runner had to deliver information and needed items to and from members by hand. The runner also retrieved items like messages, books and newspapers, ink and writing quills, parchment and paper, candles and coal oil, and food and water from the members. All of these had been stolen from their white master's libraries and kitchens.

The other ten members participated in decision-making, information-gathering, and systematic prayers and rituals. Thus the SSSPBHCB was an efficient underground organization that served the purpose and intent of The Twelve.

The SSSPBHCB was formed in 1787, the same year the U.S. Constitution was contrived. Its founding fathers were ten black ministers. For years, the ministers had observed the actions of the lawmakers as they drew up laws and changed them as white needs prescribed. What the lawmakers saw as the natural due process of law, and necessary amendment of laws—improvements for wealthy whites only—the members of SSSPBHCB saw as "a deliberate practice of chicanery operating at the efficiency of raw genius."

The following quote comes from the foreword of The Sacred Secret

Society for the Preservation of Black Heritage and Its Cultural Birthright 80-page handbook. It clearly states why the organization was formed and why their resolution positioned them as it did. It reads in part as follows:

> We, Ministers of the Sacred Secret Society for the Preservation of Black Heritage and Its Cultural Birthright, are hereby dutifully formed and ordained by Heaven for the sole purpose of preserving the Black Race, its culture, and heritage, as it has been earmarked for annihilation by certain members of the white race, that race of people who are inferior in the matters of expressing love for its fellow man.
>
> We, The Twelve who are The Talons of God, are scholarly men of an amiable sort. We are by no means deceived by the ingenious whites who periodically conjure abstract decrees which propagate laws—white lies—for the advancement of certain whites only, thereby castrating the Black Race of its ability to think, sterilizing the Black Race of its ability to believe in a loving God, thus depriving the Black Race of its strength and spirit and vigor to generate its own thoughts on matters that pertain to liberty, life, and justice.
>
> We The Twelve have seized this occasion, December 25, the year of our Lord 1778, to save not only the black man, our people, but the entire Black Race for generations to come from mental and emotional annihilation by the aforesaid white race.
>
> Our message and actions are empirically based on 147 years of study, which began in 1640, when Mr. John Punch, a black run-away slave was recaptured, along with two others who themselves were white, with the former being unjustly and more severely punished than his white companions, and personal observation and experiences that amount to more than 1070 years, the wisdom of Methuselah—which is the number of years that total the existence of the founding members of The Sacred Secret Society For The Preservation Of Black Heritage and Its Cultural Birthright—and words that have been extracted from decrees that document laws— white lies—that clearly states that the white lawmakers of

America and England are willing to do anything, stopping at nothing, to preserve their perceived power of control over the minds and lives of blacks with the easily heard, seen, and understood intent of controlling our bodies through the craftily devised institution called slavery—barbarism at its worst. Such whites have foxily created the aforesaid institution and decrees with an impure purpose, a debased hate for the Black Race, and selfishness of the most deadly kind, which murders the mind, body, and soul of black people without regard for the well-being of future generations, not even their own.

Those twelve ministers knew the white lawmakers would continue their pattern of making and changing laws without consideration for how such laws affected the lives of blacks, as they were intentionally created for the good of whites and purposely designed to destroy the minds of blacks and thus control their souls. They knew that a race war between blacks and whites was inevitable and imminent. They also knew that blacks did not have a knell of a chance to successfully fight against whites in an all-out war. That would have meant the wholesale slaughter of the black race, including Africa.

WAR OF THE GENES

THE TWELVE DID NOT WANT WHAT they believed about the developing race war to become a reality, yet they accepted the facts as they presented themselves and recognized the war as it loomed on the horizon and threatened to engulf the colonies. They decided to wage their own war, a war that would not be fought in open fields, as the whites were accustomed to. In order to keep whites unaware that a war had begun, their war, The Twelve's war was to be the greatest war any race of people has waged or ever would wage. It was the war that was to be fought in the white man's home, the war against his genes.

As stated on page 3 of The Sacred Secret Society for the Preservation of Black Heritage and Its Cultural Birthright Handbook, The Twelve believed the life of a race was in its blood, a belief they derived from their study of the Old Testament as it dealt with the issues of bloodline and blood sacrifices. It was their opinion that white hatred, as it was formulated against blacks, was in their blood—the blood of all whites and that the blood of whites could only be cleansed through what they called gene purification. Here, I quote from page 30:

> The Lord created the black man first, then the white. The icy hate which flows in through the veins of the white race is only thawed by it mixing with a warmer and suitably tamed blood.
>
> When our Lord created His white children, He placed them in a land that had a climate that was cold and damp, Europe's. In that climate it was difficult for the white race to keep warm; their inner climate, their blood, was as the outer climate, cold.
>
> In an attempt to warm themselves, whites became very active, adventuresome, warring. They roamed the whole of Europe, exploring her many frigid regions and waging war against each other. Their attempt to keep warm failed, for

they did not realize that their cold blood was indigenous of Europe and thus naturally the cause of their cold nature.

Nonetheless, their efforts to warm themselves continued, and that carried them into other lands and countries. But as these people were under a law of nature, they could not keep their cold blood warm by fighting each other, as they were the sons of God and were created with cold blood.

On the other hand, the Lord placed His black children in a hot climate, Africa. Thus, we are of the hot-blooded; a race that is filled with passion and love and a sense of family. Differing from our white brothers, we Africans are warm-blooded, and that causes us to be of a restful, peaceful, and serene nature.

Because our blood is warm, our people had no need to go tracking all over the world, trying to heat their blood, as did our white brothers. Food and game were plentiful in Africa, and as things were, her black children could lie in the hammock and eat from the vine.

If our white brothers, who are cold-blooded, are to experience warm blood, we are to conclude that their help must come from us, the warm-blooded Black Race.

Therefore, men of the Black Race are obliged, by natural law, God's law, and not man's, to systematically infiltrate the ranks of whites by impregnating their cold-blooded white woman with the warm-blooded seeds of their loins. Thus white women will give birth to warm-blooded children. And these will grow up to be men and women who will be less apt to roam the world making war with their dark-skinned brothers and sisters, pillaging their lands, desecrating their burial sites, despoiling their forests, and teaching beliefs about a god that they themselves do not respect or love, as this is the case with the whites who are still proselytizing the world.

In respect for their sacred position, the Black Race has been given by God black women who are to be kept pure in order that blacks do not become defiled through the white race's impurity, and as for the matter of black purity, it is of the utmost importance. Black women are not to be contaminated by white blood, the seed of white men, as the black men are chosen by our Lord to purify the blood of the white race with their black offspring.

Again, I state that the SSSPBHCB understood that blacks were not prepared to fight an all-out war with whites. As revealed in their handbook, they understood that whites waged wars for the said purpose of killing people and destroying their culture.

Pages 33 and 34 of The Sacred Secret Society for the Preservation of Black Heritage and Its Cultural Birthright show a chart that illustrates their strategy for what they call the Holy of Holy War.

Unlike the freemasons and other secret societies and brotherhoods, the SSSPBHCB was not open to a larger membership. The twelve men who made up the organization were all over the age of eighty, and obviously their major concern was experience and wisdom and not numbers. They did not seek recruits to be board members as page 3, paragraph three, of The Sacred Secret Society for the Preservation of Black Heritage and Its Cultural Birthright Handbook states:

> We, the generals of our Lord, are not dependent on the strength of numbers to win this war. The Holy Wars of the past were fought and won by the few men who had been chosen by God. Was it not the eight, Noah and his family, that God spared the world? Was it not the two, our father Abraham and his son Isaac that God used to build a nation? Did not our Lord God choose only twelve to war against those who opposed His Son, Jesus?
>
> We the aged and chosen are filled with the wisdom of life, are men who have been delivered from the uncontrolled desires of youth. We are generals of the Lord's army. Lest a man no longer seek the selfishness that travels with the young and inexperienced, such a man who is under four score years cannot participate as an active board member of this fraternity.
>
> We the chosen, descendants of the Isherman, are hereby solemnly sworn, and by ordination to dignify the Lord's purpose for His people, black people, to carry out His Righteous Judgment, as it is delivered by the learned, against

those who purport to destroy the Black mind.

Pages 57 through 80 of the handbook of The Sacred Secret Society for the Preservation of Black Heritage and Its Cultural Birthright give details of how The Twelve were to conduct their war of genetic annihilation of the white race. Since they were all over eighty years of age and were free from what they termed the four deadly sins of youth—immaturity, strong drink, desire for womanly companionship, and greed for money—they themselves could not conduct the act of genetic annihilation.

Their plan was to have younger black men impregnate white women. That had to be done without those young men realizing that their acts were for the greater purpose of purifying the white race and saving the world from white genocide. In order to get the young black men to carry out their plan, the handbook states:

> We, the twelve generals of our Lord's earthly army, hereby swear to adhere to the following decree as it was delivered to the presiding member of the Sacred Secret Society for the Preservation of Black Heritage and Its Cultural Birthright on the fifth day of December, the year of our Lord 1778: You shall pray. Daily, your prayers are to be offered unto the Lord as the burnt offering of the moving wind. The breath of your God shall come upon the young men and move them to life. They shall have relations with those women whose skin is of the clouds, barren of warm blood, as the Lord God formed in them icy blood. And the Lord God Jehovah shall give you the victory.
>
> You, our Lord's chosen, The Twelve, are to pray four times a day. Daily your prayers are to be faithfully offered and heard and answered.

You are to pray

1) The prayer after sunrise, 6:00 a.m., shall be the request for the Lord's breath to soften the hearts of the young men, as they are to become bulls in rut, and their great hunger will be for the cloud women.

2) The prayer at high noon, 12:00 noon, shall be the request for the Lord's breath to soften the hearts of the cloud women, as they shall become the heifers in heat, and their great passion shall be for the bull who shall consume them and stoke their loins' faint fire.

3) The prayer of evening, 6:00 p.m., shall be the request that the bull and heifer mate and that their mating increase over the years yet to come.

4) The prayer of night, 12:00 midnight, shall be the prayer of thanks that the Lord has given favor to the mating of the bull and heifer, as the veins of their sons and daughters are to flow with the warm blood of the fathers.

The Lord God Jehovah gives you the victory.

You are to fast

1) You must fast the fifth day of each week.
2) The whole of every third week of each fourth month.
3) You shall not eat meat.
4) You shall not drink strong drink.
5) You shall not have relations with women.
6) You shall not look upon the appearance of any man, woman, or child whose skin is as the clouds during fasting.

Obedience gives you the victory.

I have now revealed to you the name and purpose of the one organization that was established by blacks for the salvation of the black race and world unity. You are among the few individuals who know that such an organization existed during slavery and continues to operate today.

THE OLDEST MEMBER OF THE SSSPBHCB, the scribe, wrote the twelve handbooks and transcribed one copy each of the Constitution of the United States of America, the Declaration of Independence, and the Holy Bible.

It took one year for the scribe to transcribe the Constitution, as it was interpreted and changed to the Constitution of Black Americans.

The Twelve believed white's constitution was written by whites and for whites and was composed of laws that were written for whites only. It was structured in ways that the laws could be amended and improved for the wealthy whites as white needs warranted. The Twelve's version plainly states in the opening comments:

> The white lawmakers, those who wrote the Constitution of the United States of America, ingeniously designed that document of pseudo laws in ways that the laws can be changed as needs and time direct. Spurious architecture is its internal framework, with bogus limitations, as they, the laws, are not to be applied to the black race—people of color.
>
> Thus the black man's every turn will be thwarted before their efforts to demand equality can be completely formulated, hatched, and heard, before they are given active will on behalf of the black race. The Constitution keeps them in one form of slavery or another.
>
> Therefore the white lawmaker's ingenuity will always achieve their end, as they have desired it.

It took the scribe another year to transcribe the Declaration of Independence, as it was reinterpreted and changed to the Declaration of Independent Black Americans.

The Twelve believed the white Declaration belonged to the white race, and not the black race. They said it was plain to see that the white men who wrote it clearly stated that the whites of America were declaring themselves a free people who had won freedom from Britain and were thus independent of British control.

Mind you, the white men who had decided their voices were to be the voice of all Americans, blacks and whites and Indians, of this great land clearly presented in their Declaration of Independence twenty-seven printed facts that legally gave them a human and Godly right to rebel against the king of Great Britain because of his "history of repeated injuries and usurpations," which he plainly states "all having in direct object the establishment of an absolute Tyranny over these States." (These are direct quotes from that infamous document.)

The opening words of the Declaration of Independent Black Americans are as follows:

> WHEN, as in the Course of the lives and event of Black Americans, it becomes, and has become as such, that is of an absolute necessity for this People to dissolve the Political Atrocities, which have been brought on by White Americans, Lawmakers, and Slave Owners with their counterpart, another, Great-Britain, and to assume, among the Powers of the Earthly Life, the separate and equal Station to which the Laws of the Lord over Nature and of The GOD of Nature entitle them, a Decently Humane Respect to the Knowledge of Humanness presupposes that they, the People of Color, should declare the Causes which inspire them to Bring Whites to the Integration that will but Annihilate their Heinousness and Deviousness by way of Gene Warfare.
>
> We present God's Truths as the evidence that Black Americans are equal to White Americans in being teachable; aspiring to develop the natural abilities of intelligence, cognizance; and being superior in willingness to change and forgive; and that they are endowed by the Creator of All men.

The Holy Bible was transcribed in ten years and was interpreted and changed to The Wholly Bible of God. The Twelve believed that if the black race were to survive in the New World they needed an updated version of the white man's King James Bible. If not, the white race would continue to use their Bible as a weapon of destruction to destroy the souls of blacks (people of color) for all time to come.

The opening words of The Wholly Bible of God are as follows:

> We The Twelve recognize the Holy Bible as the Word of God, the Voice of God, as it was spoken to the men of old.
>
> That ancient recording of God's love affair and estrangement with a chosen people, an episode of enormous proportions, has led the faithful of the past and present into His open arms and protective bosom. Yet that fallen child whose skin color is of the clouds has taken liberty of deciphering its contents as he saw fit and proclaimed his interpretation to the unwitting masses for control. He has imposed his will upon the credulity of others through dishonesty, fraud, and trickery.
>
> The Twelve Generals are hereby elected by the Lord God to give the Holy Bible its truer meaning. Such meaning comes from the one and only transcribed copy of The Wholly Bible of God.
>
> The Wholly Bible of God was laid on the minds and hearts by the Spirit of God of The Generals of the Lord. Such a copy as this is therefore and is now and henceforth known as The Wholly Bible of God, the Lord's inspired and revised version of His Holy Words.
>
> These words, the Lord's present-day word, His Holy Words, apply to Abraham's seed and progeny—people of the black race—in this era of time and present condition of bleak affairs, slavery, for those children of the Holy Priesthood, men and women who will dutifully give unswerving dedication and complete loyalty to the task of giving present day meaning to an ancient map, the Lord's Holy Words.

I myself never became a member of the SSSPBCB, but I do own original handwritten copies of the handbook of The Sacred Secret Society for the Preservation of Black Heritage and Its Cultural Birthright, the Constitution of Black Americans, the Declaration of Independent Black Americans, and the only copy of The Wholly Bible of God. The day the scribe wrote the last letter in his last book, his autobiography, Black Man of the Cave, his eyesight failed him, and he lived the remainder of his life blind and in the cave.

How these books came into my possession is a story by itself. I shall not share that mysterious occurrence at this time, for it shall be saved for a later time, a very special occasion.

THE ROAD TO FREEDOM

A BLACK MAN KNOWING HOW to read during slavery was like a mule giving birth to a colt: a miracle. A slave having time to read, to say the least, was a greater miracle; it was a near impossibility. But I made ample time to do just that, read. I used every waking moment I could tear from my demanding responsibilities to read whatever book lay about. I read every printed word as I would see them here and there. I especially read and reread the worn book I kept from the view of everyone.

The worn book I speak of was given to me in the year of 1829 by Mrs. Beulah Sandridge, the solemn wife of Ol' Captain Vincent B. Sandridge. That kind and gentle lady, God bless her soul, gave me two of the most valuable keys any man, black or white, could have received during the turbulent times of slavery. Those keys were teaching me to read and write. The keys were two earthly instruments that opened certain doors that were locked to blacks, doors on the path of a slave's journey to true freedom.

Do not think Ol' Captain Sandridge favored such going on. She and I had a difficult time when it came to my lessons, but we managed to pull things off. Ol' Captain Sandridge loved drinking and gambling more than eating and sleeping. In an attempt to satisfy his enslaving need to possess more than he could use in a lifetime, and in his need to prevail over others, he spent most evenings away from home, going from one gambling house to another. While he made his rounds, Mrs. Beulah took me into the parlor and locked the doors, preventing the house slaves from walking in unannounced. There she gave me reading and writing lessons. She taught me to write my letters and numbers on a slate board she kept hidden under a pillow on the sofa. My reading lessons were from the first reader.

One night while Mrs. Beulah and I were having lessons, Ol' Captain Sandridge came home earlier than his usual time. A fight had broken out at a gambling house down in Deadman's Hollow, where Mr. Tommy Moon had shot Mr. Jack Dobson in the chest, and his brother, Frank Dobson, in the back for cheating at cards. Mr. Jack Dobson died the next day, and his brother, Frank, was paralyzed from the neck down.

When Ol' Captain Sandridge arrived home, he discovered the parlor doors were locked. And that angered him. He yelled at Mrs. Beulah and pounded on the doors with his fists. She pushed me behind the draperies, but did not open the doors soon enough. In his drunken stupor his anger boiled over into his feet, and he kicked the doors like a madman. I peeked from behind the draperies and saw the doors fly off their hinges. One spun to the left and fell over a chair, and the other spun to the right and fell on the end of a table, and flipped it into the air. The table flew over Mrs. Beulah's head, slammed against the wall, and landed on its top with its legs jutting up toward the ceiling. Two massive paintings, one of the old Captain's father, the other of his grandfather, dropped off the wall, crashed forward, and were impaled on the table's legs. And he became irate.

Ol' Captain Sandridge cursed and accused Mrs. Beulah of entertaining another man. He was so drunk that after he had slapped her around and punched her to her knees, he fell full-face against the hardwood floor. His head bounced like a child's water-filled balloon, and then lay to the left side.

I stepped from behind the curtains and ran to the door. I stopped and looked back. Mrs. Beulah took hold of the arm of the sofa, pulled herself up. She staggered a bit and removed something from beneath a cushion. She staggered toward me, stopped, and stood astraddle of Ol' Captain Sandridge. She held the object to her breast. Her swollen eyes and bloody nose and mouth caused her to look like one of the creatures from a cheep Horrors of The Night book. She lowered the object to her side, stepped over Old Captain Sandridge without looking down, and came towards me. I was frightened.

Mrs. Beulah stopped within a hand's reach of me and did the oddest thing. She kneeled at my feet and said, "I've had my eyes on you for some time now. You're not like the other darkies. I've noticed how you study things when you're in the big house. The others, their eyes are always pointed at the floor. You look at things with a familiarity. Here, take this," she said and shoved the object into my hands, "Maybe you can use it."

Fear rose from my stomach and paralyzed my tongue. My feet were stuck to the floor, my body frozen in the present limits of slavery, but my mind awakened to the future. Thoughts of the possibilities, of what could be, filled me with joy. Then my emotions pushed me back a step or two. Uncertain of what to do, I leaned forward again. Her eyes widened, and she winced and reeled back. I stepped back. I looked down at my hands. The thing she had shoved into my hands was a book. I held a book that was the color of a thousand Washington apples, the brightest red, the most beautiful book I had ever laid eyes on. Its pages whispered, "Nimrod. Nimrod." And my innards screamed, "Freedom! Freedom!" Those two words, Nimrod and freedom, rang in my ears like new church bells.

"This book will help you, Nimrod," she said. "Never let anyone know you have it. Its words were written more than three hundred years ago, but its message is still true today. I discovered the Red Book a few years ago. If I had read it and lived by it, things might be different for me today. But who knows if what I am saying is so? Maybe God.

"But, anyway, it's too late for me. You're young, honest, and hard working." She paused. "For some reason, you seem to be different from the other darkies. I think you may have a date with destiny, one you won't be able to shake, no matter how hard you try. If you study the Red Book and do what it tells you, you just might do some important things for your people." She paused again and then continued, "Why am I babbling like this? Just read the damn book."

Mrs. Beulah turned, and walked from the room. The sound of sniffling trailed behind her.

I believe Mrs. Beulah's kindness came from a sincere and loving heart. Yet it was her misfortune to have been married to Ol' Captain Sandridge, just as it was his great fortune that she had married him. I always thought it strange that he never seemed to remember anything about the nights of the beatings. As far as I knew, when he came to his senses, he never asked Mrs. Beulah about the black and blue bruises that landscaped her pale face, a face that was framed by flaming red hair.

As Papa-horse would say, "Time has a way of catching up with those who hurt others. Even when they think they've slipped past God, Miss Time always catches them by the seat of the britches." And he was always right.

Time did catch up with Ol' Captain Sandridge. One night after he had gambled the whole day at Miss Lucy's gambling house, he decided to quit and head home. While playing blackjack with Ol' Captain Sandridge, the Gulley Boys, the meanest men in the county, lost money and land to him. They wanted to play one more hand with an IOU, but he refused their request. After their efforts to bully Ol' Captain Sandridge into playing another game failed, they left and waited for a more suitable opportunity to even the score.

The talk was, Ol' Captain Sandridge left Miss Lucy's house and stopped in the woods to take a piss. The Gulley Boys seized this opportunity to regain their losses. They jumped Ol' Captain Sandridge and beat him terribly, and laid him up for six months.

The house slaves said Ol' Captain Sandridge was unconscious the first week. The second week he talked out of his mind. He said things about his father, Colonel Wallace Brigade Sandridge, and cowered in retreat pleading for mercy. The third week he screamed all night about being attacked by blacks with red eyes. He screamed for them to stop beating him. And the fourth week he came to his senses a different man. He never took another drink of whiskey, he talked to his wife and children instead of yelling, and he was kind to his slaves. It was even said from that time on he gave his slaves the day off on the Fourth of July and Christmas. There were rumors that he had told his slaves that he would free them before he died, but they never saw that freedom.

As usual, Papa-horse was right when he had said, "With most folks, a man's bad outlives his good. People are slow to forgive, if ever." The whites who knew Ol' Captain Sandridge before he was beaten never accepted him after he became a changed man, though the old slaves who slaved under his charge said his changes were genuine.

Ol' Captain Sandridge was bedridden for the six months. After he died, the farm went to Mrs. Beulah. But she was in no way capable of operating the farm, and turned things over to the youngest son, Master William Sandridge. He was the only child to attend college, and the only son who did not become enslaved to whiskey.

While Master William Sandridge did not enslave my body in chains, the fetters of slavery held me captive as he proclaimed himself to be my master. Yet it was clear for me to see through his actions that his mind and heart, as was the case with all slave owners, did not have impunity to being enslaved to something. My belief was slave owners themselves were enslaved to different unseen masters, though they were unaware of their own plight. I shall demonstrate shortly through the examination of several well known white men that what I say is true. Thus freedom could not come to blacks and poor whites by way of those men's needy hands.

When Mrs. Beulah gave me the Red Book, I was just learning to read, or call words as it were. I read from the Red Book every night, and within a month my reading skills and comprehension had greatly increased. When I read from that book, I felt I was being ushered through the portals of opportunity, down the halls of fate, and into the spacious chambers of freedom.

Reading filled my mind with words. Words gave sound and expression to my thoughts, feelings, and ideas. Reading provided my mind with knowledge. Knowledge increased my thinking ability. My thinking ability increased my understanding, and understanding became my constant companion.

Reading the books of the white man gave me my first taste of freedom. Whenever I would read, the shackles of ignorance fell from my mind, down around my feet, and soon disappeared. The knowledge I fed my mind caused it to roam the north, south, east, and west without a bloody whip licking at my back. My ravenous appetite for reading and love of knowledge gave me insight into the anatomies of animals, plants, and man. I learned to strip the white man's world of its trappings of illusion.

Through reading, I traversed the open seas and visited the countrysides of Europe. I walked into the homes and sat in the studies and looked over the shoulder of men such as Homer, Socrates, Sir Thomas Overbury, William Shakespeare, John Donne, John Locke, Washington Irving, Phillis Wheatley, and one of my all time favorites, Gerhard Dorn, the alchemist, and others.

There were many alchemists who looked upon alchemy as a scientific way of changing matter into other forms, like changing certain minerals into gold. But according to Mr. Dorn, as I understood his life's work, his interest was to use alchemy to discover transmutation. He believed people could develop their psychological and spiritual faculties, gain inner freedom, and live a life that was not to be touched by the human frailties that plague all men. He was of the notion that one's mental forces are more important than their material possessions. Reading him, I came to share his opinion that the transmutation of one's mental-force meant a man's essential nature could be changed to a higher form, which would allow him to live the mystical life that is housed in his heart, mind, and soul without his having to have thoughts or put forth efforts to do so. Not only is such a thing possible, but it takes place naturally, to some degree, for all people whether they know it or not.

As I understood things Mr. Dorn believed, and I am of the opinion that he was right, the legends about the philosopher's stone was a tale that was supposed to lead spiritual initiates into an understanding of how to use their mental forces for the good of mankind. And as I read about him I found myself there in the room beside him, and listened as he mumbled to himself, and found that enlightening. He spoke about Hermes Trismegistus, who was the founding father of astrology and the discoverer of alchemy. He spoke of how the ancient Egyptian people believed Hermes was a god, whom they called Thoth, the scribe of the gods who was the great-great, the greatest-great, the fount of wisdom. The people of Greece also made him a god.

I was drawn especially to Mr. Dorn's works, as they were similar to the African Isherman's teachings and way of life. The Ishermans, like Hermes, did not believe in casting pearls before swine. They held their teachings as sacred, spirit-filled secrets. According to them, swine were any group of individuals who were organized for the purpose of controlling God's less fortunate. And that was the case with white Christians and their churches, with America's lawmakers, and with African tribal leaders: those who sold their black brothers and sisters into slavery. As white Christians and their churches used religion and the Holy Bible to conquer countries and nations, the Ishermans believed the white man's churches would someday crumble from within. The aftermath would leave them wrestling with their ingrained devilish beliefs and a strong desire for the use of African's love-filled mystical knowledge.

My most recent studies led me to visit the office of the Jewish professor, Dr. Sigmund Freud. In my opinion, he too was leading people to the inner freedom that all men thirst and hunger for.

Through his books, Three Essays on the Theory of Sexuality, The Interpretation of Dreams, and The Psychopathology of Everyday Life, I discovered that he, too, had read Mr. Gerhard Dorn's work and broadened its meaning. Reading those men's books and visiting them through my imagination, I was armed with the one power wealthy whites, slave owners, and lawmakers did not want me to have: knowledge—book power.

Books provided me with the new understanding and insights that permitted me to dissect the white mind and its emotional temperament. Papa-horse's constant teachings about the importance of getting the emotions under control and reading, especially the works of Mr. Dorn and Professor Freud, awakened me to the fact that we blacks had to first understand what whites believed and the way they thought if we were to deal with them successfully. Not only did Master Sandridge have his own medical books and other books, he also received his mother's extensive library after she passed. As I grew older and wiser, it became easier for me to take books from his library to read and study without his knowing.

As it was common for slaves to steal food from the garden, orchard, smokehouse, and kitchen, so did I steal books from the library. I read them at night and took them to the field during the day. Whenever we were going to work a new area, I went out the night before and found a perfect hiding place for the book I was reading. During the day, when I had to relieve myself, I went into the woods where the book was hidden and read from it. I went so frequently, just to read, that the other slaves made fun of me, saying, "Nimrod's bladder's bad, and he gots the fluxes. Must be 'specting." All in all, I devoured every book my master owned, some 2,054 books I would say. And I returned each one, unscathed.

Because of the teachings I received from Papa-horse and my natural inclination to use herbs, I was drawn to Mr. Dorn's ideas and writings about the healing powers of plants. On one occasion, as I read his words, my mind left my body and traveled back to the 1500s. I stood in his laboratory and watched him work. I was there when he translated the ten treatises of Paracelsus and watched as he added his own remarks. I watched as he built the fire beneath the furnace to heat the elements in the holding vessel. I was there when he wrote

Chemical Philosophy (Theatrum Chemicum, Vols. I and II). Here I quote Mr. Dorn's opening words, and thus derived my complete understanding of the white mind:

> Chemical philosophy teaches the latent forms of things according to their truth and not according to their appearance. Access to this chemical philosophy is double, namely through opinion and experiment. Through opinion you form an idea of what is to be investigated, and the experiment is the verification of the former.

Book knowledge provided me with facts, and Mr. Dorn's work gave me permission to express my opinions and the right to experiment with whites. Personal experience provided a solid foundation for the facts, opinions, and experiments to stand on. My opinions, experiences, and experiments gave me insight into the spiritual aspects of both black and white men, opening the door of understanding and allowing me to deal with my black and white brothers.

Spiritual insight raised my thinking above the harsh realities of slavery. From that heavenly view, I was permitted to peer into the heads of the wealthy whites and slave owners, to see their souls and desires as they were formed and expressed internally. I saw that their motives were hitched to a mule team of hatred for blacks, greed for money, uncontrollable desire for sex, and a relentless need to be in the power position of all situations. They were driven to fill their wagons with more goods than they needed. Their mind was never satisfied with the knowledge they had. They always needed more. They could not control their desire to conquer the things around them and possess things they were not entitled to own, like land and people. Like hogs, they consumed whatever and whoever was in sight. Thus their greed created an emotional indigestion that kept them spiritually sick. As they took in more knowledge than they knew how to handle, they turned this country into a scary and dangerous place to live, filled with racist groups, overly religious groups, oppressive government, and war machines that would one day be capable of harming all races the world over. Reading led me to the ultimate freedom.

BOOK POWER

AFTER MRS. BEULAH'S DEATH, Master Sandridge took total control of the Sandridge farm. Her extensive library remained in the big house under his care. She knew he loved books and would take care of hers, and she gave him specific instructions on how to care for them. She told him, "Never allow anyone other than Tessie to clean and dust in the library. And make sure she moves the books from one shelf to another every two weeks. Books like to be moved, you know."

The day Mrs. Beulah died her children were out and about, doing things that pertained to the farm. As she lay dying, she sent Tessie to the field to get me. I walked into the bedroom and without hesitating she said, "Here, Nimrod, help me from the bed. I want to go to the library. . . son." I lifted her and held her as she walked slowly.

"I want to be with them," she said. "They're my only children now. They've never abandoned me. Always here when I need them."

"Who are you talking about, Mrs. Beulah?" I asked.

"Talking about my babies, Nimrod. Look. See them? They're on the shelves, all around. When I'm here in the library, they surround me with good feelings and thoughts. I live here."

I sat her in her favorite chair at the window, and tied the gold draperies back. The sun flooded the room with its summer warmth. She took a deep breath, and the burgundy chair's plush padding enfolded her thin body.

She looked up at me and said, "Sit. Pull that chair up. Sit close. I know what you've been doing, Nimrod. I know you've been taking my babies. My books. You've been reading them at night and in the field during the day when you're supposed to be taking care of work. The very first time you took one of my books, I knew it. I had ol' Tessie watching and following you. She told me everything. But I must say, you always took special care of them. You and William were the only ones that gave them love, like me. When we love books, they love us back. They give us life. That's all," she said, "you go on back to work now."

I walked to the door, turned, and looked back.

"No need for that," she said. "Nimrod . . . just don't ever let William know you've been taking the books. Stealing knowledge ... now go on. Get back to work."

Master William found Mrs. Beulah that afternoon, sitting dead in her chair with three books in her lap and surrounded by hundreds of books. She died with her children, her babies, her books.

Master Sandridge had his mother's library and his own, too. A grand library. He also loved reading the newspaper, and there were three he frequently read and kept next to his favorite chair. Whenever I was in the big house, and no one was around, I read from his books and the newspapers. One newspaper was The Liberator, a freedom paper. It was my favorite, a newspaper that was written by a Mr. William Lloyd Garrison, an abolitionist who lived up north.

Mr. Garrison filled the pages of The Liberator with a lot of preaching about the emancipation of blacks and their right to be free. But his emotional, save-the-world jargon did not convince me that his religious fervor led him to view blacks as being equal to whites. When I read The Liberator, I felt something of great importance was missing. His concern for the black man's freedom seemed devoid of compassion. Because of my dealings with Ol' Captain Sandridge and some other whites, I felt that Mr. Garrison's words and motives were less than virtuous and based on his personal pain and guilt. I had my reasons for judging him as I did, and I will now present this matter in the clearest possible fashion and thus present a free white man who was not free.

As I quote here, Mr. Garrison's warning to the slave owners was, "God in his time not long delayed would revenge the genocide they were committing against blacks. That God, in his time would cause the land to be plagued in blood." I felt Mr. Garrison spoke those emotional laden words out of religious fear of a god who was Himself in pain and angered by puny men.

Papa-horse said, "The man who crows about his religion like a rooster on a fence post is to be watched more than he's to be listened to."

Mr. Garrison stated in The Liberator that he was, "raised up as a child under slave-like poverty." I well understood this from personal experience. I was a slave, but slave-like-poverty and the poverty of a slave were two different animals.

For Mr. Garrison to state that his living conditions were slave-like can be compared to a wealthy black man saying, "I'm now equal to whites." His words insulted me, not because he was white, but because he used blacks and the issue of slavery as disguises to cover his self-righteousness and his self-imposed poverty, to strike out at the wealthy whites and slave owners. My opinion was that his need to help blacks was motivated by his need to soothe his guilty conscience with the notion, "I'm helping the poor black man."

And please do not think that what I am saying applies to all whites who desire to help blacks. By no means am I saying that. That would be like saying, "All blacks are loving and kind to each other." This is not true. Both black and white races are in need of understanding and help of some sort. But I do say it was obvious to me that Mr. Garrison lived in poverty because he lacked the initiative to educate himself in the ways of making money. Otherwise, had he gotten his mind and ass in gear, his living conditions would have been different!

Did Mr. Garrison not realize that he was a white man who had all the rights and privileges that were afforded to whites? His brand of poverty was different from the poverty that slaves experienced. A slave's poverty was based on racism and zero opportunities. The kind of poverty Garrison suffered could not, per se, have caused him, or any white person, to know the poverty we blacks knew. I say he had no right to speak on and compare his situation to the matter of slave-like poverty. He was out of line when he implied that his experience gave him insight into the plight of the black slave. His slave-like poverty was lived on a street that had a crossroad of opportunity. Our slave poverty was lived on a road that ended at a cliff of racial discrimination and zero opportunity. Not only did we suffer from material poverty, we also suffered at the hands of whites that hated us because of their confusion about the most basic law of the Bible: "Love God and thy neighbor as thyself."

Common sense and plain thinking told me that material poverty could not make Mr. Garrison receive blacks as his equal any more than his being white made him a free man. Mr. Garrison, like most whites, was a slave himself. Only his slavery was a different kind. I say that Mr. Garrison was enslaved by his poverty thinking and self-pity.

And once more, I do not want what I present to smack of racial intolerance, nor be misunderstood when it comes to the issues of race relations, so I shall give several quotes from Mr. Garrison's work that show his attempts—failed attempts, in my opinion—to show himself to be fair and just in matters of black and white equality. Thus I expose the emotional grief and personal pain behind each of his grievances.

The concept I now present may be difficult for you to accept, and that I well understand. When Papa-horse first presented the notion that whites themselves were slaves during slavery, I thought that was an outlandish impossibility. Nonetheless, I calmed myself, opened my mind, and Time carried me to a place of readiness. And it was then that I was prepared to listen and brought that new insight into focus.

Being ready to listen to ideas that were not my own has been a most difficult thing for me to do. I believe this is true for most people. It took Time to make me ready to come to the conclusion that Papa-horse was right. Today I can see that wealthy whites and slave owners were themselves slaves to many ills. And I do believe this point will become clearer to you as my story develops. For it will show the clear distinction between the two freedoms and also shed light on the matter of whites being enslaved. When Papa-horse said, "It takes stories to live, and stories can create the man," he spoke a truth.

Honesty and fairness move me to admit that there were whites who spoke out against the enslavement of blacks because they loved their black brothers. They were the individuals who knew how to love people. I know this to be true because I have had white friends since childhood. Yet I continued with my stand. I know in my spirit that Mr. Garrison's religious fervor came not from a heart that was filled with love for blacks but from a mind that was filled with an unhealthy fear about God's coming wrath against sinners, his painful upbringing, and personal guilt.

Please permit me to explain further.

Here I quote Mr. Garrison, who wrote, "While I was a child, my mother first made me aware that slavery was wrong, pointing out that it violated the very spirit of Christianity." I note here that he says that slavery violates the spirit of Christianity. And I say that slavery was wrong because it caused whites to deal with their black brothers in ways that were inhumane and unloving. I say slavery was wrong because it caused whites to look on their black brothers as being less than their animals. I say slavery was wrong because it caused whites to live as if they themselves were godly and their black brothers as if they were devils that deserved to be punished without mercy. I say slavery was wrong because it was a way for whites to rape blacks of their fundamental rights to live like human beings. Thus, I say that slavery violated the spirit of Christianity, the spirit of Hinduism, the spirit of Buddhism, and the spirit of any one of the thousands of religious organizations ("Isms") and their canons. Slavery was the one institution that allowed the slavers to act as gods and swat at the enslaved as if they were gnats.

Did Mr. Garrison indicate that slavery was wrong because he loved his black brothers who were equal to him and his white brothers? No. Not once.

I say that if any man approaches the immoral issue of slavery, whites lording it over blacks, on the basis of the spirit of Christianity, he leaves his heart out of the matter. Besides, was it not Christians who enslaved blacks, and not heathens? If one is to speak out against the slavers and their savage acts, of enslaving others, I say let it come from a heart that knows love and not from a head that is faintly familiar with a few eccentric facts.

Please allow me to put it this way. In the beginning, when the American Paradise was founded, Christian whites proselytized blacks, as they did the Indians and people the world over. At that time, these proselytizing Christians were living under English law. So were black Christians. They were to receive the same privileges granted to white Christians, which meant they could be indentured servants but not slaves. As I so clearly pointed out earlier, wealthy white Christians saw progressive blacks emerging from their indentured servitude and acquiring their own land and servants. It was then that they passed the laws that stated that only nonwhites could be slaves. Their trickery kept us from owning land and enjoying the amenities offered to white Christians.

Need I say more about their brand of Christianity?

Mr. Garrison went on to write, "After my father left us, never to return, we suffered from searing, slave-like poverty." Here he tells us his father, a white man, left him and his family in slave-like poverty.

I tell you, Mr. Garrison was speaking of slave-like poverty because of the personal pain created by his experience of fatherly abandonment. Mind you, I sympathized with Mr. Garrison, as I am sure that his having to grow up without a father was painful. I know this, for I never knew my father or my mother. But what Mr. Garrison, like all slaves, needed was more than my sympathy; he needed true freedom.

Mr. Garrison wrote, "Oh, the rottenness of Christendom! I am forced to believe, that, as it respects the greater portion of professing Christians in this land, Christ had died in vain. The orthodox churches are a disgrace to Christianity, heathenish, filled with apologies for sin and sinners of the worst sort, predominately corrupt and servile, connivers with slaveholders. The religion preached and practiced in this country is an oath-taking, war-making, man-enslaving religion, and I want nothing more to do with it. I advocate a 'Come Outer' stance and urge my fellow abolitionists to renounce all churches and all government because they are corrupt and sinful to the core. All must be dashed to pieces."

Although I agree with much of what Mr. Garrison wrote, I also say that he was moved by the emotionalism that sprang from his personal pain.

I ask you to note that Mr. Garrison's comment on his "slave-like poverty" was simply an afterthought that fell from a narrow fissure in his mind. It came from the pent-up revenging anger that he held against his father, the wealthy, and his fellow Christians, even though he himself was part and parcel of Christendom and her churches.

My opinion is that Mr. Garrison's personal pain was the night oil that spurred his religious intensity and highly wrought emotions of emotionalism. Thus his anger-based beliefs rallied a cause and he struck out against religion and government, the twin beasts that failed to rescue him from a life that was devoid of the loving care and protection of a father. His proneness to surrender to that sort of temperament caused him to blame his father, the church, wealthy whites, slave owners, and the government for his unhappiness. His accusing and blaming nature led him to relieve himself of his personal pain and guilt by attacking others.

Papa-horse said, "When a man closes his eyes to his pain and guilt, he sees it in others." I say our Mr. Garrison's concern for blacks grew out of the pain of his abandonment and the white-race's guilt.

Mr. Garrison's religious prejudices and self-righteous piousness come through the pages of The Liberator, where he wrote, "We would use the north's superior moral power to compel southern slave owners to reform themselves and free the slaves."

Well, I say, the brilliance of his personal "northern superior morals" outshone the sun when he dealt with a Mr. Frederick Douglass in a less than honorable way. (I intend to expound on this matter shortly.)

Papa-horse said, "Don't only listen with your ears. Listen with your ears, your mind, and your heart." What he meant was, first, hear a man's words with your ears, next, understand the words with your mind, and, third, feel the meaning of the words with your heart. This is what I did with Mr. Garrison's words.

Why am I railing against our dear Mr. Garrison?

Well I tell you that my life as a slave taught me to examine the motives of all men, blacks and whites, especially those who want to help. If their motives were honorable, I accepted their help wholeheartedly, but if their motives were otherwise, I resisted them with the stubbornness of a bull. Mr. Garrison was just one white man who had ulterior motives when helping slaves. I know this, for I have dealt with many of them and have been dutifully burned by their undisclosed practices. On the other hand I remind you there were also whites like Mrs. Beulah, a white woman, who taught me to read, write, and count. She gave me my first book, the Red Book, which set me on a path that leads to truth and God, a journey to true freedom. This is the journey you must take if you are to be happy and live in peace. The Red Book opened doors I did not know existed, doors that can never be closed by slavery or death.

The day Mrs. Beulah gave me the Red Book, I wanted to grab her and squeeze her like a son hugging his mother on Christmas morning. I am forever indebted to that kind, loving, and generous lady.

Papa-horse taught me that I should not judge others, that judging should be replaced with what he called reading the signs. He taught me to ask the five most important questions a man can ask: the what, when, where, how, and why of life. Some of these questions are: What is the meaning of this thing? How will this affect me today and tomorrow? Where will this lead me? When will this harm me or benefit me? Why is this person doing what they are doing and saying what they are saying? He said, "You can never ask a question and not get an answer. If you ask questions about the meaning of a thing you'll get an answer and gain understanding. There's meaning in everything that happens. Ask questions: questions lead to answers, answers to understanding, and understanding leads to true freedom. And that's a law of life, my boy." Therefore, how could I not have examined Mr. Garrison's words and motives?

Now, I shall get back to our Mr. Garrison. In time, my feelings about Mr. Garrison's motivation were proved correct. I say what I am saying because he once had a serious altercation with the one man, a black man, who had helped him the most, the run-away slave Mr. Frederick Douglass. It was at that time that he showed his true color. Before I go any further I must state as plainly as I can, I am not saying that Mr. Garrison was any more vile or evil than any other man; I am saying that he was like all men at that time, and we all needed to be set free from our slavery to our personal demons. My argument is about his demons and the fact that whites were not free because they were white, had material wealth, or wrote laws. (I shall further show that the lawmakers were slaves too.)

As things were, Mr. Douglass worked with Mr. Garrison in Rochester, New York. After some time had passed, Mr. Douglass wanted to start his own black newspaper. Being the noble and honorable man he was, Mr. Douglass talked to Mr. Garrison about his plans for owning his own paper. Mr. Garrison promptly told him, "They (meaning blacks) already have a newspaper, The Liberator."

Mr. Douglass responded by saying, "I have in mind a paper that will be owned and operated by a black man. That way, whites will see that blacks are intelligent enough to successfully operate their own businesses."

Mr. Garrison, not wanting Mr. Douglass to proceed with his idea, prevailed against him and was successful, as Mr. Douglass was persuaded not to start the paper at that time. Thus Garrison prevented that former slave, who had helped him, from performing as his equal and becoming a businessman who could think for himself and wanted to carve his own purpose out of his life.

Why, I ask, would Mr. Garrison stand in the way of Mr. Douglass starting his own newspaper? I say the answer is quite obvious. Mr.

Garrison was looking out for his own best interests, and not those of Mr. Douglass and the slaves he purportedly wanted to help. Mind you, Mr. Garrison not only grew up in poverty, but as a young man in his twenties and the proprietor of The Liberator, he was still living below the means of wealthy whites. In their eyes, he was poor white trash. I propose an additional point in the form of a question: is it possible that he refused to help Mr. Douglass because every three out of four readers of The Liberator were black?

I answer with a resounding yes. Indeed that was a factor. Since blacks were the majority of Mr. Garrison's readers, his financial difficulties would have been compounded if he had lost one reader to Mr. Douglass's newspaper.

As God would have such matters to work out, Mr. Douglass later began his own newspaper, The North Star. And true to his nature of opposing those who did not support his sentiments, Mr. Garrison turned against Mr. Douglass. (Mr. Garrison was not a bad man or an evil man. Like all men during the time of slavery, he was a confused man.) In time, The North Star and its black founder became a testimonial of success. I never read The North Star, but I heard it was similar to The Liberator in that it was composed of articles written about the hard-working blacks and whites who struggled to free the slaves. Besides, reading The Liberator gave me more than enough reading about the concerns of the first freedom, which is paper freedom. What I needed to read about most was true-freedom. That came from the Bible and the Red Book.

Although Master Sandridge did not dare keep such business as The North Star in the big house, there were occasions when I heard him talk to Mrs. Beulah about Mr. Douglass and his paper.

And as for problems, The Liberator created enough problems for Master Sandridge, as neighboring farmers thought it was a gross sin for him, a Southern gentleman, to read such a paper. But he was the best doctor in those parts (in fact, the only doctor), so they left him alone. I must admit that I was puzzled why he, a slave owner, read The Liberator. As time passed, my question was satisfactorily answered.

Papa-horse was always right. He taught me that true freedom could not come from The Liberator, The North Star, or any signature of the most powerful man in America, the president. "None of that sort of foolishness will free you boy," he said, "nor can any man. Not even the president. Freedom, true freedom, comes from the inside of a man."

As I said, it took time, but I learned that Master Sandridge and other whites was just as much a slave as I was. They were also in bondage as were the blacks they held as slaves. Whites were in no position to grant freedom to blacks. Most of them, like most blacks, had no clue of what the word "freedom" truly meant. Thus, to believe a signature, on paper, would give freedom to blacks was absurd.

The word "freedom" held no real power, no clear meaning for the whites that made the laws that had to do with freedom; they made them and broke them when matters suited their interests. The lawmakers were the individuals who made things difficult for blacks and poor whites.

Papa-horse said, "Men can't write laws that give freedom. Slaves can't give freedom to slaves. Those who lead the people to believe that they can, their words are like vapor rising from warm manure on a cold day."

THE TRUTHFULNESS OF PAPA-HORSE'S WORDS came true. Whites being slaves was proven true in 1865 when the Civil War—the war that caused whites to kill whites, brothers to kill brothers—ended. The war lasted four years and claimed over 800,000 lives. Their history (his-story) books do not say much about it, but white men raped and killed white women and killed white children. They were like farmers at hog-slaughtering time. They killed each other without remorse. Southern slavery and Northern inequality caused white Republicans to fight white Democrats. Northern and Southern whites continued to kill each other after the war had ended and on into the heart of Reconstruction.

In 1865, states of the South passed black codes, and, as Mr. Garrison stated in The Liberator, "This was a way of keeping former slaves in subservient positions." In cornbread talk, there were Southern and Northern whites that did not want freed-slaves to be free. But then again, how could we slaves expect them to give us what they themselves did not have, freedom?

Before President Lincoln signed those Proclamation papers in 1863, the word that buzzed among the slaves on the Sandridge farm was, "The freedom is a-comin'." It caused everyone's heart to swell with a joy that had never been experienced.

During that time Papa-horse told me, "Nimrod, listen. Listen to what I'm telling you. Even if the president signs those papers, slaves won't get what they're searching for, nor what they need, which is true freedom."

"How do you know?" I asked.

"I have that feeling that rises from the depths of the soul," he answered. "When the president signs those papers, slaves will go from being just slaves to being just freed slaves. Whites can't give you the freedom you want, son. Someday they'll be forced to give you the privileges they enjoy, but they'll never give you true freedom. Nimrod, you must understand the difference between privileges and freedom, between paper freedom and true freedom."

"But those privileges will be a beginning," I said, "and this time you might be wrong!"

"You know, Nimrod, you're right. That'll be a start. I wish my feelings were wrong. But I do have reasons to speak as I do. Listen to this and you'll understand what I mean."

Papa-horse then proceeded to tell me about the time he stood on a ridge that overlooked an open field. He watched as whites from the North and whites from the South killed each other. The story he told me about the Civil War was horrifying. He said it went like this:

————

IT WAS A DREARY DAY. A mass of gray clouds had squatted near the earth, hiding the blue sky and the sun from view. The naked trees swayed in the cold breeze. The air reeked of impending death.

I had left the Johnson farm and was returning to the Sandridge farm, a pleasant walk. My attention was not on the narrow path. The silence became filled with the awful sound of repeating gunfire.

I lay on the ground, and crawled in the direction of the noise. The closer I got, the louder the gunfire, cannon explosions, and screams became. I reached the edge of the ridge and there they were, hundreds and hundreds of men and boys in an open field, massacring each other. It was a frightful sight to behold.

No one hid behind trees. They were squared off in the field, face-to-face, shooting each other at will. I lay there and watched the most beastly sight one could ever witness, the wholesale slaughter of human beings on a grand scale. Those men and boys took aim with their long rifles, squeezed the triggers, and fire and smoke leaped out. Lead balls whistled in the air. When the hot lead bullets made contact with their targets, the enemy heads and body parts exploded. It was butchery without mercy. Men and boys were felled like saplings hit by the sharp ax. Running horses clumsily stumbled and fell to the ground, and became thrashing piles of muscles. The air was filled with a yellowish cloud. It rose toward heaven. The foul smell of gun smoke hugged the land like poisonous water. The screams of men and horses were muffled by the loud cry of angry guns and cannons. The men on the front row kneeled and fired their rifles. When they reloaded, the second row fired and did the same. Then the third row, and so it went, an action that was repeated again and again. Cannon balls rained from the sky and ripped through whatever stood in their path. Some landed on the blood-soaked ground and tossed men and horses into the air as a reaper tosses dry hay into the wind. The bloodbath left man and beast lying in red puddles.

From early morning, through the night, and well into the next day, the carnage continued. Men slaughtered men without concern. The butchery was so great that those who were still alive couldn't stand, walk, or run without stepping on the dead bodies of enemies, neighbors, cousins, friends, brothers, and sons.

———

PAPA-HORSE'S STORY PROVED that his words of wisdom were correct, and he was right again. Whites could not give blacks what they did not have, and that was freedom. Those civilized whites had left their children, wives, and parents to go off and war against other civilized whites. That war was not fought over the immoral issue of slavery, as some blacks were led to believe. It was the war that was fought over the issue of wealthy whites maintaining the legal right to own blacks as personal property.

The only thing that was civilized about the Civil War was that wealthy whites did not force blacks to participate in murdering each other over the ownership of something they were not entitled to own, the lives of the human beings they wanted to control forever.

After I heard Papa-horse's account of watching civilized whites kill each other over a matter that was wrong, downright evil, I could no longer use reason or logic to deny the truthfulness of his words about slavery and freedom. But I must admit that a remnant of the belief that paper freedom was of first importance still lingered in my mind, for I did not want him to be right. Only that mistress called Time, personal experience, maturity, and earned insight were the remedy for that ill attitude and incorrect belief.

Two years after President Lincoln signed the Emancipation Proclamation, a Congress group in Washington passed the Freedmen's Bureau Act and the Civil Rights Act. Their supposed intent was to help the freedmen, so-called freed slaves, move from slavery to freedom. The Liberator stated that "by law," lawmakers were guaranteeing blacks equal rights with whites. But how could such a thing be true? As all whites did not share equal rights under that same Constitution. All one had to do was look at the conditions of poor whites, and he would plainly see that they did not fare much better than black slaves. If ever there was a group of people whom wealthy whites treated like animals, other than blacks, it was the poor whites, the scorned, the filthy, and the wretched of the white race.

The laws that were scribbled on paper by that Congress group could not, and did not, give freedom to blacks or poor whites. As I have said, the white lawmakers and the wealthy whites made the laws and changed them as their needs arose, and that was the reality of things.

The Republicans' Fourteenth Amendment, another of their white laws, was supposed to make citizens of their black slaves. It was supposed to keep the states from discriminating against the so-called freed slaves and prevent whites from denying them their fundamental rights as Americans. A blind man without glasses could see that that nonsense was not going to work. But as strange as it was, many of my black brothers, being as hungry for freedom as they were for food, did not understand what the real issue was. Those white lawmakers were simply inventing laws that were intended to take blacks on the wild goose chase that would lead them back into the slave conditions they thought they had escaped from. But there was one major difference now. The new form of slavery was to be subtle and worse, an invisible slavery that would enslave the mind.

Lawmakers were the great deceivers. They were not to be trusted. Their deception was so well-organized that some of my people, slaves down South, were of the opinion that slaves up North had the freedom they longed for. And this led hundreds of thousands of southern blacks to migrate to northern cities, where they soon discovered that northern inequality was as equally horrible as southern slavery.

Anti-black attitudes were as common up North as they were down South. Many northern whites hated blacks with as much passion as southern whites. Freedom could not be found in northern states any more than it could be found in southern states. Freedom was not geographical; it could only be found inside.

Having read the above evidence, as it came from different sources, Papa-horse's teaching, and personal experience, I came to the conclusion that certain wealthy whites, slave owners, lawmakers were hardened by tradition and were not going to give paper freedom to blacks or poor whites. It was also obviously true they surely could not give true freedom to slaves, and it was not within the power of the American government to create laws that would make men free. As Papa-horse taught me, gaining true freedom was my own responsibility, and with God's help I would someday become free.

The Civil War caused white brothers to kill each other. Years earlier, my black brothers had been guilty of the same heinous crime. The American Revolutionary War saw blacks fighting against blacks. How do I know? Reading. By now it is obvious that I love reading and cherish my book collection.

During the Revolutionary War, General George Washington kept written records of the war's progress. Being the intellectual historian he was, and a general who sat behind the lines, he spent most of his time in his tent reading about wars of the past and writing in his journals.

As fate would have it, Colonel Wallace Brigade Sandridge, my master's grandfather, had fought with Washington in the Revolutionary War. In the course of a sudden retreat, Colonel Sandridge took—stole—one of Washington's journals from a trunk. The title was, Journal of War. And if you have not guessed it already, I am the fortunate owner of that journal, and it is a prized catch in my collection. (I will share the details later.)

Towards the end of his Journal of War, Washington wrote these words about the war:

March 9, 1778

The weather is dreadful, a reflection of this damn war, and my hope of the war ending in six months has not turned out as expected. By now I had hoped the Crown's army would have fled back to their King like dogs with tucked tails. Yet my troops, which once numbered some 23,000 men, have dwindled—mostly deserters—to 18,000. Thus my optimism has waned and my over confidence has weakened.

If we are to win this dreadful war, we have no choice but to build a regiment of Negro soldiers, positioning them at the front lines, and praying that Congress will favor such a decision. If not, we the American people will remain enslaved to the British Crown, under the ruler-ship of King George III.

—GENERAL GEORGE WASHINGTON

In 1765, King George III presented his colonies in North America with the Stamp Act, taxation to be collected by British tax collectors. Wealthy whites and lawmakers rebelled against the tax by refusing to pay it. In 1768, King George III sent four thousand troops to America to enforce English laws. British soldiers shot five men in the streets of Boston, and the first man to die was a run-away slave named, Crispus Attucks. White Americans decided to fight against the king's army, hoping to gain their freedom from their British oppressors. On April 19, 1775, the American Revolutionary War began. George Washington and other wealthy whites and lawmakers had grown weary of Britain's constant stream of taxation and negligence of responding to the laws they were drawing up in the New World. In October of 1775, George Washington, the future President of the United States of America, gave his recruiting officers this order, "Bar black Americans, free and slave, from enlisting in the Continental Army. Americans will find man power elsewhere."

The British governor of the colony of Virginia, Lord Dunmore, devised the ingenious scheme of turning slaves and slave owners against each other. He made it known to blacks and whites that he would grant freedom to any and all blacks that joined the British army. Lord Dunmore himself was a slave owner. From the start, it sounded like a noble thing for blacks to do. Right? And that was exactly what blacks thought. Black Americans joined the British army by the thousands, ready to fight wealthy whites, slave owners, and lawmakers, believing they would gain freedom through the white man's war. The British were quick to provide these rambunctious recruits with uniforms and rifles. They even inscribed the rifle stocks with the words, "A fight for Freedom." Finally, or so it seemed to the blacks, they would gain their freedom from their cruel masters by fighting along side their newfound friends, the British.

The Continental Congress was supposedly fighting the Revolutionary War for the rights of man. Yet, the rights of blacks could not be a part of the war, as it would cause Congress to appear to be an institution of lying hypocrites. So in April of 1776, not wanting the people to think that slavery was an issue in the war, they called for a wartime halt of the slave trade. But the educated and the learned were not blinded by their hypocrisy. Blacks and whites spoke out against their sanctimonious act of temporarily stopping the slave trade. The Reverend John Allen, a white preacher, said, "You patriots, you pretending voters for freedom, for while you are fasting and praying, none importing, none exporting, resolving and pleading for your rights, you are continuing this law, cruel inhuman and abnormal practice of enslaving your fellow creatures."

On June 28, 1776, Jefferson presented his rough draft of the Declaration of Independence (of which I have a hand written copy) to the General Congress for corrections. Let it be known that Jefferson, a thirty-three-year-old crème de la crème of Virginia aristocracy, held more than two hundred human beings as slaves. It is believed that the original changes made to the Declaration of Independence were made by Jefferson himself, but some say the changes resemble Adams's handwriting.

On July 4, 1776, the American Colonies' Declaration of Independence declared the colonies to be free of British rule. In part it read (and please note these words underscored the Colonies' "abnormal practice of enslaving . . . fellow creatures" as they had been so eloquently presented by the white preacher, Mr. Allen):

> When, in the Course of human events, it becomes necessary for a people to advance from the subordination in which they have hitherto remained, and to which the Laws of Nature and of Nature's do entitle them, a decent respect to the opinions of mankind requires that they should declare the cause, which impel them to change.
>
> We hold these truths to be [sacred and undeniable] self-evident, that all men are created equal and independent; that

from that equal creation they derive in rights inherent and inalienable, among which are the preservation of life, and the liberty and the pursuit of happiness; . . .

None of what that Declaration said included blacks and poor whites. Jefferson knew what he and the other wealthy whites were doing was wrong, for he later told a friend, "If there is a just God, we are going to pay for this."

Washington had predicted that the war would be over in a few short months, but, by 1778 the American Revolutionary War was in full swing, and his men were deserting by the thousands. He knew if Americans were going to win the war, he desperately needed more men to fight against the British. Responding positively to his prayer, Congress agreed with him and promised to give blacks their freedom if they fought with the Americans against the British. So he changed his mind (but not his heart) and began to recruit a regiment of black Americans—free and slave. Now we had slaves fighting on the side of the British and slaves fighting on the side of the Americans.

And what was that?

Black slaves fighting against black slaves.

What were the results?

The British were defeated and the war was over.

What came of Congressional and British promises that black Americans would gain their freedom?

Well, the British shipped about three thousand blacks to an island, where most of them died of starvation. The British themselves went back to Europe.

And what do you think happened to the blacks that fought on the side of the Americans?

The blacks that fought on the side of the British, the ones who were not permitted to board their ships, were severely punished or killed by the white Americans. The others, those who fought on the side of the Americans, went back into slavery. And the wealthy whites and the slave owners and the lawmakers went back to business as usual.

Africans had sold their black brothers into slavery, white Americans bought them, and the American army and British army used them to fight their self-seeking war.

PERSONAL CHANGES

⸙

AS A CHILD I WATCHED WEALTHY whites, young and old, strut around in their freedom. That caused me to desire it with a passion that was greater than my will to live.

Between the ages of three and eight, I would lie in open fields and daydream about what it was like for whites to be free. My infant mind ran wildly with ideas like wearing new shoes, having a real bed to sleep in, and eating good food. I even had thoughts about owning a pony. As I grew older, my desires began to include things like owning land, a cow, and a rifle. When I reached the age of eighteen, I had thoughts about marrying my sweetheart and raising children, having my own family.

The lessons I learned from Papa-horse and the understanding that came with time and maturity showed me that the things I wanted, things that pertain to freedom, were natural, and all people were entitled to them, I felt that I would have them one day. But Papa-horse told me, "Son, nothing in life is free. You can have freedom, the things, and the stuff you dream about. But there's a price to be paid." I had always wanted material things and was willing to work hard to get them. When I was old enough to know what true freedom was, I was also willing to pay the price to have it.

With help from Papa-horse, I soon came to understand the price that had to be paid meant that I would have to make personal changes, the changes that are made inside. Papa-horse said, "The way you deal with others, the way you treat yourself, and what you believed about God are the keys to true freedom."

My first serious lesson in paying the price for true freedom came as a lesson in forgiveness. And as I sit here at my desk, thinking about that lesson, it becomes a relived experience, one that is as real today as it was when it happened many years ago.

Papa-horse and I sat on the banks of Tims Ford's Lake, our favorite fishing spot. At the time I sat in a sinkhole of deep depression. The lesson came through the death of my best childhood friend, Tom, who had been killed by the white slave driver, MacHenry. It was August, and the sun had baked the soil into a hard, cracked pattern. The roasted air hung around our bodies like a warm, damp blanket. Ol' Captain Sandridge had given MacHenry orders to have the field slaves clear an additional thirty acres of land, which were to be planted in cotton as the two adjacent fields were playing out.

We began work before sunrise, and it was not long before the air was humid. MacHenry had his mind made up that we would work without food or water through lunch and supper. Everywhere you looked, you saw nothing but elbows and butts. Before noon, everyone was soaked in sweat, including MacHenry, who sat in the shade and watched us break our backs. Young and old slaves pulled up weeds and chopped down trees. We burned the weeds and stripped the trees for use around the farm. MacHenry forced us to work as if there were no tomorrow. Around noon, the sun turned up its heat. Old men, women, and young children passed out like poisoned flies.

Those thirty acres of land were black soil, rich with minerals, some of the best bottomland in Tennessee. Years before, Ol' Captain Sandridge had had fruit trees, apple and peach and plum, planted between the two cotton fields, and now they were heavy with mouthwatering fruit. When it came to his fruit trees, the old captain was meaner than a nest of hornets. No one, not even his children, were allowed to eat from them.

But that day, Miss Sarah, the Ol' Captain's only daughter, went from tree to tree and plucked big red plums from the low hanging limbs. That was nothing strange for her to do. In fact, her one passion in life was to do things her father had given orders not to do. Miss Sarah got into more trouble than any child reasonably should have.

Whenever the older slaves saw Miss Sarah coming, they would step aside and whisper, "That little Miss Sarah, Lord bless her soul, the child is tech'd in the head. All her parts ain't working. She thinks with her eyes and heart, you know." When she was but just a little girl she would strip herself of all clothing and walk through the slave quarters with a halfcocked smile.

Tom and I watched Miss Sarah. That girl filled her turned up dress tail, exposing her tiny fluffy patch of blond hair, with big juicy plums. The dress tail got so full that plums spilled onto the ground. She never looked down. She crushed the plums under her feet as she meandered from one tree to another. After she had gone from tree to tree, she plopped to the ground as if there was not a bone in her body, and plums rolled in all directions. She leaned against the tree. With her dazed stare, she looked at Tom and me. After a few minutes had passed she began to stuff plums into her mouth. Plum juice ran from the corners, over her chin, and down her dress. She did not spit out a single seed. She continued to stare at us and stuffed in more plums. Then she looked from side to side, flashed her twisted smile, and held up a plum.

We were hungry and thirsty. But I said to Tom, "Tom, it's not a good idea. MacHenry won't let us. We can't go."

Tom looked around and said, "MacHenry ain't around. I's can make it 'fore he knows anythang 'bout it. I's be back before a dog can scratch a flea. And that be with some big juicy plums for me and you."

"Tom, not this time. Don't do it. Things ain't right. I can feel it."

"Nimrod, you's my best and good friend, right?"

"Yeah, Tom."

"But I thanks you let them feelings get between you and stuff too much. Like I's said, I's can make it. Um gone come back carr'in a big juicy plum jus' for you. Y'all see."

"Tom, wait!" But before I could say anything more he had crawled off and disappeared into the tall grass.

Tom reappeared in a clearing, but disappeared again. The bushes behind Miss Sarah seemed to move. I did not dare call out to Tom. He was too far away and I did not want to alert MacHenry. I held my breath. Again, Tom appeared and disappeared in the thick undergrowth. I looked and waited for Tom to reappear. There was nothing. Then suddenly MacHenry got up and walked off.

The weeds moved again. Tom crawled from a tall patch of weeds. He stopped and looked around, then crawled under the fence and sat down in front of Miss Sarah. She looked at him with those glazed blue eyes. Her smile slid to one side, the same smile she smiled when braving Ol' Captain Sandridge's orders.

Miss Sarah looked over at me, frowned, and asked him, "Y'all like juicy ones, Tom?"

"Yessum, I like them a whole mess, Miss Sarah."

She looked at me again, and said, "Well, y'all's the lucky one, Tom.

Here take this." As Tom reached for the plum, Miss Sarah shoved it into her mouth. She chewed and gulped it down. Tom stared. She raised her knees, pulling her dress up. Her legs relaxed and parted. She looked at Tom, and then searched her dress for another plum. She raised her hand and held the biggest and reddest plum I had ever seen. She looked over at me, and her smile grew.

Tom reached for the plum and she drew it back, then hid it behind her back and laughed. Her shrill laughter pushed Tom away. She held the plum up again, smiled, and rested back against the tree, her legs still apart. Tom moved close again, on his knees, and reached for the plum. She dropped it between her legs and motioned for him to pick it up. He did, and she smiled. Tom smiled back.

Tom curled his leg beneath his butt and sat on his foot. He raised the plum to his mouth. The grass behind him moved. When the plum touched his lips MacHenry stepped out of the bushes, grabbed him by the ears, and yanked him to his feet. Tom screamed like he was set on fire. His mother, Miss Emma, and the other slaves ran over to the tree. When she reached Tom, she dropped to her knees and pleaded with MacHenry.

"Please! Please, Mr. MacHenry. Sir, don't y'all hurt my baby. He ain't nothin' but a child."

MacHenry said, "This 'child,' as you call it, got to pay for this here infraction. The nigger broke a rule, Emma." He smiled.

"But I can make up for it, if y'all let me."

"You know that won't be justice, Emma. My God says, when the law is broken, eye for an eye and tooth for a tooth. Tom gotta pay, and pay is what he's gonna do. You hear me? I say pay!"

Miss Emma grabbed MacHenry's leg and pleaded. He spit on her head and shoved her away with his foot. Because of her persistent pleading, he spouted Bible verses, and cursed for more than five minutes. I wanted to pick up a rock and throw it at MacHenry's head, but all I could do was just what the adults did. I watched, and said nothing.

When MacHenry had regained his senses he let go of Tom's ears. His hands were covered with blood. And blood was running down the sides of Tom's face.

MacHenry turned and yelled for Big Jake to come and take Tom to the slave quarters. Big Jake was a tall, muscular, light skinned black man with white folks' curly brown hair and green eyes. He would fight at the drop of a hat. He seemed to take delight in doing whatever whites ordered him to do. Not only did he follow MacHenry's and Ol' Captain Sandridge's orders to the letter, but his cruelty went beyond the call of duty. I remember the time when he and other slaves had been trying all day to move a stump out of a field. Big Jake wanted water. The slave who was bringing the pail moved too slow. Big Jake dismounted his horse and beat him. The slave was ninety years old, and he died that night.

Big Jake walked up to Tom and grabbed his ears. Tom screamed louder. He dragged Tom away kicking and screaming and locked him in the smoke house.

Whenever MacHenry had been reprimanded by Ol' Captain Sandridge, he would call down Big Jake, and Big Jake would lash out at the other slaves, especially the dark skinned ones, including me. Once, after he had been shamed in front of others by MacHenry, he beat me without a cause until blood flowed from my back and legs. Every day up to his death, Jake harassed the other slaves, threatening to "beat the life out of us" if we did not respect his position as the "nigger slave driver." Slaves were the victims of cruelty from both sides: blacks and white.

MacHenry ordered the slaves back to work. At the end of the day, after sunset and the air had cooled, he ordered Big Jake to tie Tom to the whipping tree, and gather the slaves. The tree was a good-sized pine; a man could hug it, and his fingertips would not touch, and a perfect circle of bare earth surrounded it. The side where the slaves were tied was smooth and dark. The blood of slaves had soaked into the ground and killed the tree and grass long before I had been born. The area was always charged with the odor of death.

Big Jake rode into the slave quarters, yelling and waving a stick, acting like a man who was rounding up cattle for slaughtering. He pushed and shoved us. Through the amber light of the torches we watched him tie little Tom to the tree. Tom was as docile and quiet as a lamb. He stared at his mother, who had cried all day and was weak. Women surrounded her and kept her from falling to the ground.

Tom looked at Big Jake and begged for water. "Big Jake, can you give me some water? I's thirsty now. My inside's dry."

Big Jake crossed his arms over his chest, and looked away.

Nothing moved. The people, the trees, the air were still, all except for the shadows that lay on the ground. They bobbed and swayed. Silence was everywhere. It had descended on Franklin County, unthreatened and unmovable. Then suddenly a bloodcurdling cry came from the dark woods and took on the color of the torch's flames. Wide-eyed slaves searched the woods for its source. A night owl leaped from a tall pine and flew toward the moon.

Tom seemed determined to defy his fate. As if to say, "They ain't gonna break me, I'm leavin'," he looked at his mother and the others. When he looked into my eyes his dry lips parted in a faint smile. Then he turned his face toward the woods.

I was so scared for Tom my vision blurred and helplessness scrambled my mind, and my body was numbed by fear. That night, Tom became the bravest person I had ever known.

MacHenry always brought his wife and children, a bottle of whiskey, and the Bible to the whippings. He stumbled into the gathering and leaned against the whipping tree. His wife and children stood to the side. With the Bible secured under his left arm, the whiskey bottle and the whip in his hands, he gave his usual speech about his power and authority. He took a long swallow from the bottle, and stepped back. The whip coiled at his feet. He raised his hand above his head and released the hissing snake, as he called it. The whip struck out and bit sharply into Tom's naked body in the middle of his back. Tom jerked, twisted, and turned. Blood squirted from the wound. The whip recoiled. Another lash. He jerked twisted, and turned. A quote from the Bible about God detesting the thievery of blacks came from MacHenry. Another lash. The whip snapped against Tom's skin. The blood flowed. MacHenry quoted from the Bible and had another swallow of whiskey. The whip lashed out at Tom's bleeding back again, and again, and Tom's body jerked and twitched with each lash. MacHenry saw that Tom was not going to plead and beg, so he snapped the whip with greater fierceness. Blood gushed from Tom's broken back, ran down his buttocks, legs, and soaked into the ground.

The sound of the whip on wet flesh and Miss Emma's crying filled my ears with the reality that was common for slaves. My heart sank into my stomach. She had shed enough tears for Tom, for herself, for all present, and for generations of blacks to come. Though Tom did not cry aloud, I knew each whimper was a scream that crept from his spirit, a cry for God's help. Or death. I covered my ears and turned away, but his silent screams soaked into my hands and reverberated in my soul.

Tom's silent screams ceased.

Miss Emma screamed, and I turned. Tom's limp body was slumped against the tree, reaching towards the ground for rest.

MacHenry was so drunk and possessed by rage he did not know that Tom had died. He continued to beat the lifeless body until he went weak, dropped to one knee, and panted like a racehorse. Minutes passed. Mac Henry pulled himself up, took a dirty rag from his hip pocket, wiped his face, and looked around. He spat on the ground at Big Jake's feet and said, "Bury the nigger. We can't have coyotes smelling around here, can we? He that lives by the sword dies from it. And he who steals, dies for that. Let them who sow, reap the rewards."

The pathetic thing about MacHenry's biblical quotes was that he could not read, and so he repeated bits and pieces of what he had heard Reverend Smith say at church.

After babbling for more than an hour, MacHenry walked away, his family marched behind him, everyone except Billy Ray, his eldest son. Billy Ray helped Kato and Jimmy remove Tom's body from the tree and bury it. Later that night, his father rewarded him for his acts of love and kindness with another death, Billy Ray's.

Billy Ray, Tom, and I had been friends since we were old enough to walk. We spent hours playing and swimming at the lake. We did all the boy things that came to our minds. On moonlit summer nights, we raided Old Man Johnson's watermelon field. We took the biggest watermelons to the edge of the field and ate them with our hands, and spat the seeds at each other. After getting our fill of watermelon, we walked home with our arms draped over each others' shoulders, soaked in sweet, sticky juice, seeds clinging to our arms, chests, faces, and hair. During the winter, we made traps for rabbits and hunted squirrels with slingshots. In the spring, we caught butterflies and pulled off their wings, we caught grasshoppers and pulled off their hoppers. We poured water into ant mounds and stomped them as they ran out. We were boys pretending to be brave adventurers.

A week after Tom was buried, Papa-horse and I got up at sunrise and went fishing at Tims Ford's Lake. Though the trees glowed with sunlight, everything was made dreary by our memories. I knew my friends would never feel a breeze sweep across their faces. Nor taste the sweetness of fruit again. My heart longed for Tom. The sound of his voice awakened me during the night.

Papa-horse and I sat on the damp bank. After several failed attempts to engage me in conversation, he laid his fishing pole to his side. He looked at me, and asked, "What's ailing you, son? Your thinking is so loud you're scaring the fish away. It's time to talk about your feelings. Let them out. If you don't, your ears will grow as big as cornmeal sacks, and you'll float away."

"Papa-horse, I'm sad. MacHenry killed Tom. It's not right. He's the devil, and I hate him. I hope he dies in his sleep."

"You do?"

"Yes, sir. If he died tonight, that'll be all right by me."

"Maradh, let's talk in our African tongue. The Isheman's."

"Yes, Rekesh," I answered.

Whenever Papa-horse said lets talk in African I knew it was time for a lesson. Papa-horse spoke a number of languages, but he only taught me the Isherman's. He said it was closer to the original language than any of the others.

"I understand the anger and pain you're feeling, son. But remember this. If you forgive your enemy, you take away his power. You set yourself free. Yes, MacHenry's actions were cruel and uncalled for. He took the God-given gift of life from a child who had the greater portion of his stretching before him. Yet, what is most important to you at this time is that he robbed you of a dear friend.

"Losing a friend is one of the greatest pains you will suffer," he continued. "A man will meet hundreds, even thousands, of individuals over the course of his life, but he is blessed if he meets one true friend during his journey. And if he loses that friend, it creates a pain that will last for the remainder of his life. But, Maradh, you lost more than a friend. You lost the friend who was greater than a brother. Tom, a true friend.

"I want to assist you to use your pain. It can help you gain true freedom. Your grief for Tom is good, yet you must not get stuck in that grief. God and Tom are telling you to move on with your life, and live as God created you to live. You must discover the work that God chose for you to do. And only you can do that particular work. You must come back, move from grief to rejoicing if you're to leave your mark on the world. That way, others can benefit from your having been here. I say that's what God and Tom want you to do. From the outside it appears as if MacHenry took Tom's life because of a plum. But that wasn't the real reason."

"Why did he kill Tom? He was hungry and thirsty."

"My son, it's time you learn what men like MacHenry really are."

"What are they? Devils?"

"No, not devils. They're slaves."

"Slaves? Slaves like me?"

"No. They're slaves of a different sort, with different kinds of masters."

"What kind of slave is that? They're white people."

"The kind of slave is not as important as what they're slaves to."

"You mean who his master is?"

"Yes. MacHenry's master is different from the master you know."

"Who's his master? Is it Ol' Captain Sandridge?"

"Yes and no. You must realize, Maradh, even Ol' Captain Sandridge has a master. The master I'm talking about controls MacHenry and Master Sandridge."

"What master can tell Ol' Captain Sandridge when to come and when to go and what to do? I would rather see this master than swim and fish. If any man can be master to Ol' Captain Sandridge, he's awful powerful."

"He is powerful. Very powerful. But he's not the kind of master you think he is. He's the unseen master who makes slaves of people all around the world. This master controls the young and the old, the rich and the poor, the blacks and the whites. Anyone who has closed his mind and heart to God is in danger of becoming a slave to this master."

"Where is he? Is he here? On this farm?"

"Yes, he lives on this farm. He's everywhere."

"What's his name?"

"He's called Ignorance of Love."

"Ignorance of Love?"

"Yes, Ignorance. Ignorance of Love."

"Is this master mean like MacHenry and Ol' Captain Sandridge?"

"Ignorance of Love is the meanest and the most evil master there is. He's every man's enemy. When Master Ignorance is in control of a man, that man harms himself and blames others. And if that man is in control of a group of people, a family, a church, or a government, all the people suffer.

"MacHenry is ignorant of love and compassion, and this causes him to be a slave to hatred and revenge. Remember how he quoted the Bible while he beat Tom?"

"Yes. He does that all the time."

"Well, the Bible is a book that represents the God of love. But MacHenry didn't show any love for Tom, God, or himself. When a man doesn't love God and himself, it's easy for him to kill others, even his own. MacHenry killed Tom because his master's control over him was greater than his compassion for a child who was hungry. But his slavery to Ignorance did not stop him with just killing Tom. The other things he did later that night show how great a control his master has over him. But the worst thing about Mac Henry's slavery is that he doesn't know he's a slave." Papa-horse paused. "But there's other unseen slave masters, too."

"Who?"

"Ol' Captain Sandridge's slavery to Ignorance causes him to be enslaved to the slave masters, Whisky and Greed. When he's under the control of Whisky he's mean and cruel, not only to his slaves, but also to other whites, including his family. His master forces him to do the unthinkable to his wife, daughter, and sons. His acts of cruelty to his children create a pain in their hearts that will affect them for the rest of their lives. And that pain will be passed on to his grandchildren. His greed for money causes him to find ways to take things from those who have less. Mac Henry's slavery to Whisky made it easy for him to kill your friend, Tom."

"But I heard that Ol' Captain Sandridge and other whites can go to church and get forgiveness. Is that true?"

"It's true that God forgives Captain Sandridge. But it is also true that the law of you reap what you sow will visit him, regardless. And besides, his preacher, Reverend Smith, he's enslaved, too. He's a slave to Religious Ignorance. He teaches the people his fear-based belief about the cruel three-headed god that lives in heaven. And since the people can't question his teachings, the people become dependent on him and not on God. He's a man who hates blacks and favors slavery because of his ignorance of Godly love. He believes that slavery is the necessary evil that allows whites to live as God created them to live, the good life with servants. His slavery to Ignorance causes him to believe that blacks are like cattle and horses, animals to be domesticated.

"Ignorance of Love is the great slave driver who has a far-reaching power that can cause humans to hurt each other, animals, and the land."

"Rekesh," I asked, "can we kill the slave driver, Ignorance?"

"Yes."

"How?"

"Not long from now, you're going to have a dream. The dream will answer your question and keep you on the path that leads to true freedom."

"Does that mean I'll have food to eat like Ol' Captain Sandridge and live in the Big House?"

"Maradh, listen closely," Papa-horse said. "Captain Sandridge is not free because he has food and lives in a big house. As I told you, Captain Sandridge is a slave. Except he has a different master. While you're a slave to Captain Sandridge, he's a slave to Ignorance, Whisky, and Greed.

"Where your stomach is hungry for food, his heart is starving for love. Where your mind is hungry for knowledge, his mind is filled with guilt. Where you're crying yourself to sleep at night, Captain Sandridge is drinking himself into a drunken stupor. Maradh, you must learn the difference between paper freedom and true freedom."

"Which freedom does Ol' Captain Sandridge have?" I asked.

"The first freedom. Paper freedom."

"Is that because he's white?"

"No. All whites don't have paper-freedom. Poor whites, whites like MacHenry and his family, they don't have it. They suffer poverty like blacks do. They're mistreated by the wealthy whites; whites like Master Sandridge. It can be easier for some poor whites to gain material things than it is for blacks, if they work hard. But if not, they suffer poverty the same as blacks."

"I want both," I said. "Paper freedom and true freedom."

"You can have both. But you must develop your listening skills and gain the second freedom, true freedom if you want to enjoy your life. Paper freedom will permit you to get material things, but true freedom will bring you peace and happiness. Without peace there's no happiness, and without happiness there's no life."

"What's true freedom?"

Papa-horse tapped my chest with his index finger and said, "True freedom is the happiness and peace that's inside of you. You can only experience that freedom when you discover it's there. Inside. True-freedom is like living in a dream all the time. Do you remember how things are when you're dreaming?"

"Yes. But when I have nightmares, I'm afraid."

"Well, I'm talking about the dreams where everything turns out right and you feel peaceful. If you're running from a bad dog, in the end you discover the dog is friendly. Or if you leap off a high cliff, you begin to fly. Or if you're chased by a bad man and he catches you, he can't hurt you. Somehow you always escape the bad. In those dreams, nothing harms you. You live inside a protective bubble. You're in the care, love, and protection that come from the inside. That's the freedom that God created, and placed in the head and chest of all men."

"I want that freedom, Rekesh, but I want the freedom that Ol' Captain Sandridge has too."

"Maradh, take your enemy's power. Kill him!"

"But how, Rekesh!?"

"By loving him and forgiving him."

Inexperience and not listening, the two great enemies of all human beings, hindered my progress when it came to the journey of true freedom. They made me crave paper freedom more than true-freedom. Over the years, I have suffered many painful experiences, some of which I believe could have been avoided had I listened to and followed the instructions I received from Papa-horse.

So I tell you, listen. Listen even when it hurts. That way you may be able to learn without so much suffering.

Papa-horse further proved his point about Master Ignorance being a slave driver when he reminded me of what Mr. Garrison had done to his infant son. Mr. Garrison's, child was sick with sinus. Out of desperation, Mr. Garrison, under the control of the slave driver Ignorance, tried to heal the child by putting him in scalding water. The poor baby died. It is true that Mr. Garrison's intentions arose from love, and he meant the child no harm. But his slavery to Ignorance caused him to do what most folks today would consider an unbelievable and barbarous act.

You and I can reason that Mr. Garrison did what other people were doing at that time, as they were uneducated in the ways of modern health and medicine. But it remains that his efforts to help his son came from ignorance. Papa-horse's point that some whites were slaves to Ignorance (as were blacks) was true then, and is true today.

Mr. Garrison's ignorance cannot be explained away, and even if it could, that would not bring the dead baby back to life. But that was not all. Papa-horse also reminded me of what I had read in The National Intelligencer, the other newspaper that Master Sandridge kept in the big house.

According to The National Intelligencer, President Jefferson had gone blind in one eye. The report stated that the president had trouble with nerves on the side of his face, and the eye had swollen. In an attempt to help the president, a doctor lanced his eye with a hot metal lancet and blinded him. The ignorance of the doctors and the president regarding how to deal with the problem of nerves cost the president an eye. I say that was barbarism in full sway. What those civilized men could have done, had they not been blinded by their racism, was to have sought the aide of his slaves. President Jefferson, I am sure had them as did other presidents, wealthy white, and lawmakers. It was common for slaves to have a good working knowledge of healing plants and herbs, which were spoken of in the Bible as being for "the healing of the nations." Had the president and his doctors been willing to make changes in their beliefs about healing and the intelligence of slaves, the slaves could have directed them to the proper healing plants for the nerves and swelling. Who knows, the President's eye might have been saved.

Slaves received their knowledge of healing plants from their ancestors, who had received theirs from generations that stretched thousands of years into the past. We used specific herbs for specific ailments. For instance, when you are suffering from gas, bloating, or constipation, Cascara will alleviate that problem. Agrimony heals the liver. Red Clover, the plant with the beautiful red blooms, will cleanse the blood. White Oak bark clears up congestion. Black Cohosh and Blue Cohosh are good for problems that plague women once a month and when they are in the change of life. Black Walnut kills internal parasites. White Pine stops the flux. Echinacea is good for all infections and the nerves. Peppermint tea reduces fever and is good for digestion. Wood Betony is good for nerves, delirium, headaches, and worms. Wild Lettuce works wonders when there is pain. Willow is for pain and wounds. If one suffered from poor eyesight, he would make a tea of Eyebright and drink it two to three times a day. There are many other herbs that are used for healing.

Where it was common for us slaves to have a working knowledge of healing plants, it was the opposite for many whites, especially the wealthy whites. When they came from Europe, they brought many of their churchy traditions and beliefs. They were not willing to change those old world beliefs for new ways of thinking. One such belief they held onto was the belief that herbs were a form of witchery that was connected to charms, spells, magic, and sorcery. Their fear, their enslavement to ignorance of the use of herbs, kept them away from certain healings. The president's slavery to ignorance, not having a working knowledge of the medicinal properties of herbs, cost him the hefty price of one good eye. When that sort of thing chanced a man, Papa-horse said, "No matter who the person is or what his situation may be, when Ignorance is his master, he suffers. And if he's master over others, they suffer, too."

And I say there is no way of knowing how much and in how many ways the people of this country suffered because of President Jefferson's ignorance in other matters. An entire nation was at the mercy of his good and bad decisions.

Papa-horse believed that all men were under control of the slave driver called Ignorance. I must admit that much of the suffering I experienced over the years came from my own ignorance. Outer suffering has forced me to work hard at making inner changes. One such occasion was when I was accosted by a Mr. Duvall Little. I learned a lesson about the importance of controlling my emotions. Prior to that I was ignorant of that need.

It was the year 1841. I was eighteen years old, stood six-feet four inches tall, and weighed 245 pounds. My master and I had traveled down to Bridgeport, Alabama, for a load of building supplies. When we rode into town, the white women and children scurried from the street as if they had seen a wild animal. Men who walked along the dirt road stopped and stared, and those who sat in front of the few buildings stood and gazed at us.

Master Sandridge stopped the wagon at the general store. A group of five or six boys gathered at the corner of the building and watched as we climbed from the wagon. Master Sandridge told me to wait outside while he went in with the list. After he had been inside longer than I thought it should have taken, I walked up to the door and looked in. The glass was so dirty, I could not see inside, so I turned to go back to the wagon. That's when two white men grabbed my arms and shirt and began to pull me. I resisted, and they pulled harder. I had no idea what they were up to, so I planted my feet on the ground. They stumbled, ripped off my shirt, and tumbled like boys rolling down a hill. They came to a stop and sat upright. I flexed my shoulders, chest, arms, and they gawked. The big one, Mr. Little, jumped up and started to come at me. The smaller one yelled for more help. And me, being eighteen years old and for the first time feeling my own strength, I was excited.

Mr. Little reached and grabbed my arm again. I twirled it up and back, and thrust it out, and he flipped like a rag doll. He hit the ground with a thud, dust flew up, and he bounced on his bottom. When he stood up and turned, his face was aflame. He stared. Without a blink, he crouched and began to circle to my left. I crouched. He stopped. I stopped. Without warning, the little fellow and the three recruits jumped me from behind. I stumbled forward but kept my eyes on the big fellow. I regained my balance, twisted my shoulders sharply, and dipped to the right, then quickly to the left. They flew in all directions like water flying off the back of a shaking dog. I faced the big fellow again. He crouched, circled to my right, and smiled. I smiled and rubbed my hands together. We stood face-to-face and smiled. Then he did the strangest thing. He stood upright, put his hands on his hips, and laughed. I thought he was having as much fun as I was, so I laughed too.

When I woke up in the back of the wagon, it was obvious that Master Sandridge and I were headed back to Deckard without the building supplies. The storeowner had refused to sell them to him and said, "You don't have your nigger under control."

Later that night, Papa-horse told me the story of The Little Prince of Change, a story I had heard and loved since childhood. It helped me to understand what I had done to inflame the incident with Mr. Duvall and his friends. I saw that I was strong outside, physically, but weak inside, emotionally.

Papa-horse and I were in the hayloft and he sat down behind me. He removed a wad of moist herbs from his pouch, and put it on the large lump at the back of my head. He patted it gently and asked in the African tongue, "Son, what got into you, today?"

"I just wanted to have some fun. And I thought they did, too," I said.

Papa-horse laughed. I turned and looked at him, and we both laughed. I told him what had happened and he laughed harder. He sat beside me and said, "Son, you're at one of those stages of life."

"What stage is that?" I asked.

"The one where you're becoming aware of bodily changes and physical strength. Emotional changes are taking place inside of you, too, but you're not aware of them. If this newfound physical strength and body changes are combined with uncontrolled emotions and are not carefully bridled, they'll cause you to do things you shouldn't do. For instance, the thing you did today," his words were mixed with laughter. "You have moved into the time where you must stop and think before you say and do things. You can't allow your emotions to rule your actions. If you do you'll make a lot of avoidable mistakes."

"Like what?"

"Like the thing you did today with Mr. Little."

"I just wanted to have some fun. I thought they did, too. That's all."

"I know, son." He could not stop laughing.

I smiled and asked, "What do you mean?"

He continued to laugh and several minutes passed before he answered. "Nimrod," he finally said, "do you remember the Spanish story, 'El Principito Del Cambio'? 'The Little Prince of Change'?"

"Yes, it was one of my favorites. But what does it have to do with this stage of life you're talking about?"

"Well, son, you're in one of those stages, and this story can be helpful if you listen with a new ear. I've told it many times. Now that you're eighteen, it's time to tell it again."

"What can it do this time?"

He laughed and said, "Why don't I just tell it again? And this time you can listen for its moral with a new ear, one that's eighteen years old. Believe me, you need to hear it again."

"I enjoy your stories and I love my books," I said, "especially my Red Book."

After he had gotten his laughter under control, he told me the story.

———

"ALGÚN TIEMPO ATRÁS, A LONG, long, time ago there was El Principito, the little prince. El Principito lived in a big casa, a house, made of stones. The stone house sat between a field and the woods. The field was to the right of his casa, and the woods to the left. The little prince's house had two rooms. The room on the right was the eating room. The room on the left was the sleeping room.

Every morning El Principito would wake up early and go to the eating room and have breakfast: arepa de choclo con queso, chocolate, huevo y pan. And every morning, his favorite food was on the table in the center of the room. After breakfast, El Principito went outside to play in the field. The field was big enough to play in and small enough to work in.

There was an old man. The old man lived in the field and worked in the field. Every day, El Principito walked to the center of the field and played. Every day, the old man stood in the field and worked. El Principito and the old man never talked to each other. It was as if they didn't see each other and couldn't hear each other.

The old man always said, "This field is too small to work in. It's not big enough."

El Principito always said, "This field is too large to play in. It's not small enough."

Every day at twelve o'clock, El Principito went back to his casa to eat lunch: arroz, patacón, yuca, guaraná. His favorite foods were on the table, which sat in the center of the room.

After lunch El Principito went outside to play in the woods. The woods were big enough to play and small enough to work in.

There was an old woman. The old woman lived in the woods and wove in the woods. Every day, El Principito walked to the center of the woods and played. Every day, the old woman sat in the woods and wove. El Principito and the old woman never talked to each other. It was as if they didn't see each other and didn't hear each other.

The old woman always said, "These woods are too small to work in. They're not big enough."

El Principito always said, "These woods are too large to play in. They're not small enough."

Every day at five o'clock, El Principito went back to his house to eat supper: pescado, arroz con coco y agua de coco. His favorite food was on the table, which sat in the center of the room.

After supper El Principito went to bed and dreamed. Every night he dreamed he was el camaleón, the chameleon.

Every time el camaleón touched something different, he changed color. He touched a black table and he turned black, he touched a white plate and he turned white, he touched a yellow bowl and he turned yellow, he touched a red spoon and he turned red.

Every day and every night was the same. El Principito, the little prince, would sleep, dream, wake up, eat, and play. He would eat breakfast and then go play in the big field. He would eat lunch and then go play in the big woods. He would eat supper and then sleep in his bed. And he would dream about being el camaleón and watch himself change color every time he touched something different.

Every day was the same. All the same. Until one day.

One day, while El Principito was playing in the field, the old man spoke. The old man of the field asked the little prince, he asked, "'Hey! Little prince, who are you?"

"Me?" asked El Principito.

"Yes. You," said the old man.

El Principito said, "I'm El Principito, the little prince. Hey, old man, who are you??"

"Me?" asked the old man.'

"Yes. You."

The old man said, "Well, I'm the old man of the little field. El Principito, why are you in this field that's too little?"

"I come to this big field to play games, old man," El Principito answered. "Old man," he asked, "why are you in this field that's too big?"

"I live and work in this little field, El Principito."

That day, the old man and the little prince had a long conversation about games and work and life.

The next day, not the same day, but another day, while El Principito was playing in the big woods, the old woman spoke to him. "Hey! Little prince, who are you?" she asked.

"Me?" asked El Principito.

"Yes. You."

El Principito said, "I'm El Principito, the little prince. Hey, who are you, old woman?"

The old woman said, "Me?"

"Yes. You."

"Well, I'm the old woman of the woods that are too small, El Principito," said the old woman, "why are you in these woods that are too little?"

"I come to these big woods to play games," El Principito answered. "Old woman," he said, "why are you in the woods that are too big?"

"I live and weave in this little woods, El Principito," the old woman answered.

That day, the old woman and El Principito had a long conversation about games and weaving and life.

At bedtime that night, after supper, El Principito said his prayers and went to sleep and dreamed.

He dreamed he was el camaleón, the chameleon. Every time El Principito was el camaleón and he touched something different he changed. He touched a black table and he became a black man. He touched a white plate and he became a white man. He touched a yellow bowl and he became a yellow man. He touched a red spoon and he became a red man.

Early the next morning, El Principito awoke from his dream. He climbed out of bed and stood in the middle of his house, between the two rooms. He stretched and stretched and reached his right hand out the window on the right side of the house. He held the hand of the old man of the field. Then he stretched and stretched and reached his left hand out the window on the left side of the house, and he held the hand of the old woman of the woods. El Principito held hands with the old man and the old woman at the same time.

El Principito smiled and became the old man and the old woman who played to enjoy himself, worked to feed himself, and wove to clothe himself. The child who became an adult. The prince became a king. The individual became the human race.

————

I WAS ASTONISHED AT WHAT I heard. "My God!" I exclaimed, "It sounded like a different story with a different meaning. How does that happen?"

"What did you hear this time that makes it a different story?" Papa-horse asked me.

"It's saying the Little Prince is a part of the Old Man of the Field and the Old Woman of the Woods at the same time. He's a brother to all humans."

"Yes, that's right. And what happened this time that made the story different is simple. When you heard the story before, you were a younger fellow with less experience and limited needs, and you listened with younger ears. Today you're older, and your needs are different. You have more experience and your listening skills are improved."

"You mean I hear more?"

"No."

"What do you mean?"

"Your hearing is the same. You don't hear more. But experience has sharpened your understanding, and your listening skills are sharper, keener. You have a greater understanding of the moral of the story. A clearer understanding of its meaning than you had at earlier stages of your life. It's like hearing it for the first time ... again."

As I think back on that story and that time, I say at this stage of life that we are alike, as shown in the following poem: Similarly Alike.

We,

The human race,
With our differences,
Are much alike.

We
Resemble each other
In many ways—
Similarities of
All races
We are much alike.
Differences
Make us alike,
More alike than different.

In the beginning
We are all born from the immortal:
We feel pain and pleasure,
We laugh and cry,
We dream and lie,
We live awhile.
But in the end,
The flesh succumbs to the mortal,
And we are both
The moth and the candle:
Fluttering wings
And ashes,
Cold wax,
And melting changes.
We rush into the flame.

In the end
We lay our head against life's bosom:
We
All
Die.

NOT SKIN COLOR BUT SPIRITUAL ISSUES

TODAY I AM OF THE OPINION that the issue of some whites—the wealthy whites, slave owners, lawmakers in particular—not being capable to love blacks was neither a skin color nor a racial issue, but a spiritual matter. We can look back at any point in America's history and witness the fact that whites fought and killed each other from the very beginning, and the same held true for blacks. But my point of argument is this: whites and blacks that sold their brothers into slavery were not capable of loving with the heart. The love niche, a small opening deep within the human heart, had not been opened to love from the inside to the outside, and men who had not gotten in touch with God. I grant you, this sort of love is not easy, for we all must struggle to open that space and learn to love everyone. That means, loving without motives.

What I am speaking about here, brothers loving brothers, takes a lifetime of hard work and constant struggle. It seems to me that our wealthy white brothers, slave owners, and lawmakers were way behind in this sort of work. They seem to have been preoccupied with procuring the things of the world and gaining the power that comes from having money, material goods, and control over other people's lives, rather than the power of love. Though I believe this to be true, the truth of the matter is that racism was and still is a real problem and will be a serious problem for generations to come.

Those who have their mind set on selling and enslaving others must be cured of the contaminating disease called racism. This cure must take place before they can even consider loving all men as equals. Then the world can know peace. Racism and greed are the sicknesses that created the ills of the Americas.

RACISM, LIKE ALL ISMS, CAUSES people to hold on to their doctrines as though they are the absolute truth. People become possessed when their doctrines are not based on love for God, others, and self, and that causes them to develop hatred for those who are not a part of their brand of Ism." Papa-horse said: "Isms are spirits that herd people together in doctrines of falsehoods, and falsehoods are contrived and promoted as The Truth by men who claim to be chosen by the Most High God.

In my opinion, most of us can deal with what is true with limited success, but none of us, through no amount of reasoning and logic, can devise truth. Truth is of God. I say the racism and greed of today are America's hardening-of-the-heart disease.

Although I do not adhere to the tenets that white Americans are white devils, I do believe that white racists are possessed by evil devil spirits, which possess anyone whose actions are less than loving. These whites that I speak of are not going to accept what I say about their being enslaved by that spirit, or their being enslaved by anything, but all whites, at some point in their lives, are going to feel the pain stored in their hearts and inherited from murderous, slave-owning ancestors. The truth of my story brings this fact and other facts to the surface of reality.

On the other hand, some blacks and poor whites are not going to accept what I say about the second freedom, true freedom, being the real freedom that should be sought by all people. Their desire for material goods causes them to be consumed by the notion that paper freedom can give them all the joy and happiness they need in this life.

The importance of gaining true freedom over paper freedom is paramount if one is pursuing happiness. Here I am moved to say, that Thomas Jefferson should have inscribed his 1776 Declaration of Independence that for freedom to be a part of the American experience, people must be free inside.

The long-lasting physical, mental, emotional, and psycho-logical scars slavery left on the black and white races need a strong readiness and persistent work to develop the inner man if any of us are to experience true freedom. It is going to be very difficult for blacks to move beyond the pain that the white racists implanted in our hearts during slavery. I believe the race-based pain that was inflicted on innocent black people who were herded together in cramped living quarters, forced to work from before sunrise to after sunset, and fed less than dogs ate will take generations to effectively deal with and heal.

Papa-horse said, "Just as a man inherits his parent's eye color and skin color, he also inherits his pain. Time is the Great Healer. She is the only healer."

Nonetheless, I hope that all humans will some day come to the readiness to love each other in spite of our external differences like the color of our skin. We must open the valves of suppressed and overt hatred if we are to release the pain we have stored and carried since childhood. The pains of racism—emotionalism and possessiveness—will continue to be passed on as generational curses and affect each succeeding generation. That racial pain will explode into a devastating catastrophe that will inevitably cause new scars and create the racism that can destroy all mankind.

The racism of future generations will far exceed what we have thus far experienced in slavery. If we do not come together as a single race, not only will racists on all sides continue to kill each other, but their children will kill their own family members, as was demonstrated in the Civil War, except that the killing will happen with more frequency and a greater fierceness. Everyone will continue to suffer from the ills of this dreaded disease and be filled with a greater hate, a stronger racism, which will become the world plague that spreads to all continents, countries, and cultures. Our children's pain will become so great that they will kill their parents, their playmates, and themselves. Our world will be a scary place to live. This poisonous hate will affect our food, water, and air, making them unfit to eat, drink, and breathe. Thus, peace will become a shibboleth; a proverbial saying that describes the diehards, a nickname for dreamers of change, and a mere slogan of the weary.

In spite of my pessimism, I am convinced that my story will demonstrate to some people that the saving grace that can keep humans from racial self-destruction is the true freedom that Papa-horse talked about. In my opinion, the human race will be saved one individual at a time, and not in groups or organizations. Leaders who present organized religion and political factions as the means for saving and changing the world mislead themselves. They also mislead the people they preach at. Thus we have the proverbial blind leading the blind.

Please understand me: I do not mean to imply that religion and government are not needed. They are. Religion, the service and worship of God, provides man with different ways to seek God's purpose for men and the world. Government, which is God's management of human affairs, provides man with procedures for accomplishing a greater end. But man cannot successfully create such agencies through his thinking. He cannot find spiritual insight and write orderly laws that benefit all people equally.

Even when a man begins to promote a cause he thinks is from God, more often than not, it becomes contaminated by his personal motives. This is true when his motives are sprinkled with desires for personal fame and success and power over others.

Every individual who has made a valid statement to the world about freedom, peace, and happiness had to first have had a healthy love for God, his own freedom, and that of others. That puts him in the position to pass the Word to the world and let others know that it is possible to attain the lofty goal of living in true freedom.

MY STORY

IN THE MID 1800S, I was the first black man in Franklin County, Tennessee, to be put in charge of his master's field workers. All the other slave owners had white bosses or black drivers, the most ruthless poor white trash and meanest blacks they could find for the job. Those men did not give a second thought of killing blacks or anyone else who stood between them and their pinch of pseudo-authority.

My master, William Sandridge, was a good man in his own right, I once convinced myself.

On the Sandridge farm, we farmed cotton and corn, raised hogs, chickens, and cows, and trained some of the best walking horses in Tennessee, just as his father, and his father's father had done. Master William received his first hundred and fifty acres of land as an inheritance when he lay waiting in his mother's womb. This was one of the many privileges of being white.

Master William Sandridge's father, Ol' Captain Vincent B. Sandridge, was about as tall as a blackberry bush and built like a bale of cotton. He married a tall, very pale-skinned woman with flaming red hair, a sculpted beauty, Miss Beulah Mae Davenpoint. On the one hand Mrs. Beulah was the sweetest person in the world, and Ol' Captain Sandridge was as mean as a trapped rattlesnake. I believed his short stature had something to do with his anger, alongside the fact that he was enslaved to whiskey, gambling, and wanton sex.

Master William Sandridge developed an obsessive need to do things different from his father. Master William did not want his slaves beaten, so he put me in charge of the field slaves. But although his slaves were not beaten with the whip, he still beat their minds and murdered their spirits daily with his emotional and verbal insults.

When you get caught up in an important thought time slips past you like milk pouring from the corner of a nursing calf's mouth. That was what happened to me the morning I stood in red lice field. I was lost in thought, and before I knew what had happened, a squeaky voice called out, "Nimrod, Nimrod!" I looked around but saw no one.

My thoughts drifted again.

Then I suddenly felt a tug on my pants leg. "Nimrod!" the voice squeaked, "Nimrod, Nimrod. Master Sandridge wants you up at the big house." I looked down. Little Josh's smile stretched from one ear to the other. I stooped and wiped the sweat from his smooth, coal black brow and looked into his dark brown eyes. My mind leaped into the future, to a time where I saw living conditions improved for some blacks, and worse for others. Then my thoughts turned back to an incident I had read about in The Liberator back in 1831. I must have been around nine years old.

A Mr. Thomas R. Gray gave a detailed report of a slave that, with the help of other slaves, killed more than sixty white men, women, and children. His name was Nat Turner. Nat Turner lived in Jerusalem in southeastern Virginia. From what I read in The Liberator and heard Master Sandridge tell his wife, Mrs. Carol Jane Sandridge, about the incident, Nat Turner was a highly intelligent black man. It was reported that when he was a child he had been given a book to play with by an adult slave. Instead of playing with the book he somehow taught himself to read. The Liberator quoted his master, Mr. Benjamin Turner, a Methodist preacher, as saying, "His intelligence was of a superior kind." After Nat Turner had taught himself to read, when he was eight or nine years old, his master encouraged him to read the Bible so he could save his soul. Not only did he read the Bible, he went a step further and committed the Old Testament to memory. Then he became a preacher to blacks.

When Mr. Benjamin died, his son, Mr. Samuel Turner, put Nat Turner to work in the cotton fields with the other slaves. I imagine that that one act was the spark that ignited his anger, which became the consuming flame that burned in his mind. In my opinion and experience as a former slave, Nat Turner, a black man with "superior intelligence" could not keep his hot temper from plotting revenge against the whites that recognized his superior gift and nonetheless treated him as though he were superiorly inferior. In 1822, Mr. Samuel sold Nat Turner and his wife to two different masters. Being forced to live apart from his wife and children turned Nat Turner's fiery anger into a burning whirlwind of rage. For Nat Turner to do what he did, including axing innocent children to death, his emotions must have become a roaring fire of hate that burned out of control. Nat Turner and the other slaves tried to gain freedom through force, which led to their demise.

Back then, I believed that kind of unrest and burning desire for freedom, "insurrection," as whites called it, would continue to spread until blacks and whites all over the country were forced to see that true freedom was what we all needed. Today, there are still some blacks and whites that have not gotten the message that all men must be free, and if there is to be peace on earth, personal freedom must be experienced by blacks and whites, by everyone. The particular whites I refer to think they are superior, and the blacks I refer to act as if they are inferior.

Josh tugged at me again and said, "Ol' Master Sandridge gone be mad if y'all don't get a move on it, Nimrod."

I strained to keep from laughing. I knew what Josh really had on his mind that morning, and it was not work. He and the other boys had been sneaking off to Beaver Creek to swim. Spring had arrived, the sun was rising earlier each day, and fast approaching its summer's zenith. What healthy child could resist the temptation to swim in the cool waters of Beaver Creek? It flowed quiet and lazy-like and formed a good-sized pond on one side. All the kids, black and white, went there to swim. They would run to the edge of the bank, holding onto the end of a rope that was tied to the limb of an oak tree, let go, and splash into the cool water.

Josh tugged again.

"I can handle Ol' Master Sandridge," I said. "You go on back to the field. We got plenty of work to do before dark. And don't you and the others go stopping at Beaver Creek." I knew Josh was not listening to me. His mind was on having fun with his friends, and that desire was stronger than any words I could speak.

Josh looked at the ground, a sheepish grin crossed his shiny face, and he said, "Yes, suh, Nimrod. I's won't."

In an attempt to hide my laughter, I turned my back and pretended to watch the red-tail hawk that circled above. Josh took a few steps backward, toward Singers Ridge, the area where field hands were clearing land for the new cotton field. He turned and walked off, made a sharp turn behind the pine trees, and ran like a scolded dog for the creek. I watched Josh and had myself a good laugh as I headed for the big house.

Mindful of Josh's words, I decided to take a shortcut by going through the Lonesome Bend trail, a beautiful and mystical track of land that lay at the heart of the Sandridge farm. Lonesome Bend like any plot of land of that sort had its tales. The old slaves told the children "hant" stories about Lonesome Bend. One such story was about a headless, one-legged man who came out at night and limped around, searching for his head. It was said that the man had been hanged by his master for looking in the eyes of a white woman. The weight of his body tore his head from his shoulders, and a bobcat chewed off his left leg before the master allowed the other slaves to bury him. Another story was about the floating lantern. At night, when there was no moon, they said you could see a lantern floating in the air with no one carrying it. And there was the one about the crying baby, which was told when the children had been rowdy during the day. The baby's mother was not permitted to nurse it because the slave owner's wife forced her to feed her baby instead. So one night, the slave mother's baby died of hunger. The dead baby cried and screamed from late at night into the early morning because it was hungry.

Stories like these were told to the children to keep them from going out at night. They also discouraged the adult slaves from taking the Lonesome Bend shortcut unless they were in a group.

Papa-horse and I saw Lonesome Bend as a spiritual haven, a place where the soul was refreshed and the spirit fed. Its heavy growth of trees towered above the other trees on the farm, and the leafy undergrowth, countless flowers, and healing plants kept it fifteen degrees cooler in the summer and fifteen degrees warmer in winter. It had a spring-fed pond with the best sweet water in the county. At certain times of the evening, the water became agitated and you could see it bubble up from the bottom. That was why we called it Dancing Pond. On windy days, the sun's rays seeped through the swaying trees and shone in shades of green, yellow, and white. I saw those rare occasions as light shows from God. On days when it was hot, you could see water droplets floating in the air like wispy clouds. Lonesome Bend was a paradise for me, the place where my soul found comfort and healing from the brutal life of being a slave. When I was there, I became lost in thoughts about God, love, and freedom.

That day, as I headed for the big house, I walked under the protective covering of Lonesome Bend. The sun was on the rise, its heat on the increase, yet the cool air of Lonesome Bend hugged against my sweaty skin. I stopped and took my shoes off. My aching feet were soothed by the thick green ground cover that carpeted the narrow path. Each step seemed to clear my mind. A lively moss crept up the side of trees. The haunting smell of flowers and herbs filled my lungs with new life. The path snaked in and out of the undergrowth—I felt enlivened. I thought about Master Sandridge and walked faster. As my feet came to rest on the cool moist grass, each step planted in the middle of the trail, one behind the other, in a smooth rhythm, my mind drifted far beyond the coverings of Lonesome Bend, the Sandridge farm, and beyond slavery. My emotions peaked. I walked on clouds. Ahead of me, a streak of brilliant sunlight waited in my path. I stepped into the light and my pace seemed to slow to a turtle's crawl. I felt as if I had stepped into a dream. My thoughts strayed into the past, back to the good times of my childhood, the spring of 1829. Papa-horse had blindfolded me and taken me to Lonesome Bend, the Birthing Garden, as he called it, for the first time. He stripped me of all clothing and said, "It's time you rediscover the freedom that's inside you, son. Time to take in knowledge that'll start you on your journey of life, the road to freedom."

"Okay," I said, "I'm ready to go. Will it take long? Is it far?" I did not realize that the journey he was talking about was not the kind I had in my young mind.

Over the years, Papa-horse took me to Lonesome Bend to teach me about the art of listening, the trap of emotionalism, the power of choice, the power of love, the two freedoms, obedience, and God.

Looking like a plucked chicken, I romped around in the nude, and Papa-horse sat with his back against a tree. He watched as I investigated shoots of grass, flowers, sprigs, insects, and everything I got my hands on. Afterward, he bathed me in the waters of Dancing Pond and told me stories about the Motherland, Africa.

After my first visit to Lonesome Bend, Papa-horse took me there regularly. He taught me the knowledge of the ancient ones, the Elders of the Isherman, descendants of the mighty Zulus, the Nguni people of southern Africa. He told me how they hid themselves in the jungles and were left behind when Africans began to sell their brothers and sisters to the whites.

The Ishermans lived in southern Africa for five thousand years before they migrated to Sudan. Papa-horse said they were the most powerful people in the known world. He said the Ishermans' form of rulership, their government of king, queen, and priesthood, taught their people how to live a balanced life through bringing the opposites together. They believed God created opposites in all his creations. If people studied until they understood, all people would discover how to live as they were created to live without prejudice and with love for all.

Papa-horse said, "God created man with great powers, powers that are deep within each man. And man is to live like God, in God's image, here on earth."

The Ishermans searched for balance by studying the opposites in everything: day and night, hot and cold, up and down, right and left, front and back, right and wrong, good and bad, man and woman, and the black and white races. They believed opposites gave order to human living when they were understood and respected. They believed if one saw the opposites in people and races as good or bad, or weaker or stronger, that was a serious mistake that created separation. As Papa-horse said, "The house that's separated in purpose is a house that's on the path of destruction, becoming prey for the enemy. And everyone in the house will suffer."

Papa-horse said the Isherman people studied the opposites for the purpose of learning how to interact with each other and other races. At that time, men and women, races and cultures, government and religion were not separated. To prevent gender separation, boys and girls were taught at home to work with each other in harmony and peace. Peace was the foundation of their society. All relationships and dealings were measured by the feeling of peace. The person who was not feeling peace was doing things the wrong way. Once they realized that they were not in a state of peace, they were to stop what they were doing and search for the cause of their lack of peace.

People of different races came together and shared cultures, ideas, and customs, which created understanding. Government and religion did not exist back then as they do today. There was only one way of ruling and worshiping: God's way.

Laws, rules, spiritual rituals, and beliefs were forms of worship and prayer, with prayer being the first and final say in all matters. No one made a decision without first praying. Love and forgiveness were the foundation of the two opposing systems of religion and government, and men, women, and races.

The Ishermans approached earthly life as if it were the second phase of a continuous journey. They prepared their children for this journey of life by teaching them about the different stages of life that we all experience. From birth through age six, their children were encouraged to believe in mind power, fantasy, spiritual powers, and the mystical world. They learned about the realities that are common for children during the early years of childhood: speaking without palaver, seeing and talking to invisible people, talking to plants and animals, stepping out of the body, and flying to other places. The children developed their natural God-given abilities through the arts of dancing, drawing, painting, sculpting, and most of all playing. From age seven to twenty-one, they learned reading, writing, and math. From age thirteen through eighteen, they were required to seek the unknowable through a personal relationship with God and were responsible for personal meditation and prayer. They meditated three times a day and prayed without ceasing.

The Ishermans believed individuals died each night at bedtime and were reborn at sunrise or at awakening. Papa-horse said the death process took place at the end of the day, and one needed to spend an hour looking back at their good and bad deeds. Thirty minutes was spent thanking God for that day's blessings, and thirty minutes were spent asking for forgiveness. Rebirth took place in the morning, when a message was taken from a gold container that was kept at the head of the bed. The message was read in silence and reread aloud for thirty minutes, then meditated on for thirty minutes.

Copies of those sacred writings were kept in all Birthing Gardens, which were a part of every home and all public places. No one was ever without an opportunity to get a needed message. I imagined those gardens were like Lonesome Bend: filled with flowers, herbs, trees, ponds, and waterfalls, perfect places for reading, meditating, and healing.

Beyond the age of ten, individuals spent their lives practicing the spiritual truths they learned. The Ishermans believed God was in constant communication with every individual, telling them what to do and how to do whatever they were doing. Individuals were to listen for his voice and messages in books, art, conversation with others, signs, and incidents. They believed that a person's beliefs should change like the seasons. If an individual's beliefs, attitudes, and actions were the same at age twenty as they had been at fourteen, the individual was stuck in emotional quicksand, and if his beliefs continued to be the same at age thirty as they were at twenty, the individual was spiritually dead. Yet the individual could be resurrected from spiritual death, if they were, willing to pay the price, as Papa-horse said. When they reached the age of thirty-five, they had reached the stage where life would attempt to force them into a rebirth and a new beginning. After an individual was thirty-five years old, he or she was prepared by the elders to begin what they called the Cross-Over, or the death of the sleeper.

During the Cross-Over, the individual only ate fruits, vegetables, nuts, and grains. He prayed all day, and bathed in herbal baths three times a day for thirty days. Afterward, he reported to the Isherman elders. The senior elder dressed him in a black gown and covered his eyes with red silk. The twelve oldest elders, men and women, led the individual into the Holy of the Holies, deep into the heart of a special cave. The individual had to lie on the ground, on his back, and the twelve elders sat around him in a circle, prayed, and chanted for three hours. After that, there was total silence for four hours. Then the elders took turns telling their portion of the special story, "Death of the Sleeper."

This is how I remember Papa-horse telling it to me:

Way, way back when, when the world was small, every night the old men and women in the remote village of Muimbahwha gathered the young men and women around a big fire and told them stories about the Twins. When the young men and women were children, they enjoyed the stories and believed they were true. But when they became young men and women, they didn't believe the stories are true. So each night after the old men and women had told their stories, the young men and women gathered under the banyan tree to do the things they called fun. They drank the sweet wine of the star fruit, touched each other's naked bodies, and laughed at the old people's crazy stories.

What the young people didn't know was the old people had done the same things when they were young.

And there were the Twins, a brother and sister team whose names were Life and Death. The young men and women of Muimbahwha didn't know Life and Death personally, but the old people did. The young people only knew the stories they had heard and laughed at.

One night, the night of the full moon, after the old men and old women had told their stories about the Twins, the young people left and sat under the banyan tree and drank sweet wine, touched each other's naked bodies, and laughed at the old people's stories. Finally, after they had gone home, and were in bed, they fell fast asleep. And that was the night that Life and Death came to visit all of the young men and women of Muimbahwha.

Death was thin and frail. She had two big, black, almond-shaped eyes that pierced the soul. These eyes sat above a broad flat nose. She also had long, white, stringy hair hanging below her shoulders to her hipbones. She had twelve long fingernails, six on each gray hand that curled like a lion's claws. Her two broad, gray, scaly, flat feet had three fat toes each, and her two tiny, gray, thin wings were attached at her hips.

That night she decided to visit the village of Muimbahwha. At three o'clock in the morning, Death rose from the ground, flew straight up into heaven, and fell back to the earth. She slammed into the center of Muimbawha and made a loud noise like the sound of a hundred broken church bells. The air smelled like a thousand rotten potatoes.

All the old people were awakened. They sat up in bed. Then they walked the floor and began to pray.

All the drunken young people remained asleep and snoring.

Death entered a house, the bedroom of a young person, and held a frail hand to her ear and listened for the sound of snoring. Then she put her head close to the sleeper's face and smelt his breath. If the sleeper's breath was strong with sweet wine, she held a bony hand close to the sleeper's ear and moved her fingers as fast as a mosquito's wings: buzz, buzzz, bizzz.

If the sleeper was thirty-five years old and too drunk to fan her away, Death kissed him on the jaw. If a bump rose where she had kissed him, she had not done her job. She bit him and bit him until there is no bump. When there was no bump, Death knew she had removed the sleeper's soul. She then flew out the window.

In the light of the full moon, Death searched for a dandelion. When she found one, she dug a hole beneath it and spat the soul into the hole. If the soul of the young person tried to escape, she spat again, in his eyes, then spread her tiny wings and farted gray smoke into the hole. Then she covered the hole and flew away. She repeated her actions with all the young people who were thirty-five and too drunk with sweet wine to fan her away.

The soul remained in the earth for five to twenty years until it became older, wiser, and sober from being alone in the dark. Then it was ready for rebirth. If the soul was ready to live as one who was born again, Death's brother, Life, came and paid him a visit.

Life, who was delicate and charming, had one round, shiny eye in the center of his face that could light up the soul. He had two large lips, seven long arms, six strong hands and one gentle hand, two large butterfly wings, and he glowed like a million or more stars.

Life swooped from the sky like an eagle. He circled Muimbahwha twelve times as fast as he could. He made the sound of chimes and filled the night air with the smell of roses. Then he hovered over the center of the village.

Life flew to the first dandelion and lit on the ground. He smelled the dandelion. If it smelled like a rotten potato, he flew off and found another dandelion. If the next one smelled sweet, he kissed it with his large lips. Then he held his big round eye at the center of the flower, and the bright light of his eye shone down through the stem. The sleeping soul saw the bright light and was awakened. The soul stretched and yawned. It followed the light up through the stem and came out. Life embraced the soul with his six long arms and wiped the dirt and sleep from the soul's face and eyes with his seventh hand. He kissed the soul with his large lips.

The soul took a deep, deep, deep breath and turned into a bird. Life stroked the bird's feathers with his six strong hands, and covered them with a special powder that was dry and oily. Now the bird became the Ba-Soul.

Life released Ba-Soul from his embrace. The Ba-Soul looked into Life's shiny round eye and began to glow like a star. Then the Ba-Soul gently pecked at a finger on Life's seventh hand, pulled it off, and preened its feathers with it.

The Ba-Soul flew high, high, high. It flew as straight as an arrow up into the sky. Ten miles up, the Ba-Soul stopped flapping its wings and fell to earth. The Ba-Soul fell fast, hit the earth hard, and went deep below earth's surface.

It entered Death's smelly abode. The Ba-Soul wrestled Death to the floor. Then the Ba-Soul grabbed one of Death's toes with its claw and ripped it off, and it flew up and out of the hole and went back to the village.

The Ba-Soul searched each house until it found its body, then it set Death's toe on its body's head and set Life's finger on its body's chest. Then it sat in the mouth of the body like it was a nest.

Life checked every dandelion for a sleeping soul by smelling them. He released all the souls that were ready for rebirth with a kiss. All the young people who were reborn became kind, compassionate, happier, wiser, and loving. All the young people who were not reborn after the twenty years continued to sleep. Their bodies wandered through life without a soul and they were mean, angry, revengeful, and cruel to everyone.

So, when you see a dandelion that has a short stem, smell it. If it smells sweet, leave it in the ground. If it smells like a rotten potato, close your eyes, hold your breath, and pull it out of the ground. That way, the trapped soul may see the sunlight, find its way out, and return to its body. Maybe.

Papa-horse said all the Isherman people knew this story. Most of them benefited from its message.

As a people, the Ishermans were forever moving into the unknown and seeking knowledge about God and his purpose for human beings. They believed all people were on a personal journey to the true freedom that is inside us.

Papa-horse told me, "Don't fear the unknown. Anticipate it. It will lead you to God. You won't find God in a church building. Nor will you find God in the Bible. Use church gatherings to be inspired, and inspire others to seek God. When the Bible is properly understood, it becomes a map that leads to God. God is in you. When you find God inside you, you find true freedom."

My experiences in Lonesome Bend, with Papa-horse's assistance, led me to the Unknown Knowable, to God, my purpose, and both freedoms. Each experience was the beginning of change, and change was the one thing that kept me on the journey to true freedom.

My walk through Lonesome Bend had presented me with another uncommon experience. When I stepped beyond the protective shade of the trees, the midday sun splashed against my cool body. I felt like I had been dashed with a wash pot of scalding water. I was weak and drained, I felt lightheaded, my knees buckled, and I stumbled. I grabbed a sapling to steady myself and walked slowly until the dizziness passed.

As I walked toward the big house, I realized the sun had reached high noon. I had lost time. Puzzled, I tried to figure out how it could have happened. Three hours of my life had vanished, and I had no remembrance of what had happened. I do not mean I simply lost track of time. I had lost Time herself. It was indeed a strange occurrence.

But before I could draw a single logical conclusion from my fuzzy mind someone yelled at me.

"Boy, where in the blazes have you been?"

I looked up. Master Sandridge stood at the edge of the porch, staring down at me like a screech owl getting ready to make a meal of a field mouse. His eyes locked in on mine, and mine on his.

"It's been three hours since I sent Josh to fetch you," he said. "What in tarnation have you been doing?"

Ol' Dr. Sandridge, as the white people called him, did not scare me. He was nothing like the other slave owners. His bark was worse than his bite. I knew him to be a kind man with a good heart, though he was enslaved by his fear of the white society of Franklin County. As Papa-horse said, "Right is right and wrong is wrong. All people are the same when it comes to matters of good and bad. Everybody has his good and bad. The worst white person has good, and the best black person has bad." All in all, Master Sandridge had his good.

I did not know what had happened to me, so I could not give an immediate answer to his question. I could not answer at all. I opened my mouth and stammered like a baby bird begging for food. My lips just slapped together, and Master Sandridge stood and stared. He was more confused than I was, as he knew me to be a dedicated and hard worker who was never tardy.

He set his sweaty glass of lemonade on the table and said, "My father would've had you flogged to an inch of your life for such negligence," he said in his teaching voice. "For such arrogance on this farm would've jeopardized the family's respect, not only among the people of Franklin County but the surrounding counties as well. You and the others belong to me. I own you like I own this land. You're my property."

Whenever Master Sandridge reminded me, a slave, that I was his property I thought it was a strange jester. As far as I was concerned, those reminders were signs that he did not have true freedom. I saw Master Sandridge as being the slave he was, a slave to fear. He feared what other slave owners would say about his showing kindness to blacks. That fear showed its ugly face on more than a few occasions. (I speak of Master Sandridge's slavery, yet I do not want you to misunderstand me. He, a white, had privileges and benefits I did not have, but his privileges did not make him free.)

During my years as a slave on the Sandridge farm, I watched my master and other slave owners live without knowing they were slaves. The way they lived showed their fear of each other and their bondage to traditions that had been passed down from generation to generation. I saw that they did not have the true freedom Papa-horse talked about. The significance of Papa-horse's words and lesson about true freedom, and whites being slaves to unseen masters, rang true to my ears and eyes every day. Whenever I saw them show a lack of respect and love for each other and their families, I saw their slavery. How could they give us blacks, and poor whites freedom?

Papa-horse said, "A man's words aren't as important as the meaning of the words. Look for the meaning in his actions." I saw white slave owners living as slaves.

I apologized to Master Sandridge for being late. I said, "Master Sandridge, I don't know what happened. I lost time. But it won't happen again."

"That's the most plum-fool thing I've ever heard of, Nimrod. People don't lose time. They lose track of time."

"I know, Master Sandridge, but it happened."

He leaned against a column and put one hand in the pocket of his white jacket. He looked more confused than ever. Being at a loss for words, he did not know what to do next. He walked off a few steps, turned, and made one of his usual remarks. "I expect you to remember this, and don't allow it to happen again!" These words were more for him than me.

Then he motioned for Sadie, a house slave, to clear the table next to his rocking chair. Sadie bowed her head, jumped to attention, and hurried across the porch with the shuffling walk that was common for house slaves. When she reached the table she stalled and moved the items on it back and forth, watching the master out of the corner of her eye and giving him time to regain his composure. After a moment or so, he stood straight again, filled with an overabundance of self-respect, and started toward the door. As he reached for the door handle, his wife, Mrs. Carol Jane Sandridge, poured out the door like a beam of sunlight breaking between dark clouds. Her tall slender body, hidden in the coverings of her southern belle dress, caused her to glide across the porch as if stepping to the music of an invisible orchestra.

"Hello, darling," Master Sandridge said to her. "I trust your nap was restful."

"Yes, thank you," she answered.

"Nimrod, hitch up the wagon," Master Sandridge barked in his half-commanding, half-asking voice. "Me and Mrs. Sandridge will be leaving shortly for the grits mill." He had different voices for different occasions, and I knew them all. When he was ahead on a business deal, he spoke in an authoritative voice. When he was wrong and felt guilty, or was outdone by me, his voice was less demanding and more asking. And when he was sickly, he spoke in his whimpering, puppy-dog voice.

During slavery, it was not wise for a white man to give the appearance that he was generous to his slaves, and Master Sandridge walked as close to that custom as possible. In fact, there was a time when slave owners had to beat their slaves in a correct way, using considerable force to create one-inch whelps in the flesh. If a slave owner were seen or reported by another white for not beating a slave hard enough, other slave owners would give him a lashing. Although

Master Sandridge did not have his slaves beaten, he still had to deal with his slaves in ways that displayed his complete authority and total control.

"Yes, sir, Master Sandridge," I said, "I'll take care of it."

Master Sandridge removed his hat from the chair, folded his hands behind his back, and strutted off as if he owned all of Franklin County. He and Mrs. Sandridge went into the house, and the screen door creaked closed.

Miss Sadie, that proud black woman, straightened her back and lifted her chin. She looked down at me from the porch, and I stared up at her from the ground. We watched each other's nervous movements. Those large almond shaped eyes sparkled like stars. My toes curled. My soul moved with joy.

Miss Sadie kept her long thick hair covered with a white headwrap, the crown of an enslaved African queen. Her full lips painted a permanent smile on her smooth, coal-black face. No man could look upon her glaring beauty and not be weakened and fall into submissiveness. My heart melted in my chest, slid down a pant leg, and overflowed onto the green grass.

Then my attention was diverted from Miss Sadie's beauty when I heard Mrs. Sandridge say to Master Sandridge, "You've been at it again with Nimrod, I see." That was a common mistake. Whites often discussed private matters in the presence of slaves as if we were not present. Or maybe they thought we did not understand what they said because of our poor pronunciation and broken English. Whatever their reasoning, they talked to each other as if we were deaf and dumb. Though they treated us that way, it was not true, for we heard and understood the things they did not want us to understand. We called it white ignorance of black intelligence. Their ignorance of our intellect and their practice of disrespecting our intelligence gave us opportunities to know the things they wanted to keep hidden from us. A case in point is their many and varied means for making money and reinvesting that money in deals that caused them to earn greater profits without working. Papa-horse called the practice sowing with little efforts and reaping great profits.

Have you ever wondered why so many blacks own barber shops today? Well, I can answer that question. During Reconstruction, it was common for blacks to work in barbershops, cutting the hair of wealthy white patrons. While those white men were in the barber's chairs, they discussed ways of making successful business deals, and where and how to invest the profits. Not only did the black barbers listen to those discussions, but they were also wise enough to use the information for their own benefit. Many barbers became prosperous businessmen as a result of wealthy white's white ignorance of black intelligence.

So you see, we blacks were quite ingenious when it came to surviving poverty and slavery. And while I am mentioning survival, I must tell you the story of Irene, the Four-Foot Giant. It was customary for the old slaves to tell stories to all children, black and white, but this story was among the few they told only to the slave children. This true-story was about one of the most amazing women, slave or free, to have ever lived. It went like this:

———

ONCE THERE WAS A SLAVE WOMAN, by the name of Irene. Irene was a short, feisty woman who married herself a big, tall slave named Bow Jack. Irene and Bow Jack had six children: Kato, Thomas, Peter, Nancy, Little Prissy, and Daniel.

Irene was the most determined slave woman in all the British colonies.

One day, Irene and her children watched their master tie Bow Jack's hands behind his back and beat him until he was unconscious. She said in her mind to her spirit self, "no more. I would rather die," she said, "and lay in a cold grave than continue to live as a slave and work in my master's hot fields. I shant take it anymore."

That night Irene pretended to run away from her master's farm, but she didn't really run away. She hid.

The next day when the old master discovered that Irene was gone he was fighting mad.

"She's a runaway," he said to his driver and two other slaves. "I'll have her back on this here farm before nightfall. Get the dogs. Let's go, boys!" And they headed into the woods and toward the north.

But what he didn't know was, Irene was still on his farm hiding in his barn. And, thank God, she was a little, bitty-ittsy, tiny woman. She was hiding in the small, cramped, crawl space between the floor and ceiling of the hayloft. She was just pretending to be gone.

Bless her soul, Irene, lived in that cramped space for more than seven long years. Every day she looked out through a peephole and watched her family come and go and slave in that master's fields. And once a day, every day, her family took turns to bring her food and water.

Soon the old master got tired of searching for her and paying the white Night Crawlers to find her. He was satisfied that he would never see her again.

Then one bright moonlit night, Irene crawled out of hiding. That same night, she and her family put a piece of bread and two strips of dried meat on a rag and rolled it up. They kissed each other good-bye, and she headed north.

For six years she and her family didn't see each other. For three years she worked hard, saved all her money, and bought her own farm. For the next three years, she worked that farm by herself and earned more money. Then one day, when she has enough money, she sent for her husband and children. They came to her little farm, were reunited, and lived as a family of free people.

———

MISS SADIE'S SMILE GREW, AND I was charmed like a bird caught in a cat's stare. Her passionate filled eyes made me feel loved.

Then I heard Master Sandridge say to Mrs. Sandridge, "That damn nigger is going to be the death of me," and Mrs. Sandridge said, "William, dear, I've told you time and again. You mustn't look at Nimrod as you do the others. He's different. His abilities set him apart from most slaves."

I could not see Master Sandridge's response, but I felt the heat of his anger radiating through the walls and leaping out the windows and the doors. Whenever Master Sandridge and I had had a skirmish, that dear lady made it her business to try and console him.

"That very well may be," Master Sandridge said. "But he's got to understand that I'm in charge of this farm and he's just a nigger slave I've put in charge of my slave field hands. And I'll be damned if he thinks, for one minute, that I'm going to share my property with him.

The nigger's got another thought coming." When he said he was not going to share the farm with me, I wondered why he would say such a thing.

"Why don't we have a bite to eat?" Mrs. Sandridge said. "Then we'll be refreshed and ready for our trip."

Master Sandridge had a successful doctoring practice in Decherd, Tennessee, and he and Mrs. Sandridge also owned grits mills in the neighboring counties of Grundy and Marion. They were preparing to go to the mill in Marion. Their trips took them over the rugged trails of the Monteagle Mountains during the harsh winters, through the early spring rains, and during Tennessee's sizzling summers. They traveled to the mills and ground corn into meal for families that were scattered throughout the county.

Master Sandridge yelled for Sadie to come into the big house to prepare something to eat for him and Mrs. Sandridge. Miss Sadie and I said our good-byes (our eyes spoke of the unattended longings of our hearts that our mouths dared not speak aloud), and she went inside.

I headed for the barn. The walk gave me time to think about the experience I had had in Lonesome Bend. I did not understand how it was possible for a man to lose time. I needed an answer. An overwhelming desire to talk with Papa-horse came over me. I prayed that he would be at the barn when I arrived.

But when I reached the barn, Papa-horse was nowhere around, so I began to hitch the horses, Jim and Nell, to the wagon. When I turned to buckle a harness, there he was. He appeared in his usual manner, from nowhere, and without a sound.

"When're you going to wake up to who you really are, son?" he asked.

I looked over my shoulder and smiled. I was happy to see him, but did not want to show how much.

Papa-horse, no taller than a Bantam rooster wore a sweat-stained straw hat that lay on the right side of his head, partly covering his snow-white woolly hair. The carved lines in his face were as deep as fertile valleys. His beard looked like virgin cotton set against a moonlit horizon. When he talked, his old corncob pipe flopped up and down in the corner of his mouth. His gnarled fingers looked like the twisted limbs of an oak tree. The fact that he never wore shoes, summer or winter, made his tiny feet to look like crusted paws. And his beady-eyed stare pierced your soul when he looked into your eyes.

"You're going to have to listen to what God's telling you, Nimrod," Papa-horse snapped, "or else you'll find yourself in a whole mess of trouble, staring Mr. Death in the eyeballs. And that'll happen because of some powerful illness you'll bring upon yourself."

Papa-horse's warning caused my mind to retrace my walk through Lonesome Bend. I wanted to discuss that walk with him, but I had to hitch up the horses. I worked faster, going from one section of the barn to the other.

Determined to get my full attention Papa-horse was between the horses and me faster than a snapping turtle could close his jaws. "Nimrod," he poked his smelly pipe in my face, "you must listen to what I'm telling you. You didn't come into this world just for yourself. You have a purpose for being here. God called you to live and do specific things while you're here. And if you're going to live in true freedom, you must listen to wisdom. There're reasons that you and the others are slaves in this foreign land." That last sentence caught my attention like a rabbit snared in a trap. "Black people aren't supposed to be in this condition. They're here because of one problem. The same problem you have now."

The truth of his words rang in my ears like notes on a tuning fork. What he said was correct, but I was not ready to accept that truth. When I was a young man, something in me wanted him to be wrong. I wanted things to be different for me. I thought I was special. Papa-horse's words stirred me with thoughts from the past, thoughts that slipped beneath my mind, lifted me, and carried me back to the time when I was five years old. He took me fishing one day.

———

"PAPA-HORSE," I HAD ASKED him, "can I go fishing with you?"

"Do you remember any dreams?" he asked me.

"No, sir."

"Then you're not ready."

"Papa-horse, all I want to do is fish. What do dreams have to do with fishing?"

"No, son, it's not time yet. You must be patient. The time isn't right for you to jump into the deep waters of life. When you're ready to fish, you'll remember your dreams. Dreams reveal the real man."

————

BACK IN THOSE DAYS, Papa-horse's answers to my questions were posed as questions, told as stories, or given as replies that did not make sense to me. That was the way of the old Africans, the Ishermans, their way to teach truth. And I was ready for anything but truth. Papa-horse said on many an occasion, "When you're ready to learn something new or gain understanding, God will provide you with the specific teacher you need at that time." He was a master teacher and storyteller, and I was not a master student. But as I grew older and matured, I developed an appreciation for his way of teaching. Out of the hundreds of stories he told, there were several that stood out in my mind. Those stories were like bright red apples hanging at the top of a tree covered with shiny green leaves.

"Nimrod," Papa-horse said in his gruff and rattling voice, "where did you go? Are you listening to what I'm saying? Can't you see what I'm trying to do for you?

"Yes, Papa-horse." I did not dare tell him I had been daydreaming.

"I'm trying to give you what's yours, son."

"I thank you kindly, sir, and I want it. But right now I have to get these horses hitched to the wagon. Master Sandridge and his wife are waiting for me to make things ready for their trip to the grits mill. There are folks who are depending on them. They have to eat just like everybody else, you know. But, sir, I do have a question. I need to do this one thing more then I'll be ready."

Papa-horse shook his head. I smiled and kept working. After I had completed my task, I turned to tell Papa-horse about my experience in Lonesome Bend. He was gone. Like a breeze, he had appeared and disappeared.

I loaded empty gunnysacks into the wagon and thought about what Papa-horse had just said. "Blacks aren't supposed to be in this country, except for the one problem that brought them here, and that's the same problem you have." My stomach sank and my chest felt hollow. I knew what he meant, and I knew the problem was going to be a difficult one to overcome. It had to do with the one lesson he repeated to me daily. He always said, "If you're to learn anything, learn that all you'll ever learn will come from listening. Listening is a road that leads to the two freedoms."

I led Jim and Nell outside. The sun bounced off their shiny coats, and I was reminded they were the most handsome horses in the county. Both had been broken and trained by the number one horse breaker in Tennessee, Papa-horse. I was the only person he had allowed to watch him as he worked. He said, "The secret to breaking a horse is not to break him. If you deal with these animals in ways that allow them to understand what you expect, their joy will be to comply with your wishes. They have a great capacity for companionship. Lead them. Do not break them."

I climbed into the wagon and thought about some of the important things Papa-horse had taught me through object lessons: the importance of uniting the mind with the heart, the power of choice, the power of love, the need for honesty, and the necessity of listening to and obeying God's voice.

Here I want to ask you a question. I do not mean to impose, but if I am to share the good of my lessons with you and my descendants, you need to answer this question. The question is, what portion of your pain and suffering comes from your poor choices?

During the time I was being taught by Papa-horse, I did not want to answer that question, yet one of Papa-horse's object lessons set this question squarely before my eyes. I was faced with the answer and this was how it came to be.

I held the reins in my hands and gently snapped them on the horses' backs. The wagon jerked forward. My mind drifted. Thoughts from the summer of 1833, a time I will never forget, rushed in and filled my senses. Papa-horse and I were in the barn. That was the time when he was teaching me that both good and bad results come from choices and the choices are determined by how well we use our listening skills. This is listening that involves the heart and mind. It is the ability to make changes. That lesson came from grooming a horse, and it happened like this:

———

"HERE, TAKE THIS," PAPA-HORSE said handing me the brush. "Put it on your hand, son."

"But, Papa-horse, this is your favorite brush."

"That's true. But if you're going to learn what I've learned, you have to do what I do, when I do it, and how I do it. All the understanding I have about grooming is in this brush. Put it on your hand."

I did as Papa-horse said and began to stroke the horse, which jerked and backed away.

"Papa-horse! Why is he doing that?" I asked. "He acts like he's been shot."

"No, no, no! Give me that brush. Let me show you how to use it, son. You should ask questions first if you don't know about a thing. Then listen to the answer and follow the instructions. All right?"

"What're you talking about?"

He held a finger to his lips, "Shhhhhh. Listen. Be like the cat. When she stalks breakfast, she's still and quiet. We must make sure nobody's close by and listening. Make sure we're alone." He looked around and continued, "I want you to open your mind and make your heart receptive. Listen for God's voice. Feel the peace and calm as it fills this barn. Stop the slave talk," he added. "Speak African. When we talk about the sacred things of life, we must speak in our tongue, Isherman."

"Yes, Rekesh."

"Good. Look into my eyes and listen closely to what I have to say. Listen with your mind and receive with your heart. It's time you learned a lesson about making choices and true freedom. When you listen with the mind and heart, the wisdom of God will lead you to true freedom. Try and understand what I'm saying, son."

I nodded and he continued.

"Now please, listen. With the mind, you think, and that causes you to make certain choices. But with your heart, you feel, and that causes you to make different choices. Whatever choice you make, whether it is from the mind or heart, you'll get results. If your choices are good, you get good results. But if your choices are bad, you get bad results. Listen closely.

"When you make choices with your mind, and the mind is

separated from the heart, you're going to make bad choices. But when you make choices with the mind and heart united, your choices are going to be good. Not only will you be satisfied with the good choices, and the good results that come from a united mind and heart, you'll also experience a taste of true freedom.

"Your ability to make choices is a personal power. When you use that power properly, it brings good results. You must learn to use the power of choice the proper way. When you do, true freedom becomes a way of life." He paused. "Now, do you understand that the choices you make create the results you get?"

"Yes. I think I do."

"Do you understand that Jim rejected your grooming because of the choice you made?"

"No. What do you mean?"

"All right, listen closely, Maradh. Son, when you started to brush Jim without knowing how to do it, that was a bad choice."

"What do you mean?"

"You didn't know what you were doing."

"How could I know? It was my first time. And you didn't tell me what to do."

"Right. You couldn't have known. But you still made a bad choice. Although grooming is a simple task, you didn't understand how to do it. Nor did you ask for help.

"I didn't know."

"That's true, Maradh. You didn't know. But the fact remains. The approach you chose could have only rewarded you with the results you received. Because you didn't know how to do what you were attempting to do, Jim rejected your efforts."

"Rekesh, you're saying I chose to fail?"

"Listen, Maradh. Listen closely. What I'm saying is the choice you made brought the results you experienced. All your choices bring results."

"I didn't plan to mess up. So what? It was a mistake."

"That's correct. It was your mistake. And that mistake came from your bad choice. Because you attempted to do something new without asking for help."

"Rekesh, you act like I suppose to know these things. I'm not old, like you."

"Maradh, it's all right, you'll learn. Let me help you. But this time, first listen to my instructions. Then follow them carefully. Okay?"

"Rekesh, I didn't know there was a special way to brush a horse."

"I know, son. That's why I'm telling you there is. Now listen. "When you don't know how to do a thing, ask questions. When you ask a question the answer finds you. Here, put the brush on your hand again. Okay?

"Okay."

"Place the other hand on Jim's neck. Now gently pull the brush in the same direction the hairs grow. Tell me, what are the results this time?"

"Sir, he's letting me brush him. I'm brushing his neck, his shoulder, and his chest. He's happy. He likes it."

"Yes, he's pleased. Jim feels your calm. He knows you understand what you're doing now and he welcomes the brushing."

"But why did he act different the first time?"

"Before, your actions were without thought and understanding. You moved quickly and harshly. You brushed against the hair growth. You brushed in the wrong direction.

"But I didn't know."

"It's all right, son. Your first attempt was out of ignorance, and Jim reacted to your ignorance. That's my point."

"What point?"

"The point is this: life does the same. There's an old Spanish saying, 'The first time you make a mistake it's out of ignorance, the second time is for experience, and the third time is because you don't care.' And we don't want them apples, do we?"

"What, apples?"

"Anytime your actions go against what's natural, you cause the results and you suffer the consequences."

"I thought we were brushing a horse."

"Yes, we are. And you're learning a valuable lesson. If you ask questions, you'll turn ignorance into understanding. And listening will bring insight. Following instructions gives the best results. Remember, if you don't ask questions before you start into something new, something you don't understand, your most difficult lessons will be listening. Asking questions and listening leads to true freedom."

"Rekesh, how can I do all that? And how do you know that's the best way? I know you're old, but I believe there might be a shorter way to freedom."

"Maradh, the things I'm teaching you are true and simple. If you're going to gain freedom, you'll have to give a lot of attention to listening. That's going to take effort and practice. If you don't listen, you'll make bad choices and suffer. That'll always be true until you learn to ask questions and listen."

"What else do I have to listen to? I heard what you said the first time."

"You're right. You heard what I said, but you didn't get the point of what was being said. That's the problem, Maradh. You hear me, but you're not listening. Son, you can do it. Listen. If you're going to be free, you must listen. Anyone with ears can hear sounds, even the animals. But hearing is not the same as listening. Hearing what I say is one thing, and listening to what I say is another thing. For instance, when you only hear what I say, you can repeat my words, and that's nothing great. Some birds can do the same thing. But when you listen to what I say, you get the meaning. You get the point. You gain the wisdom and get the good results you want."

"Sir, I don't understand. Hearing and listening is the same thing to me."

"Well, watch this, I'll demonstrate." He began brushing the horse. "Look, I'm stroking Jim's neck and he does nothing. Now watch this. I put my hand on his face, between his eyes …aha! See? Jim is nudging my hand and moving back, pulling away. Now watch what he does next. See how he flares his nostrils, and sniffs the air? Now he's moving close again. He's satisfied that everything is okay. Did you listen to his message, Maradh?"

"Dang, how can I hear his message? He didn't say anything!"

"Maradh, I didn't ask if you heard the message. I asked if you were listening to Jim's message. Sound comes to the ears as noise. Messages are understood in the mind and felt in the heart."

"If I don't hear with my ears, how can I get messages?"

"Learn to listen with your mind and heart, son. When you learn to do that you'll hear the silent points that come through messages. Messages are given by everything: animals, nature, people, and God, all the time."

"Rekesh, your words are like rain falling on a hollow log. I don't understand this lesson about listening. You'll have to teach me how to do it."

"My dear son, don't be so quick to be impatient. In due season, the rain that falls on the log causes life that's hidden in the earth to grow. I can't teach you to listen. But if you live long enough, life will teach you. I've laid the groundwork by bringing this lesson to your attention. And Mother Time and Father Experience will give you understanding and wisdom. Some day you'll come to know that your personal failures and successes come from either not listening or listening. The choices you make through understanding or ignorance bring the results you experience. Asking questions and listening are keys that open doors that lead to the two freedoms. All your experiences will come from your choice to listen or not listen."

"Rekesh, how can you say all my experiences come from my choices? If that's true, then you're saying blacks chose to live in this country as slaves. You're saying I chose to live as a slave to Ol' Captain Sandridge. How can you say that?"

"Maradh, look into my eyes. Listen. This lesson is about choices and the results that come from listening and not listening. You must understand that one of the greatest powers you have is the power to choose. As I said, your choices bring results and that is true whether you believe it or not. It's a law you can't change. Not only is there the choice of the individual, there's also the choice of the group. Both bring results, and you are a member of a group that is enslaved.

"This is not a good time to go deep into your question about blacks being slaves in this country. We'll save that for another day. There are other lessons I must share with you first. You need more time before we explore that matter. I'll explain it in detail when the time is right. But, first, if you're to live with true freedom, you must live on purpose by making choices that come from a mind that's joined to the heart.

"You're responsible for all of your choices, and all of your actions, and results. And this has to be the way if you are to be free. Come. I'll give you another demonstration. This one will show what's available to you when your mind and heart are united. We'll enter a place, the heavenly peace of the Nother World, a place that's within you. Follow me. Let's climb up into the hayloft."

Papa-horse and I climbed the ladder and sat in a corner. We sat with our legs crossed. Our hands rested on our knees, palms up. And we breathed slowly.

"Maradh," he said, "most of what you do and decide comes from your mind. You struggle and try to make things logical and reasonable. But you're going to have to change that practice if you're to be free. It's time for you to start developing your feelings, your heart-understanding. Allow your mind and heart to work together as one. That way, you can listen without being prejudiced. You can hear God's voice.

"But I must warn you that there's a price to be paid. And once you decide to pay this price, you'll discover, through great determination and constant effort that you can live in God's power. The price that must be paid is a heavy and exacting price."

"Rekesh, tell me. I can do it."

"You must give up your way of doing things and learn the art of listening. When you do, you'll hear God in you. God will tell you what to do and how to do all the things you need to do. When you learn to listen, you'll live a life that's filled with miracles. The most important thing is that you'll be happy and at peace. You'll have true freedom."

"Rekesh, what does listening have to do with freedom? Ol' Captain Sandridge ain't going to give me freedom because I listen!"

"You speak of things that aren't logical. If slaves want to be free, we have to fight for freedom!"

"Teach me how I can get the power of God. That's how I can fight for my freedom."

"Foolish boy, what is it going to take for you to understand? Your ears are open and you hear the noise of my voice, the sound. But your mind and heart are closed. Can't you hear the voice of God within you, Maradh? You must learn that you hear with your ears, but that listening is done with your mind and heart. You'll never possess God's power. That'll never happen. You can experience and live in God's power, as it is possible for all humans, but now your love is not developed enough to do that. You're not ready.

"At present your mind and heart aren't ready to live in God's power, not to mention the notion of having God's power. Your mind and heart must be free of judging, hating, wanting revenge and be filled with love and forgiveness before you can live in that power. Otherwise you would suffer more. God's power consumes and destroys all that is not of love. It purifies!"

"Rekesh, you're angry. Your words are frightening me. I don't understand. How can I do all the things you tell me to do?"

"Good. That's a question. Your first step. Now you've started your personal journey to freedom. Now you're ready to listen to wisdom and calm your chattering mind. You can never experience God's power on your terms. God's power is expressed in those who listen to that voice that's within. Your freedom isn't in the hands of Captain Sandridge. As I have told you, Captain Sandridge is not free himself. Your freedom will come from within you, not from another slave!"

"But, Rekesh, Ol' Captain Sandridge ain't a slave. No one tells him when to come and when to go. The house he lives in is the best. He don't need food and clothes like slaves do. He and the other whites tell us what to do. They live their lives and our lives. We're the slaves, not them. They have everything. We don't! How can you say Ol' Captain Sandridge ain't free? Your words don't make sense. They're not logical. No reasoning in them!"

"Remain quiet! Say no more. Listen," said Papa-horse. "You must be clear on what I'm sharing with you. Understanding will come to you when you control your emotions. From ancient times, our people have known the importance of listening with the mind and heart. Individuals who choose to use only the mind see the world in a limited material way. Many of those individuals fall pray to the Isms. And racism and materialism are two of the Isms that have trapped Captain Sandridge. He's separated from most men. He hoards more than he can use in a lifetime, filling himself with hate. His wastefulness and his greed for material things cause him to rob others of their meager possessions, even if that means killing them. His hunger for the material things has led him to idolatry.

"On the other hand, his wife, Mrs. Beulah, she tries to use her heart. She's very sensitive. Because of her sensitive way of relating to life and its difficulties, she has problems functioning in the material world. She has become trapped by a different Ism. Emotionalism. Her overly sensitive way of being causes her to feel the hurt and pain of all the world. She tries to carry the burdens of others, something she's not equipped to do, and isn't suppose to do. Her sensitivity, mixed with the world's hurts and pains, causes her to believe in strange doctrines and do strange things. She has grandiose ideas about saving the world, bringing peace and happiness to all people. Her invented religious-ideals, believing that God has called her to save the world through religious piety, lead her astray. At times she believes the world can be saved through politics. She and Captain Sandridge both go to the extreme. They haven't learned to take care of themselves. Because of their extreme ways of being in the world, they can be removed from society, and locked away to be cared for by others.

"Most people are like them. They live in the world by moving in and out of the mind and heart, thinking, then feeling. They sometimes make choices with the mind and other times make choices with the heart, good and bad choices. These people blame others when they get bad results. They blame their situations on friends, parents, masters, and God. And they're proud and brag when things go their way. But every now and then, there are a few who come to the world with a special capacity to love all people. These individuals make choices with their mind and heart. They experience true freedom.

"Listen carefully. You have this life, this one life. Unite your mind and heart by loving all people. When you do this you'll make decisions that lead to true freedom."

"I do love people. I just don't love the evil white man."

"You can only know his evilness because of your own evilness."

"You're calling me evil?"

"Did you call your white brothers evil?"

"Yes. They are evil!"

"If you can see their evilness, you're obliged to look at your own."

"Why?"

"Good! You asked another question. Whenever human beings are babies and young children, they can sense the evilness in others, especially adults. But they don't call them evil. They just withdraw. They're too young to know that they themselves have evilness inside, and theirs is called innocence. But when they're old enough to see and call others evil, that's the sign they're ready to discover their own evil."

"Oh…."

"Maradh, when you love your good and your bad, then you'll truly love. Now, relax, my son. Listen for the message that's within this reminder. Listen. Go back to the first time you straddled Nell's back. Remember how awkward it was to feel that huge beast moving between your tiny legs? For the first time in your life you felt the awesome power of the horse. That was the beginning of a new awareness. At first, you didn't know how to control that power. But with time and practice you learned how to ride. You soon discovered the secrets of controlling the horse and its power. The control came from the bit in the horse's mouth.

"Now it's time for you to discover how to use the power of a united mind and heart. Listening to God, as the voice of God speaks through different means, you'll become powerful. God's spirit will help you to get your anger and hate under control and lead you to true freedom. The mind and heart must become united as one.

"Close your eyes and sit still. Be as quiet as a church mouse. Listen for God's voice. Talk with him. Open your mind and heart, and you'll experience God's power. You'll feel it, but you'll never possess it. God does not share his power and glory, not even with the angels."

Papa-horse's words reached my intellect and sank into my heart. I did as I was told. Disbelief vanished. I became lost in the silence. The muffled sound of my heartbeat rang in my ears. God's voice filled the silence with wisdom.

———

TODAY, AS I RECALL THAT lesson, it seems like a dream, something from my imagination. Eventually I took it to heart, or should I say to mind and heart, and drastic changes took place in my life. I believe that if you will grasp the meaning of this one lesson that Papa-horse struggled to teach me, you will experience a major breakthrough on your own journey to true freedom. You will experience peace and happiness.

The significance of what I experienced in the silence is of grave importance to me. If I had not experienced the silence, the lesson would not have been meaningful. I admit that what I am about to do is impossible, but I must try, as I feel an uncontrollable urge to do so. I will now attempt to put my experience of the silence into words. I am not saying your experiences will be the same as mine, but I am saying if you are aware of some of the things I have experienced, they may help you.

This was my experience. I relaxed. My mind was filled with thoughts of receiving the limitless love that flows from God. Thoughts of being loved by God and loving others passed through my mind like water running through a strainer. Bad thoughts were caught and held. Good thoughts filled me with a calm that saturated my entire being. The good seemed to go beyond my body and fill heaven with all that I truly was. My heart was filled with love for everyone, even Ol' Captain Sandridge. That love spilled its contents into my soul and lifted me to a mountaintop of compassion. The peace of God filled my mind and heart until I could not tell where my body ended and space began. Like the air, I was everywhere. I sat in the center of life, and the material world and spiritual world blended like warm honey and butter. My senses became the total awareness of all that was.

My understanding of life expanded and extended into the past and the future and formed a perfect present: eternity. Time ceased to be a sliced pie, I was united with it, and we became the forever. I had entered the Nother World as Papa-horse had promised. I did not see them, but I felt the presence of angels. They spoke without speaking, and I understood beyond intellect. True freedom, the freedom that comes from the inside, was a steady stream of love that flowed through the trunk of my body. I wanted it to last forever. It was this experience that I referred to earlier that gave me a clearer vision and understanding of the entity man has called Time.

Then suddenly I felt as if someone had grabbed my collar and began to pull me through a dark cave. I rolled and tumbled and fell through blackness. When I had come to a sudden stop, I felt as if I had fallen from a tree and landed on my butt. I heard Mama Besta ringing the dinner bell. I was home again, in the barn.

I looked around the hayloft in search of Papa-horse. He had gone. I stood up, staggered, and fell against the wall. I braced myself on a rafter and stared at the golden sunrays that poured through the cracks between the gray boards. The hay smelled fresher, and its sweetness filled me with joy. The sound of the dinner bell, and the smell of Mama Besta's food made my mouth water. I felt hungry. I was famished. In spite of the hunger, I felt as if I had been delivered anew from my mother's womb. I was a baby who was fully aware of life's good.

The love I had felt in the Nother World lingered. The nonsense lessons Papa-horse had been trying to teach me now made sense. I understood what he meant when he spoke about the mind and the heart being united, the power of choice, the power of love, and the importance of listening to God. I thought I was ready to live every day with a sense of true freedom. But later, my dealings with whites showed me that I had another thought coming.

I brought the wagon to a stop in front of the big house. The dinner bell down in the slave quarters stopped ringing. My senses were back to normal and reality had made its sad appearance. I was still a slave on the Sandridge farm. A noise came from the corner of the porch. I looked up and was blinded by sunlight. The silhouette of a woman wearing white stood between the two large columns and swayed from side to side. I squinted and leaned to one side. Spellbound I watched her sway, repeat her movements: one thigh brushing the other. I was weakened. She raised one knee slightly above the other, and my attention was gripped by her swaying. The toes of one foot pressed against the floor and the heel rose slightly. Weakened by longing, I was caught. As if in a kiss, her thighs ever so lightly brushed each other. Mesmerized, my mind went blank.

"Nimrod, what you be looking at?" she asked.

I was startled.

Her girlish grin was as perfect as the smile on a marble goddess. The sparkle in her eyes was as clear as a raindrop hanging from the tip of a leaf after a spring shower. Her smooth skin was as dark as a pail of blackberries at picking time. Her breasts looked like twin honeydew melons pressed against a slope. Her round butt was as tight as a deerskin drum. And her short narrow waist and flat stomach was made to be wrapped by the fingers of the man who could truly love her forever.

Miss Sadie pulled her fingers through the hair at the nape of her long, sweaty neck. My heart leaped from my chest. She turned her head slightly and took a deep breath. She sighed. I wanted to weep. She was a sight to behold.

"Nimrod," she said, "I done save you what you like ... them extra biscuits from the lunch table. Just likes you likes for me to do."

"I'm mighty proud of you Miss Sadie," I said. "You're truly a saint sent by the Lord."

I jumped off the wagon and walked toward the porch. The screen door squeaked and announced Master and Mrs. Sandridge's presence. As they walked onto the porch, they were surrounded by a familiar calm, that basic earthly need that all people have, one that needs to be satisfied with true love. After you had eaten one of Miss Sadie's heavenly meals, you could not be otherwise.

They walked past Miss Sadie, and she jumped to one side. She offered Master Sandridge his hat.

"Thank you, Sadie," he responded in a voice of pure satisfaction. Then he turned toward me. "I expect the field at Singers Ridge to be cleared in a day or so." As he walked past me he continued, "And if you and the others have to work on it around the clock, I guess that's what you'll do."

"Yes, suh, that's exactly what we'll do," I said.

Master Sandridge hesitated, and Mrs. Sandridge slid her small hand under his arm and said, "William, dear, did you remember to get your glasses from the dinner table?"

"Oh, yes. Me and these glasses are as inseparable as Reverend Smith and his beat-up Bible. I don't dare leave without them."

He looked at me. I looked at him. Mrs. Sandridge led him down the steps. I followed them to the wagon and assisted Mrs. Sandridge up into the wagon seat. (Her hand was as soft as cotton, and she smelled like a bed of gardenias.)

Master Sandridge barked his usual compliments and instructions to Miss Sadie. "Sadie," he said, "I do believe you're the best cook in all of Franklin County. But do give extra care to the silverware. We're having guests on Wednesday. I'd like to put my best foot forward of course."

Miss Sadie nodded her head and said, "Yes, suh. I always does my best for you and the Missus. I'll clean that silverware right fine like, sir."

Master Sandridge climbed in the wagon and looked at me. As if he had not spoken a word about clearing that damn field, he repeated the same instructions.

I thought to myself, I declare, guilt is driving you crazy. Just as it did your sister, and the rest of your family. "Yes, suh," I said aloud.

"We must be going, dear, if we're to arrive before nightfall," Mrs. Sandridge said in a kind voice.

Doctor Sandridge flicked the reins. And with a stern, "Get up!" Jim and Nell moved forward. Their hoofs threw dust into the air that swirled behind the wagon like clouds. Miss Sadie and I watched the master and his wife disappear behind the dogwoods, reappear briefly, and vanish beyond the gate.

"Well, Miss Sadie," I said, "why don't me and you make our way into the big house? That way I can give them biscuits of yours the final test."

Miss Sadie beamed one of her picture painted smile. She grabbed hold of her floor-dragging dress and pulled it up a tad and said, "Y'all just come right on in, and make yo'self at home, Mr. Nimrod. I'll dish them up for you." Her voice was like the song of the mocking bird when it fills the morning with the joy of spring and romance.

I pulled the door open, Miss Sadie stepped inside, and I followed. We walked down the long hallway, and my lusting eyes went from the shining hardwood floor to the woodwork of the furniture, the art on the walls, and ended at the high, colorfully painted ceiling. Whenever I was in the big house, I tried to soak up as much of my master's beautiful surroundings as I could, hoping that it would vanish from his care and become mine. That act refreshed me, thought at the same time, it pained my heart. I thought about the stories Papa-horse told me about African kingdoms. He had said, "The marble floors of the African palaces were so shiny they looked like the still waters of a lake. They reflected everything: the green trees, the blue sky, and the white clouds. The king and queen sat on thrones that were made of ivory and ebony. The thrones were decorated with gold, rubies, and all manner of precious stones. All the people's concerns were treated with respect. Everyone was dealt with as an individual, a necessary and needed part of a successful kingdom."

Miss Sadie caught sight of my intrigue and said, "Nimrod, why's you be eye-ballin' this stuff? Every time you's comes into the big house, you just stare. You must be out of yo' mind. Y'all know y'all can't never have this as yo's."

I placed my hands on her shoulders, looked deep into her coal black eyes, and said in the old African tongue, "It's not so, except your beliefs makes it so."

Miss Sadie jumped back and looked around. She stared at me as if I were a purple plum hanging on a blue apple tree and said, "My Lord, Nimrod, what's you be doin'? Why's you talkin' like that? If the whites heard you talkin' in that old African-gibberish, they'd have you strung up. You gotta be careful with that. And, besides, it don't make a bit of sense no way. Cut it out."

I understood Miss Sadie's fear and felt compassion for her. She was the most loving person I knew except for Papa-horse. Her fear for my safety told me she loved me. And I loved her.

Papa-horse's teachings and my keen and observant eyes and ears had taught me that people hear what they want to hear, and their understanding of what they hear is founded on personal beliefs and experiences. That gives them their interpretation, the stuff choices are made of. And I well understood that my dear Miss Sadie had not chosen to know anything beyond her understanding and experiences of slavery. But I could not be what she wanted me to be, a part of her fear-based perceptions of whites.

I said playfully, "Ah, Miss Sadie, I'm just speaking what the Lord would have me speak." Her puzzled look, as it so often did when I was playful, turned into a warm smile. I grabbed that tiny waist of hers and laughed. She draped her arms over my shoulders, and laid her head on my chest. We both laughed.

"Come on girl," I said, "and give me what you been promising. I'm ready for them hot biscuits of yours." She looked into my eyes melted. A soothing warmth radiated from her body. I laughed harder. She laughed. We laughed until our eyes filled with tears and our toes curled in our shoes. We walked into the kitchen, side by side, hugged as tight as twin vines. We stopped between the table and the stove, faced each other, and looked into the other's eyes. Her warmth was stronger. It joined itself to me and became mine—I felt it strong. Our laughter faded. We stared at each other, and the warmth consumed us. Her faint underarm odor began to smell of the delicate scent of sex, the scent of love.

Reality faded. Her scent reached into my very soul and pulled passion from every fiber of my being. I inhaled deeply. Her scent became trapped in my nose. It was sweet. My heavy breathing pushed everything from my mind. My heart raced. The room and everything in it disappeared. My heart beat faster, our hearts beat as one, and my hands took on a life of their own and moved over her breast and buttocks. She purred like a kitten. It was music to my ears, and I moaned like a tom. She laid her head on my chest and purred again, except it became more like a whimper. I raised the back of her dress and exposed her bare ass. She rocked to the left, then to the right. I raised the side and she rocked to the left, and then to the right. I started to lift the front of her dress, but she looked into my eyes and pushed me away. We stood and stared. I sighed. She stepped back and sighed. She turned, slowly, and walked away. I watched her. I sat at the table and she went to the stove.

I watched Miss Sadie's butt as she walked away. My mind and heart had fallen down below my waist. The image of her round naked butt and the way it twitched as she walked away was trapped by my eyes and lodged in my chest. I longed to hold her, just once, all night until morning. She stood at the stove and rocked, and I knew she felt what I felt.

She said, "They're almost ready, Nimrod. And I hope you gots a appetite for them." I was awakened. I stared and watched her sway, and I thought how much I hated that things were as they were for us.

I could not live and act toward Miss Sadie as I desired. Nor could I be the man she deserved. Though life had given me the wherewithal to love her as a man loves a woman, feelings and desires and passion, my white slave owner had decided that I was better at being his slave than her lover. His cruel act of enslaving me had stripped me of my natural right to express the normal feelings that came with being in love. I could not love her the way a man should love his wife.

That beautiful black lady took those plain biscuits from the warmer, christened them with raw clover honey, and created a work of art.

I cleared my throat and said, "My, my, my, Miss Sadie, God bless your soul. You have the most beautiful gift. It's an amazement, how I wonder, you take plain biscuits and honey and butter and turn them into a feast that's fit for a king."

Miss Sadie walked to the table with her head lowered and said, "Ah, Mr. Nimrod, you is a king." Then she looked up, smiled, and said, "And, besides, you just saying that 'cause it's true."

I leaned forward, put my chin in my hands, and shook my head.

Miss Sadie's simple wit and dry humor always brought the best out of me. I laughed harder than before. When I was with her, I knew I was in the presence of royalty. Like a child at Christmas who had hoped to receive a few nuts, wished for an apple or orange, and prayed for a piece of peppermint candy, I waited for her to set the platter on the table.

As she did, a tear rolled from the corner of her eye and crept down her dark cheek. I felt what she felt. She felt what I felt. Over the years we had come to cherish the brief and infrequent moments we shared. It was in those encounters that we discovered the great pleasures that came from the rare occasions of being with the one you love, sweet togetherness. Those are the moments when one truly feels alive, the times when you know you are with your one and true love.

A TRIP TO JASPER AND BEDROOM ROBBERY

WHILE MISS SADIE AND I WERE lost in our private moments, Master Sandridge and his wife were well on their way to the grits mill. During the long drive they made light talk about whatever subjects Mrs. Sandridge dreamed up. That was her way to make conversation, that is, if there was any conversation at all. Oftentimes, the trips seemed to trap Master Sandridge between present reality and haunting memories of the past. At times he would make the entire trip without speaking a word. But Mrs. Sandridge's light talk continued.

I recall one such trip I made with them to Jasper. The week before the trip, Master Sandridge had one of his sick spells, and he was still feeling poorly. Whenever those spells came over him, he seemed to temporarily lose his mind, and Mrs. Sandridge was the only person who could calm him, so she would stay with him around the clock. I believe that if she had not done so the poor man would have died sooner.

I felt that Master Sandridge's suffering came from the haunting memories he kept stuffed deep down in his mind. They caused a heavy dose of guilt to lodge in his heart. As a slaveholder and one who believed in a supreme being, Master Sandridge had to have known that he was violating God's law to love all people. He had to have known he was wrong. As I said earlier, Master Sandridge was determined not to be like his father, in that he would not beat his slaves, but he still committed the serious wrong of claiming other human beings as his property. The last time a slave was beaten on the Sandridge farm was the day before Ol' Captain Sandridge had been jumped and beaten by the Gulley Boys.

The slave, Cato, had snuck off and gone over to the Johnson farm to spend time with his wife, Pansy. When Ol' Captain Sandridge discovered he was gone, he waited at the corner of the shack for Cato to return. As soon Cato reached for the door, Ol' Captain Sandridge struck him in the head, knocked him to his knees, straddled him, and hit him again and again about the shoulders and head. When the stick broke, the old captain went to the woodpile, and got a stick of green pine. When he came back, Cato was doubled up in a fetal position. Ol' Captain Sandridge began to beat him about the head again, and his brains poured from his skull like scrambled eggs.

Papa-horse taught that a man's present actions spring from his past. He said, "No man can plant pain and guilt in his mind and heart without reaping a crop of uncontrollable anger and a harvest of bad habits." Although Master Sandridge did not beat his slaves physically, as his father had, his tongue, his hateful actions, and his murderous attitude of white superiority beat us emotionally and killed our right to be free in any sort of way.

Whenever Master Sandridge was recovering from a sick spell, he and Mrs. Sandridge required me to be close at hand. For some strange reason, he wanted me within eyesight and hands' reach. I felt in my spirit it was because he wanted to share something with me if death came suddenly. That particular trip was the following.

————

WE WERE MAKING A TRIP DOWN to Jasper. As usual, I sat at the tail of the wagon, and Mrs. Sandridge started into her "let's have some conversation" kind of talk. It was one of those trips where Master Sandridge just sat and stared without blinking, not speaking a word. Bless her soul, she talked on and on as if the poor doctor was talking back. She rambled on about everything and nothing. After miles of riding, bouncing, and Mrs. Sandridge talking to herself, we were caught by nightfall and reached the Brownstone farm.

Aside from Ol' Captain Sandridge, Old Man Brownstone was the meanest white man in Tennessee. Those two old men had a lot in common. They both swore more than they prayed, and they hated Indians, Blacks, Yankees, and women more than they hated the devil.

When we arrived at the Brownstone farm the slaves swarmed the wagon like bees, and their larger-than-life smiles and grins and constant head bobbing made Mrs. Sandridge nervous. Old Man Brownstone yelled, and the slaves backed away, still grinning, and disappeared in about the house.

Mrs. Sarah Jane, Old Man Brownstone's wife, came out on the porch and wiped her hands on a clean apron. She had had the house slaves to prepare a meal in advance, and now she invited Master Sandridge and his wife in for a meal. While they ate with the Brownstones, I fed and bedded the horses.

After supper Old Man Brownstone, Master Sandridge, and their wives came out and sat on the front porch and talked about their concerns of the day. I sat at the far end of the porch and listened to their chatter for awhile, but it was soon lost in the night critters' performance of their evening "way down yonder in the South" melodies, a chorus that could be heard miles around. The humid night air drew more than enough mosquitoes out of hiding and kept our hands fanning our ears, necks, and ankles. The women talked about their children, knitting, and gardening. Old Man Brownstone complained about the damn Yankees, niggers, and poor white trash. Master Sandridge just listened.

After Old Man Brownstone had consumed several healthy glasses of whiskey and constant puffs on his pipe, he was in full sway. Although he knew Master Sandridge did not drink, he repeatedly poured a glass for him and himself. The pattern was that he would pour a glass for himself, gulp it down like water, then pour a glass for Master Sandridge and drink it too. Old Man Brownstone always kept a Bible close by, just as Ol' Captain Sandridge had. Like Ol' Captain Sandridge, he laid the Bible on the floor next to his chair and set the whiskey bottle on top of it. That was one of those mysteries of the illogical thinking of white slave owners, who respected no one and held nothing sacred, not even the book they claimed to be inspired by God. I believe they used the Bible as a lame attempt to cover up their guilt and hatred for blacks. One thing I came to see for sure was that they were not the all-wise race they thought themselves to be and tried to force us to believe they were.

Not only did the hatred of the white slave owners cause them to make the serious mistake of enslaving blacks, which created permanent damage for both races, but their inbred hate also caused them to underestimate our intelligence. Their ignorance of our intelligence was the instrument that enabled us to gradually carve a chunk of freedom from their decrees and laws. You see, it was blacks like Mr. Frederick Douglass, Mr. William Edward Burghardt Du Bois, Mrs. Harriet Tubman, and others who used white-ignorance to shape the beginning stages of our paper freedom. Those hard-working, faithful, and loyal blacks laid the solid foundation that you stand on today, the foundation that your children (my descendants) will build on tomorrow. White ignorance became black blessings.

So whites talked and lived in front of us as though we were deaf and blind. I can illustrate what I mean through the conversations that took place the night and morning I was in Jasper with Master Sandridge and his wife.

"My, my, Sarah Jane," Mrs. Sandridge said, "the year has flown by like a red-tailed hawk diving at a rabbit, and I'm still behind on my work."

"Yes, Carol Jane. I've got to get my sewing on the girls' dresses done, or else they'll go naked come winter," Mrs. Brownstone responded.

"Here," Old Man Brownstone said to Master Sandridge, "have another drink, William. You look a little dry around the gills."

"Thanks, Cylas. I'll set it here. That way you won't have to stretch as far."

"Mighty kind of you, William. Like I was saying, them Goddamned Yankees are robbing us of the good life. We shouldn't have to suffer 'cause them sons-of-bitches don't have walking-around sense. Hell, they don't want slaves. Dammit! I say they don't have to have none. Right? You agree, William?"

When Master Sandridge did not reply, Old Man Brownstone continued his rant. "William, can't you do more than nod your head? I declare, there're times when I wonder if you don't side with the damn Yankees and the niggers. Hell, you got to be more vocal. Verbalize your feelings! The Good Book says, God will bring to ruination those who ruin the earth. The Goddamned Yankees are at the top of his list, the sorry, good-for-nothing Indians are second, and them lazy niggers are third. And women are fourth. Of course, the women present are the exception. It's only the ones who refuse to take care of their wifely duties I speak of. Goddamn Yankees are trying to take away the only way of life we've ever known. And if they're successful, I tell you, William, we'll never see these days again. You can just kiss them and your own ass goodbye! There was a time when the niggers were happy with their lot in life. They lived as God created them.

"Slaves!

"And the Goddamned Yankees messed that up. Hell, we took them out of the hot jungles and put clothes on their bare backs. The Lord never meant for them to run around all day naked like animals and chucking spears at each other. We even taught them how to talk. Have you ever understood any of that jabbering they do when they first come here? Huh?"

"No, can't say I have."

"See? That proves it. We made them peaceful and docile—good slaves.

"Civilized!

"If you ask me," Old Man Brownstone said, "I'd say the first time a nigger ever saw happy was the first time he was locked in chains, his place in life. The Lord made them as a simple breed with simple needs, you know. Before the Yankees stuck their nose into our affairs, all them niggers needed was proper caring and such. Watered, fed, and a dry place to lay their hard, kinky heads. That's all they needed. But nowadays, hell, they seem to be discontented! Have you ever noticed that look in their eyes? The damnedest thing I have ever seen. I've never seen it before. Have you? "Huh! I say, have you, William?"

"No, can't say I have, Cylas."

"It ain't right, I tell you. It just ain't right, Goddammit. Oh, wee, wee, pardon my French ladies. I can get overly excited, you know. Speaking of excited. Honey, I hope the red flag ain't a-waving tonight. I got myself a real hard on, and I'm going to plow your field … real good. Now what was we talking about? Oh, yeah, don't you say, William? You agree? The niggers are different these days?"

" … "

"Dammit, William, I declare that head of yours is going to roll off your shoulders. Man, get that disgusting look off your lonely looking face. I say, have a drink. Trust me. It'll improve your disposition and sorts. You got to speak up about the damn Yankees, the Niggers, the Indians … and the women who don't satisfy their men. The ones who're good for nothing of course.

"Changing the subject here for just a wee bit," Old Man Brownstone went on, "I must say right about now, you darling ladies are looking as pleasing as plum pies on a prepared table. And I feel as horny as a hungry-rattlesnake in a dark feed sack with a mouse. Right about now, I could wrap myself around anything that wiggles and get some relief. Oh, excuse my bad manners, ladies. I don't mean any harm, it's just that God made us men to feel the way we do, and we just looove feeling pleased. Don't we William?"

"…"

"Well, don't we?"

"Yes. We do."

"The Good Book says, Man, fill the earth with your off springs. And I just want to do my part, that's all. And besides, William's forcing me to drink every glass of whiskey I pour. And I declare, it must be going to my head. My head! Get the point? Head! Oh, hell. Here, William, have another drink. No. Tell you what, I'll have one for both of us. Goddamned Yankees can kiss my fat ass. Eh, William?"

Disgust came over Master Sandridge's face. His head looked like an apple sitting on a mound of snow. Even I, sitting at the other end of the porch, could feel his revulsion for Old Man Brownstone. I say that revulsion was not caused by the conversation about Yankees, Blacks, Indians, and women. And it went deeper than that. It was a hurt whose roots lay in the past. As I said earlier, Old Man Brownstone was the spitting image of Master Sandridge's own father, Ol' Captain Sandridge.

I had heard Master Sandridge say to Mrs. Sandridge on more than one occasion, "I swear, that man, Cylas Brownstone is the exact copy of my father. Incarnated. His spirit will haunt me for the rest of my life. He just won't die. He won't let me live my life."

In my opinion, Master Sandridge's disgust for Old Man Brownstone was sparked by the memory of an incident that happened in 1811, when he was a child. My reason for believing this is based on a matter that was told to me by house slaves, along with the way he grimaced when Brownstone talked about women and sex. This is how they dramatized that night in the vernacular of slave storytelling.

The day, that day was coming to an ending.

The summer night was late and steamy and hot. The young child William Sandridge and his brothers lay there in the bed.

The boys slumbered in the quiet of a deep sleep and the mysteries of the cat-o'-nine tails swaying in the breeze, a kitten drowning in a well, the stone from a slingshot knocking a bird off his perch, pee poured from a tree onto the head of an old slave man and woman, fibs told about a slave child taking fruit from fruit trees. The sounds of crying filled their dreams.

Suddenly the boys was woke up from the world of dreams by the most dreadful sound, the sound that should never wake sleeping children.

They was woke up by the sound of their mothers' soft crying and the rumbling noise of furniture knocked about.

That was the night their mothers' crying filled the dark house with a heavy, endless sadness. The noise of furniture tumbled across the floor. The noises seeped through thin walls.

The old master, Ol' Captain Sandridge, was a man who suffered at the hands of many demons, demons of his own making. The old master was an evil and a vile man. A man less than a man. A man less than human.

That man beat his slaves, his children, and his wife.

He was a piece of a man who was conjured by whiskey, the water that burns hot going down the throat and boiling in the guts.

Demon whiskey cares for no man's family. It don't have no love for the one who dranks it. Demon Whiskey had the Ol' Captain under its spell.

"That whiskey-demon had led his soul many times down its unforgiving path, that path of unbridled anger and hate.

And it led him to doing what is unforgettable, thangs that leap from a heart that's filled with greed and guilt. It throws its victim into feelings that can't be controlled.

That whiskey-demon made Ol' Captain Sandridge his slave. No man is a match for the whiskey-demon. All who taste his venom are clay in its hands.

That night was the same as any night for the old master, just another night to do what he always did: drank until he lost his good mind, be a dirty skunk without a heart, and be twice as mean as a cornered badger.

After Ol' Captain Sandridge beat Miz Beulah to the floor, he picked up his bottle and started out the bedroom. But that night, she had gotten enough of his adventures of beating her until she passed out. Her desperation rose from the stomach and jumped out of from her mouth. She screamed at him. These are her very own words. "Oh, no, you don't, Mister! Not tonight! Not ever again! You'll have to go through me first. I won't permit it anymore! You'll rot in hell!"

She grabbed the old master by his arm. Then she got down on her knees and she begged. Miz Beulah cried and begged. She begged and begged. "Please, not tonight! Please, don't do it, Vincent!" she begged. "You don't have to! Have me! Take me! You can have it like you want it! Just take me, please."

He turned and smashed the bottle against the side of her face, and she was knocked out cold. It took all of a week before she came back to her right mind to walk and talk. After that she never went outside the big house again. She spent her last days crawling from bed and limping to the rocker in the front parlor. She sat for hours and cradled them books with her good arm. Just like they was her babies.

That night Miz Beulah laid on the floor and bled like a stobbed hog.

The Ol' Captain looked at her, then he got a fresh bottle and headed down the long, dark hall with his full bottle in one hand and a candle in the other. He stumbled and he mumbled. He cursed the darkness 'cause it was black. "Like the niggers," he said.

He cursed the Lord for making anythang that was black. The old master even cursed his own cursing.

That night the child, Mr. William, and his brothers heard for the first time the same thangs what we done heard for more than three years.

When Ol' Captain Sandridge came to the end of the hall, he mumbled. And then he cursed some more.

He kicked at the bedroom door. It flung open.

He went in little Miz Sarah's bedroom.

The boys got out of bed. And they crept through the darkness like they was injuns. They peeped and peeped through the halfway open door. And Lord a mercy! What they saw was what we slaves done knowed about for the whole time. The boys saw their father doing the unthankable. They saw their father taking something from their sister. Something that could not ever be gave back. They saw that piece a man rob their baby sister, Miz Sarah, of her precious sacredness. She weren't innocent no more.

The old master liked Miz Sarah's business more than he liked his wife's. He even liked it more than the slave women's. And that's why the child never got married.

Miz Sarah did her business with most every man and boy in Franklin County, black or white. Color didn't bother her none.

And that child, she could never sough any babies, neither. She just did it all the time.

We feel real bad for Miz Sarah. But we was glad it was not a slave child.

This story, told by house slaves, was not an unlikely tale. And as I said before, whites not only talked around us as if we were deaf, but they also lived their lives in front of us as if we were blind. They treated us as if we did not have the thinking faculties they had. In their eyes we were mere beast in every sense of the word.

Now, I will get back to my trip to the Brownstone's farm.

Night fell on the Brownstone farm like a blanket floating to a bed.

The music of the night critters grew louder, and Ol' Man Brownstone and the others continued to make conversation about the things that concerned whites. They talked as if I was not present. Their disrespectful conversation caused me to think about the foreseeable time when their foolishness would open doors for slaves and create paths for us to escape from their oppressive control.

We, slave men and women, listened to everything they said, and we learned from their foolishness. Because of their ignorance of our intelligence, we discovered successful ways to deal with them. We learned new ways to think, and thinking led many of us to paper freedom and some of us to true freedom. Papa-horse said, "Most won't gain true freedom because they'll get trapped by paper freedom."

Old Man Brownstone talked on and on, and Master Sandridge's head bobbed like a cork on a fishing line. The long ride from Decherd had tired him out.

Old Man Brownstone called out, "William! William, have you heard one single damn word I've said all night?"

"Oh, yes, Cylas. Yes, indeed, I agree," he answered.

And Brownstone complained until bedtime.

The next morning, field slaves on the Brownstone farm were up before the crack of dawn. They marched in lines like ants. When it came to working slaves and poor white trash, as he called them, Old Man Brownstone showed no mercy. His anger, fueled by guilt and whiskey, did not permit him to see color when it came to money and land. In his eyes, poor whites were nearer to being black than being white. "Poor white trash are half a step up from blacks and two steps from Yankees," I once heard him say.

They sat on the porch in the warm morning sun. Master Sandridge sipped his coffee and Old Man Brownstone sweetened his with whiskey.

After Old Man Brownstone had gulped down his eye-opener, his conversation began where it had left off the night before. While he cursed and rambled, I turned my attention to the things and scenes that were common to farm life.

It was a typical Tennessee morning. The sun rose from behind the dark trees and inspired everything with life, some hens scratched in the yard, and others ran to avoid a rooster's lustful chase. They ran with an awkward determination. Down at the edge of the field, at the bend in the road, a buck and three does crossed from one field to another. The air was fresh and clean and scented with the smell of a country breakfast.

The women, Mrs. Brownstone and Mrs. Sandridge, were in the kitchen, where they gave cooking instructions to the house slaves Mama Buck and Nell. Mrs. Brownstone talked at them as if they were cooking for the first time. I heard her tell them how to slice the bacon, how many eggs to scramble, the measure of milk needed for the biscuit batter. And on and on she went.

Mama Buck and Nell, experts in the culinary arts, pretended to do as they were told. This was common for slaves. Mama Buck and Nell had been cooking longer than Mrs. Brownstone had been alive. The smell of buttermilk biscuits, smoked ham, and fresh ground coffee filled the kitchen and spilled out through the house and poured out the windows and doors.

Little Miss Betsy and Miss Anna were awakened when Mama Buck called out, "Rise and shine. Old Mister Sun done said it's time for a new day."

The way she talked to the girls was gentle and loving. She wanted them to begin their day in a good mood. That way, they would grow up in their Southern traditions, and be the Southern-belles they were expected to be, gracefully lifting the sides of their hoop-skirted dresses with one hand, carrying a handkerchief in the other, and wearing a permanent smile for Southern gentlemen on their powdered faces.

"Great day in the morning. Yous sure does look beautiful this fine morning, Miss Betsy," Mama Buck said. "And, Miss Anna, yous be the pretties thang in all the county. Why, God done tried to out do his-self when he created the two of you. And Looord, is I's proud to be's with you this very fine day."

Master Sandridge and Old Man Brownstone were interrupted when Nell, in her cheerful house slave voice announced, "Master Brownstone, you and the doctor, y'all come to breakfast now. Come and get it 'fore it done gits cold."

Old Man Brownstone grunted like a pig, and Nell stepped to the side and held the door open. Old Man Brownstone rose from his chair, and Master Sandridge followed. They walked into the house, and I trailed behind. They went into the breakfast room and sat at the table, and I went into the kitchen with the house slaves and sat where my vision and hearing had clear shots into the breakfast room.

Old Man Brownstone sat at the head of the table and asked Master Sandridge, "William, I declare, is it totally necessary to have that damn nigger follow you around like a dog?"

Master Sandridge smiled.

Soon Mama Buck, Miss Betsy, and Miss Anna made their way down the stairs. They were all smiles and talk, making plans for the day.

"Of course, we must take our walk along the river," Miss Betsy said, "and have a picnic and go horseback riding." She was interrupted when Miss Anna piped up and said, "We just got to play dolls and dress up, Mama Buck. It's my favorite thing in all the world to do. I just love looking pretty. It makes me feel good when you brush my hair and tell me how pretty I am."

When they reached the bottom of the stairs, Mama Buck gave way to one of her belly-laughs and said, "We's gone do it all and more, my sweetie pies."

When the girls entered the breakfast room, Mr. Brownstone

stopped talking and smiled. Miss Betsy and Miss Anna turned cold. Sadness covered their faces. Old Man Brownstone cocked his head and said playfully, "Well, shit fire and save the matches. How's my sweet angels? You sure do look sweet this morning, girls. As sweet as honey on watermelon."

As those words crossed his lips, Miss Betsy and Miss Anna gazed down at the floor. They were as quiet as death. Only God and Old Man Brownstone knew why.

———

I STIRRED MY LAST BITE OF BISCUIT in the honey and butter, opened my mouth extra wide, and slowly placed it inside. It melted. I was thankful for good food. Miss Sadie smiled and sighed.

Night had arrived at the Sandridge farm, and I had chores that needed to be attended to. After I had bade Miss Sadie a good night, we walked to the door and I pushed it open. She grabbed my hand and held it tenderly. Her bright eyes told me her heart was darkened by loneliness. When I put my hand on her shoulder, she pulled back, closed her eyes, and lowered her head. She walked off and disappeared in the kitchen. I wanted to follow her, but felt it was best to take my leave.

I left the big house and made my rounds, checking the animals, making sure things were prepared for the next day, then headed down the path that led to the slave quarters.

The moon was full, and I was thinking about the time I had spent with Miss Sadie. As I walked, I kicked at patches of grass and enjoyed the feelings that ran through my body. After I had walked a short distance, I took the key from my left pocket, the key that Master Sandridge gave me each time he left the farm. I rolled the key in my hand. I was curious to know the secrets that it protected for my master. Papa-horse's words came to mind. "Man makes secrets in the dark, and God reveals them in the light." I looked at it and thought, 'Some day, some day soon, I will know what you know. And you may give me a river of pain, a mountain of happiness, or both.' The bright moon bathed the grass, the trees, and the buildings in its velvety blue light. I inhaled the night air deep into my lungs.

There was movement in the distance. A silhouette about the size of a child stood in the middle of the path, blocking my way to the cabins. It was covered by a flaming blue light similar to that of the moon.

The figure turned toward me. I stopped. I put the key in my pocket and took a few steps forward to get a better look. I was relieved. As Miss Sadie would say, it was a sight for sore eyes. It was Papa-horse.

My day had been a mixture of trying tribulations and great pleasures that were marked by an important and unanswered question. And I knew Papa-horse had the answer. Without uttering a word, he turned and walked toward Lonesome Bend. I followed him. In my heart I knew I would get my answer. After I had walked a short distance farther down the path, I put my hand in my pocket and searched for the key. Terror leaped from the depths of my very being. The pocket was empty. I desperately searched my other pocket, and my terror increased. Both pockets were empty. My fingers searched the folds and corners of both pockets and found nothing. The size of the pockets grew as I searched for that vanished key. I had mistakenly put it in the right pocket, the one that sported a hole.

"I've lost the key! It's gone! What am I to do!"? I asked aloud.

Master Sandridge had given that all-powerful key, the most sacred thing on the Sandridge farm, to me for safekeeping. Locks and keys were not common on the Sandridge farm. It had been that way since the Sandridge clan had first arrived from Scotland. Master Sandridge's great great-great-grandfather told his family when they arrived, "The day I have to keep my belongings under lock and key in this country, that'll be the day I'll surrender my crown of glory and faith in God to the wrath of hell."

I desperately searched my pockets for the key. But it did not reappear. I called out to Papa-horse. He turned around and said, "Don't think, don't use reason, and don't use logic. Don't hesitate. Pray. Go back to the place where you dropped it. It's there."

That was another one of those times when Papa-horse's suggestion made no sense. I was in desperate need of help, and all he did was preach to me about reason and logic.

"I have no idea where I lost it," I said. "If I did, I wouldn't need your help." Papa-horse just turned and walked off. I was left with no choice but to listen and do as I had been instructed. I prayed as I walked back to the spot where I first saw him. I stopped. I stooped down and reached towards the ground without looking. Without thinking. My hand brushed against the wet grass. I closed my fingers. And I was shocked. I held the key in my grip.

"How in heaven does he know these things?" I asked aloud. He was right again. I was excited to have found the key, but I was also flustered by his rightness. He was always right, and though that caused me to feel wrong, I knew his rightness did not make me wrong. It was my need to have him be wrong that hurt me. And I knew I needed humility as a companion.

In spite of my lack of humility and my bruised feeling, I could not control my excitement. I ran to catch up with Papa-horse. The experience fed my hunger to ask a thousand questions. I wanted to spend the closing hours of that day with my friend and teacher. I rushed down the dark trail. The cool night air flowed around my face, and thoughts of what I would learn rushed through my mind. I was eager to listen to anything Papa-horse had to say. Most of all, I wanted to know why and how I had lost time.

When I reached the entrance of Lonesome Bend, my heartbeat was faster than a jackrabbit running from ten hungry hounds. I ducked and pushed low-hanging branches out of my way and headed for Dancing Pond. I imagined how I would find Papa-horse sitting at the edge of the pond, his feet in the water, ready to reveal the secrets of life to my hungry mind and thirsty soul.

The light blue moonlight seeped through the spaces between the leaves on the trees. The trees seemed to pull their leaves back at night to let the moon bathe the garden with its healing light. The air was sweet with the smell of herbs and flowers. I walked around trees and stepped over logs and around the bushes that lined the path. When I reached the pond, Papa-horse, a shadowy figure, sat at the edge with his feet in the water.

Not one ripple danced on the surface of the water. I sat down beside him to his left and crossed my legs. My excitement was calmed by the motionless reflection of the moon, a perfect light blue ball on glassy water. My thoughts traced back to my walk through Lonesome Bend and my lost time. I closed my eyes and waited for Papa-horse to speak. He sat motionless, and said nothing.

My mind still drifted. A warm and intoxicating weightlessness filled my chest and spread through my body. I inhaled deeply. My sense of touch drifted off into the distance, and I no longer felt my bodily parts. I took another deep breath. I wanted to look at Papa-horse and tell him what I was feeling, but I was paralyzed and rendered speechless by a new sensation that filled me. My eyelids would not open. Love flowed from him and surrounded me like a cocoon around a caterpillar. I was covered by the power of love. Papa-horse also sat motionless and speechless. For the second time, I felt what I perceived to be true freedom. It rose from the remotest regions of my soul and within minutes all traces of lingering fear fled into the darkness. In those moments, nothing else existed for me except love and peace.

Minutes passed, and a white light came from Papa-horse and entered my mind through a space between my eyes. Gold and purple lights moved in and out of each other like cream and coffee. Then they were thoroughly mixed and the white light surrounded them and the calm was deepened.

Suddenly, I found myself sitting in heaven. I had passed through the portals of time and entered into the fullness of life. Eternity carried me on her wings of peace and love. I traveled without moving. Planets far ahead of me, and distance itself, rushed toward me. My mind raced with hundreds of questions, and my heart gave answers to each within an instant. In the fullness of unity, oneness with all things, oneness with life itself, oneness with God, the creator, I realized that my mind was not confined within a brain or a body. It seemed to have originated outside my body from a central location and radiated into my body, brain, and heart. My mind was not aware of distance and time. I was infinite, the vastness of the universe, which streamed from a pinpoint center and spread in all directions. I was no longer the concept of Nimrod. I was that part of God that was expressed as Nimrod. I was what God expressed as the created man, Nimrod. It was then that I understood what Papa-horse meant when he said, "Everything is from God. All things come from within themselves. God is in all things."

Material things were no longer solid, but were vapors of light. Even the colors, the music, and the fragrances I smelled seemed to be pure light. I saw the colors and heard the sounds that Papa-horse told stories about, colors and sounds that do not exist in the natural or human world. The most amazing thing was that I smelled and tasted the colors and sounds. For the first time in my life, I felt I had come face-to-face with God. I thought about Papa-horse's words, "No man can see God face-to-face and continue to live as he does. He changes forever."

I felt that what I experienced was too wonderful to be true. Doubts came into my mind, and the sensations began to fade and I tumbled down a tunnel of blinding light. The old reality rushed in and surrounded me. The trees of Lonesome Bend and the water of Dancing Pond lay before me, in full view. I felt as if I had fallen out of a tree. I kept my eyes closed, my mind relaxed.

The chirping of a cricket got my attention. I took deep breaths and listened to his melody. Then I opened my eyes and the little fellow leaped from his perch, my knee, and scampered off into the grass. The trees had a strange appearance. An unearthly feeling of a common familiarity, the kind one encounters when in love, came from them. They seemed to be communicating with each other, and with me. They spoke angel talk, which is speaking without words. It was as if they shared a sort of wisdom regarding their God-given purpose for being. The grass, the herbs, and the flowers did the same.

I thought about the time Papa-horse told me about the Ishermans' belief that all life forms communicate their own special purposes for being to each other and humans. He said, "From the beginning there have only been a few people, the sensitive ones, who can hear them, the plants, the insects, the animals, speaking of God's wisdom and glory, and their purposes for being created. And they're ones who truly listen. God created all life forms with the ability to communicate with their kind and with humans who have ears to listen. God created life, all life, for that very good purpose."

TRANSFORMATION

⤜ ⤛

AS THE NIGHT GREW DARKER AND the hazy blue moon grew brighter, Dancing Pond lived up to its name. Its water swirled and tumbled, and the moon's reflection danced. Excitement swelled in my stomach as I stared into the agitated water.

A large object at the bottom of the pond seemed to be inching toward the center of the pond. Seconds passed, and another moved. Then others. The objects were different shapes and sizes. Soon the bottom of the pond was covered with movement. For the first time I saw what Papa-horse had talked about. That experience delighted my soul.

I wanted to know what was moving, so I leaned forward and the cool water excited the tip of my nose. What I saw move at the bottom of Dancing Pond surprised me beyond a million guesses. Rocks. They were rocks. To my amazement, rocks were moving as if they were alive. Papa-horse had once said, "Everything is alive with the spirit of God. The rocks, soil, insects, plants, animals, wind, and water are alive in their own unique ways. All are created for man's play, enjoyment, and food."

Again and again, the swirling water lifted the rocks from the bottom of the pond. They were like leaves in the wind. Overcome with joy, I turned to Papa-horse. I pointed at the water and said, "Look! This is the most amazing thing I've ever witnessed. Do you see it?" I could not contain my laughter. I fell back into the grass and rolled and laughed.

When I had stopped laughing, I lay on my back looked at Papa-horse, to ask if he saw what I saw. I was surprised. I sat up. I turned and faced what I had thought was Papa-horse. Papa-horse was not there. It was a bush. I had sat next to a bramble bush the whole while, and thought it was Papa-horse.

Of all the experiences I had that night, the bush awakened in me the greatest appreciation for all creation and the Wisdom of God contained in every little thing. I understood that the abilities I had attributed to Papa-horse were mine. They were gifts God had created in me. Papa-horse's words, "All humans are created in the likeness of God," had become clearer. But I must confess that reason, logic, and false humility still blinded me. I was not ready to accept the notion that the power that created me, God, was working within me. I still had my doubts.

Then I had another experience that caused my mind's eyes to open a bit more and understand a blessing for a man like me who was in search of freedom that went beyond slavery on the Sandridge farm. A soft blue light, like moonlight, surrounded everything I could see. I looked at the water of Dancing Pond, and that light rose from it like a hazy blue mist. The rocks, grass, bushes, and trees glowed with that same light. I stretched my hands out, and they were covered with the light. I did the same with my bare feet, and the light surrounded them, too. The clarity of Papa-horse's lessons about listening and true freedom began to sink from the top of my mind down into the center of my heart and the pit of my stomach. In that moment, the thought came into my mind, If I continue on this path I will become a victim of imaginative and delusional thinking. How can this be true? It's not logical. It's not reasonable. But there I was. And there it was, a truth strangled by deadly doubt. My doubt.

I stood and reached into my pocket, and my fingers groped for the key. It was there. I pulled it out of my pocket, rolled and twirled it in my hand, and said aloud, "As the night turns to dawn, your secrets will be revealed."

I felt in my soul and knew in my spirit that someday that precious key would open a door that would be of great help to me and the other slaves on the Sandridge farm. It had to.

That night the answer to my all-consuming question, my lost time, was answered by my experience with the key. I came to realize that when feelings are tainted with emotionalism and beliefs are soiled with doubts, to lose anything, including time, is a loss of awareness.

I walked out of the thick coverings of Lonesome Bend wired. I felt as if I had smoked locoweed from Mr. Bray William's cattle farm. It seemed as if my hearing had sharpened. It was as if I could hear the slaves down in the slave quarters talking to one another, as if I could hear Master Sandridge up at the big house in a fight with Mrs. Sandridge. I felt powerfully free. Once more I had reason to think that

I was ready to live in true freedom. I looked up at the moon and heaven, and I prayed.

When I started to leave Lonesome Bend, I saw Papa-horse standing in the middle of the path. His body and presence radiated pure love. Filled with the excitement of a newborn colt, I ran toward him, eager to tell him about my experiences. As I approached, he held up his hand and said in the African tongue, "The fool brags. The wise man does not. Besides your being excited, what're you going to do with this new knowledge, son?"

How do you know what I'm going to say? I thought to myself. How?

In that moment, a moment of excitement, I felt rejected by the man I loved most. I saw Papa-horse as the meanest man alive. I looked down at the ground. But his gestures and my feelings forced me to take stock of my attitude. My anger told me that I was not ready for true freedom. My pride told me that Papa-horse was wrong, that he did not truly love me. On the other hand, there was the more sober part of me that said, 'Your experiences were but a mere fragment of true freedom. You have not scratched its lustrous surface, young man.'

I wanted true freedom all right, but my understanding and actions were proof that I was not ready for it. I thought about Papa-horse's words, "What one says is not as important as what one does. When one part of a man rises in elation, he brags. Soon another part of that same man pulls him down into despair."

All in all I knew what I had to do. I raised my head to look into his eyes, and stepped forward to embrace him. He was more than twenty feet down the trail. He walked toward the slave quarters, and I trailed behind like a whimpering pup.

"Nimrod," he said, "you must be careful, my son. Listen.

"When men first began to invent gods, their notions came through their reason and logic. They described The Creator Of Life as a larger version of themselves, a giant human. "From the beginning man has talked about God and worshiped God as though God were evolving alongside humans. As man's knowledge, intellect, understanding, and beliefs have changed, his description of God has changed.

"Men have taught that they were created in God's image and likeness, yet they did not accept their own words as truth. To the contrary, their beliefs and practices demonstrate that God, their God, was created. Was created by them, men, according to human reason and logic in a human likeness.

"Men who seek to control other men don't see beyond their personal fears and doubts. And because these men fear they will lose their perceived power, when things go against their reason and logic, they explain it away with more reason and logic. When men couldn't see beyond the horizon, they said, 'The earth is flat.' But had they used their reason and logic properly, as it was created to be used, they would have said, 'Since the sun, moon, and stars are circular, and the apple and orange are round, it also stands to reason that the earth is round.'

"The man who teaches the masses that he, the one preaching, is God's chosen one, he himself is one of those false man-made self-appointed-leaders. A leader who changes God into what God is not, into what he wants God to be, is a self-appointed spokesman who has taken the position of being a mediator between God and the people. Those leaders teach their fear-based and doubt-based beliefs about God to the gullible, leading them astray. They convey their personal thoughts, their personal commands, and their personal visions to the people as though they have squatter's rights on God's purpose. Throughout history, the lost have followed those self-appointed spiritual leaders. They have been disappointed time and time again. These man-God messengers carry atrocities of all kinds in their bosoms and heap them on the heads of the innocent and ignorant. Especially beliefs that lead to separation, war, and premature death.

"The time is coming when masses of people, great numbers of people, will begin to reason as individuals. They won't be as eager to follow the self-appointed religious leaders as their fore parents were. Those individuals will seek a personal relationship with The Creator Of Life and seek divine knowledge from its source. There will be confusion for a season. Individuals will create sects. Some will teach that God is dead. Some will build magnificent structures, churches that will house thousands of people and lead the masses into greater spiritual darkness. They will teach about a cruel, mean, and vengeful god, their god, who is a reflection of themselves, of men who are in pain, of men who do not know to love themselves or others from their brains, hearts, stomachs, and kidneys.

"Men who are trapped in their emotions and sick with emotionalism will teach people that they, the preachers, are the messiahs. People will leave their families and follow these men into death. They will take their own lives in gatherings. To an alarming rate, that will increase in the twenty-first century.

"Man will soar with the birds. He will perch on the moon. He will discover worlds that lie beyond the sun and the stars, worlds that can't be seen with human eyes. The ocean of stars that will be discovered will stretch into distances that can't be measured. The time will come when man will discover planets that will defy his all too human reason and logic. He will discover single planets that are larger than all of the oceans of stars put together and the unimaginable distances that lay between them.

"Things will change.

"Man will mix divine knowledge with human logic and reason and create spiritual travel. Man will live in the world that all men have sought from childhood, a world of magic. Yet that will not satisfy man's hunger for power and control over others. His new power, his knowledge of the unseen laws, will not give man the peace and happiness he seeks. Man doesn't know that his need to control others springs from his need to be led by God."

When Papa-horse spoke of those things I had no clue what he was talking about, and I did not question him. I was more concerned with my anger that whites controlled the lives and destinies of blacks. I was still living with the mistaken view that they had freedom, and I did not. It was obvious that my understanding of freedom was not complete. I had not come to appreciate that those whites, the slave owners and lawmakers, only had paper freedom and privileges.

Because of the things I had experienced in Lonesome Bend, it seemed logical to me now to ask Papa-horse about those things, rather than the future he had talked about. "Tonight I heard the voice of the plants," I told him. "I saw the moonlight that surrounds everything. And I felt my power. Why did it happen tonight, and not before?"

Papa-horse looked into my eyes and said, "Rekesh, tell me, what did you feel while sitting at the water's edge?"

"I was consumed by peace and love. I felt powerful."

"My son, that's it."

"What?"

"What you felt as being powerful, your power, as you believe, was the power of God being expressed in you. Freedom. The secret to having power, God's power, is love, peace, and forgiveness. That's freedom.

"Love is the power that stands behind all great men and their accomplishments. Those men listen to the voice of God, the voice that comes from within. They are granted freedom to accomplish notable deeds. Freedom itself is the greatest deed.

"What you seek, finds you. From this time forth, your senses of seeing, hearing, and feelings will be finely tuned. Your sight will show you things you may not want to see. You'll see people's sickness with a greater clarity and see their thoughts and feelings. Your hearing will permit you to hear things you may not expect to hear. You'll hear what others think, before they speak. Your feelings are going to be so sharp that you'll feel what others are feeling before they feel it.

"When one puts his attention to a thing, an idea, invention, or any task, with love, that which is loved is compelled to surrender its secret knowledge and attributes to the seeker. Actions that are carried out under the influence of love open the inner eyes, permitting that one to see God and understand God's creations. He hears God's voice throughout the day. All questions are answered. Problems are transformed into solutions. The unseen is seen. The unknown becomes knowable.

"Love gives its possessor power and ability to do the impossible.

"Once you're filled with a passion to love, loving all people, you can't be stopped. Not even by death.

"Remember this, love is the constant demonstration that God is working in and through you. Anything less than loving all people, is not love. It is powerless. It is slavery."

A cool breeze gently brushed my face. The smells of summer filled my nostrils. The moon's healing rays were reflected by Papa-horse's midnight skin. The ringing of silence echoed in my ears as we walked side by side toward the slave quarters.

I was thankful to be alive, even if it was on the Sandridge farm, as my understanding of true freedom grew clearer with each encounter. It was at such moments that I could no more hate my white brothers any more than I could hate my black brothers or myself. I felt the whites that hated blacks had enough hate within themselves. And they certainly did not need my hatred.

My thoughts traveled back to 1829, the night MacHenry, Ol' Captain Sandridge's slave driver, had beaten Tom, my very best friend, to death for taking the plum from Miss Sarah. Later that same night, MacHenry drank himself into a beating fit, and he beat his wife, Mrs. Anna, because she burned a skillet of cornbread. His oldest boy, Larry Ray, who could not bear his father beating his mother anymore, tried to stop him.

"Papa, don't hit Mama no more. She ain't done nothing wrong."

MacHenry was enraged by his son's plea, and became a mad dog. He punched the boy in the face. The boy fell back. His head hit the edge of a chair, and that broke his neck. The whites throughout the county accepted it as an accident, and MacHenry's life continued as before. He continued to beat his wife and children and drank more than ever.

Papa-horse's words about whites killing whites were true. He said, "A white man will kill his own just as quick as he will a black man. Rage and anger mixed with guilt and whiskey don't see color, nor do they respect family members. Whites can't give what they desperately need. Freedom."

When Papa-horse and I arrived at the slave quarters, the moon had begun to fade and the sun was awakening a new day. We said our good-byes, and I leaned against the fence post and watched the little giant disappear in the shadows of the early morning.

Although his words wounded my pride, the time we spent together had been healing. My soul had been refreshed by my experiences at Lonesome Bend. My mind and heart had been inspired with a new strength, the desire to demonstrate love in deeds and actions toward all. My life's meaning and purpose for being had become clearer. Papa-horse's concern and support always fed my hunger for spiritual understanding. I was like a climbing vine as I constantly reached for change. I wanted to stop judging people, as I had, especially whites. I was filled new determination. I felt God had forgiven me.

Yes, I was willing to try and forgive whites.

After I had watched the dark form of Papa-horse's body blend with the dark trees, I stepped inside my cramped hovel. The meager furnishings consisted of a bed that was too short, a table, two chairs, and a few shelves that were covered with herbs and bottles. All these reminded me that I was still a slave.

A voice in my mind reminded me that the hatred I had for whites could never set me free. Papa-horse's words, "Every change begins in the mind," told me that I was being led to a path that would lead me to freedom.

As I stood looking into the oil lamp, its dim amber light transformed my surroundings, every stick, into a glistening gold. And I then realized that though my outside was poor, on the inside, I was rich with love. Gratitude helped me to use my strong body, sharp mind, and quick wit to seek the fruits of true freedom. I got down on my knees and thanked God for what I had. I asked for his help to continue to bring me into the light. I prayed that I, a slave, might gain both paper freedom and true freedom.

I sat on the edge of my bed and undressed, then I lay back on that dreadful corn-shuck mattress and thought about the time when things would be different for all slaves and me. I believed and felt with all my heart that I would one day have money enough to buy the material things Master Sandridge had. I would also have what he did not have. I felt ready to seek the true freedom that is within all men. I closed my eyes, again giving thanks for the changes I felt were coming. I knew they were on the way. I thought, and thought, and drifted off into a deep sleep and dreamed.

I dreamed I was with two other slaves, and we were painting a house. Time was running out, and we needed to complete our task. So I shouted, to them, "Hurry up! We got to finish whitewashing this house!"

———

"HURRY UP," I YELLED, "we got to finish whitewashing this house!"

In my dream, the day was sunny, and you could see beyond the horizon. We were painting the house as fast as we could. Then the foundation and three of its walls vanished.

"We have to finish painting this house," I yelled at my helpers again, "Hurry! Paint faster."

I made one long, wide stroke with the brush, and a large section of the wall was painted. Then I painted myself into a small cramped area and was forced to slow down and be more careful. I painted toward the left side of that single wall, and then looked around its edge.

I saw blacks that were dressed up like whites. They didn't look like slaves. They stood around a long table that was covered with a white tablecloth and filled with plenty of food and drink. Children, women, and men were eating and playing together.

Another slave named Tree was painting and walked from the right side of the wall. He smiled and walked out among the people and sat on a throne. The throne was carved from ebony. The people gathered around him.

Tree talked to them with great authority. He said, "The food we's eating comes from my wise thinking and planning. We'll prosper more in coming days."

The people were delighted to hear his words. I stood up to show respect. I held the paint bucket in my left hand. A child walked up to me, looked into my eyes, and asked, "Will you paint me?"

I looked down at her and said, "Yes, I will." The child's skin was blacker than black and smoother than a robin's egg. "You go behind the house and wait," I said, and she ran toward a house that was a short distance away. I knew it belonged to her family. Her father, mother, sisters, and brothers were in the front yard listening to Tree. I looked over at Tree, and he looked at me. I felt a connection.

I turned, took one step, and I was standing behind the house with the little girl. I got down on one knee, dipped my brush in the white paint, and began painting her. Slowly I pulled the brush up and down, and back and forth across her dress, her arms, her legs, and her neck. I painted all of her except for her head and face.

Then I wondered, 'How am I going to paint her head and her face without getting paint in her eyes?' Then started to paint again. I painted her head, then her face. I moved the brush around her eyes without any problem. Then I thought to myself, 'What will her mother and father say?'

A voice answered, "Don't concern yourself with such matters."

My dream was interrupted when a squeaky voice yelled, "Nimrod, Nimrod! Wake up! Wake up! You done slept too much! It's time to be up an' at 'em!"

I opened my eyes and saw the intruder. He stood between me and the morning sun, which peaked from behind him, flooding the room and my eyes with daylight.

"Mister Red Rooster done jumped from the fence post and started chasing the hens," the high-pitched voice squealed. "And you's late, Nimrod!"

That morning was the first time I had ever missed the early-morning call of Ben the rooster.

"Nimrod, wake up I sezs!"

I sat up. "I'm up, Josh," I said, "I'm up."

"We gots to go. The others done been gone already."

"You go on, Josh. I'll join you shortly."

Josh stepped back and crossed his arms. His look raised me out of the bed. I smiled and stretched and yawned. It was a beautiful Saturday morning. Saturday was the day slaves worked harder to complete whatever task was set before them. For slaves on the Sandridge farm, it was a liberation of sorts. It was the day before whites celebrated their Sabbath, the slaves' day of promised frolic and rest.

On Sunday morning, the whites dressed in their finest clothes and gathered in the church house to listen to Reverend Smith preach about right and wrong and God and the devil. In my opinion, their church buildings were filled with white bodies that were dressed in clean clothes but housing evil hearts and poisoned minds that were possessed with evil rancorous thoughts about blacks. The inside of their church smelled of death. The beliefs there were of darkness that blinded the innocent and ignorant. How the words of the Bible could penetrate such rancid piety was beyond my comprehension. And they sang their hymns, rhythm-less dirges, without heart, which only made their spiritual plight worse, depressing, to say the least. I thought and believed that God, 'Surely you are outraged at this people's insulting attempts of worshipping you.'

I certainly thought it was cruel beyond reason that whites allowed their idiocy to inspire them to lead their slaves into those church buildings. While we listened to those dreadful dirges that whites sang as praises to God, we slaves stood at the entrance of the church and cared for their spoiled children. To make matters worse, we slaves had to listen to Reverend Smith tell the whites his contrived lies about a god who lived up in heaven. He told them if they believed in what was right and had faith in that god, he would receive them in heaven, where they would live in mansions on streets paved in gold, sit on thrones, and drink milk and honey forever. How white men could invent such practices and beliefs was beyond me. They saw no wrong in killing innocent black men, women, and children in the name of God, and then take them to their churches. How could they do this?

If any good came from whites having those Sunday church meetings, it was this: slaves had a few hours of rest from the ungodly work that was forced on them by so-called God-fearing people.

The white's Sabbath gave some slaves time to rub their aching muscles with axle grease, mend broken bones, regenerate weakened spirits, and worship the ancestral gods that had not prevented them from being led into bondage as slaves.

Slaves on the Sandridge farm fared a bit better than slaves on the surrounding farms. Saturdays found us working faster and harder, but the workload seemed lighter, and the day did not seem half as long. Saturday night came quickly and was filled with playfulness and laughter. The children played games and the older people danced and drank. Each Saturday, we lived as if that day came once in a lifetime and there were no worries.

I sat up on the edge of the bed, smiled at Josh, and forced my tired feet into my worn shoes, shoes that allowed my feet to be covered with dust when the ground was dry and became caked with mud when it rained.

When I was dressed, Josh grabbed my hand and pulled me out the door and onto the porch. While I poured water into the face bowl and washed my face and neck, he poked at a spider's web.

"We'd best be going to Singers Ridge, Nimrod," he said. "We gots ourselves plenty to get done before the day's over."

As he rambled on about what we needed to get done, I thought about him and the other boys going to the creek to swim. Laughter swelled in my stomach.

"Yes, we do, Josh." I said. "So I guess we best get headed in that direction. Huh, Josh?"

"Yep! That's right, Nimrod. We best go right now."

When Josh and I arrived at the work field, the sun and the slaves had begun their competitive race towards the day's end.

The sun moved full-steam ahead. As it climbed across the blue canopy above, the slaves scampered nonstop over the cool dark soil below and turned it for airing and planting. At midday the sun peaked and fell faster than it rose. After lunch, the slaves went back to work to claim another cleared field, another job well done. The sun sank behind the trees and mountains and painted the horizon and clouds yellow, orange, and purple. That was my signal to shout the words the slaves had been waiting all day to hear. "Round 'em up! Tonight we live like the white folks!"

Laughter echoed throughout the valley. Songs and laughter led us back to the slave quarters and made the walk seem shorter. When we had reached the quarters, we were greeted by Big Mama's customary shout, "Fetch me up them mud cats and carps, girls! We gon' have some good eating tonight."

Thanks to Master Sandridge's contrived compassion, we had a number of privileges others' slaves did not have. Other slave owners did not allow their slaves to eat any better on the weekends than they did during the week. But on the Sandridge farm, Master Sandridge permitted one or two slaves to stop work early and go fishing. The first three fish went to the big house, but the rest came to the slaves. He also allowed us to take vegetables from the garden and meat from the smoke house. Saturday nights on the Sandridge farm were like having Christmas and the Fourth of July once a week.

SATURDAY NIGHT FORGETTING

SLAVERY FORCED US SLAVES TO use our inherent, innovative, and God-given talents. With our unique collection of homemade instruments, Saturday nights in the slave quarters on the Sandridge farm were transformed from doom and gloom into our heaven on earth. So you see, we went to heaven on earth before the whites did. They had to wait until Sunday morning.

Mr. Music Man pulled out his walnut bow and dragged it across the catgut strings of his homemade fiddle. The screeching notes sang out that our Saturday-night forgetting had begun. Peanut curled his long, slender fingers into a fist, blew in them, and made soul-full tunes. Big Jim and Mouse beat rhythmic sounds from hollow logs. Bear threw his head back, held his mouth open, and beat a host of musical sounds on his broad chest.

The slaves moved into action. Dancers twirled, jumped, kicked, and leaped into the air, as if they had been shot from cannons. Children ran up and down the yard, around and around, kicking up dirt as they played tag. Men gathered beneath the big oak tree and drank whiskey that had been brewed by the master brewer, Mr. Whiskey.

On Saturday night Mr. Whiskey's tonic drew the largest gathering. Men sat in a tight circle and passed a brown jug from one to another and raised their sunken spirits to soaring heights.

I felt it was good that my people enjoyed their merriment. But that Saturday night, I felt something bad was going to happen. I felt I should be with my brothers and sisters, but I had to leave. Master Sandridge and his wife were returning from their trip, and I had to be at the big house to greet them.

As I walked to the big house, I thought about my dream from that morning. As Papa-horse would say, "If you want an answer, you have to have a question." My question about my morning dream needed to be answered.

I thought back on the time when Papa-horse had taught me the importance of dreams and understanding their interpretation. I must have been six years old. We were down by rabbit tobacco field when I asked him again about going fishing.

———

"PAPA-HORSE," I HAD SAID, "can I go fishing with you today?"

"You remember any dreams?" he asked me.

"No. I don't."

"Then you ain't ready to jump into the deep things of life, son. When you can remember your dreams, then you'll be ready to go fishing with Papa-horse."

"Huh? Papa-horse, guess what—I believe I remember myself a dream!"

"Good. Now we'll speak in the African tongue, and you can tell Papa-horse all about that dream. When did you have it?"

"This morning. Before daybreak."

"Good. Take your time and think back. I want to know everything, every detail. Walk slow, son. The lake won't wonder off. It'll be there when we arrive. By the time we cross this thicket, you'll have had time to remember everything about your dream. Just think and remember. When we reach the lake, we'll sit at my favorite spot. I'll sit under the sycamore tree, and you'll sit next to me on that large flat rock. We'll catch lots of fish. Think about your dream. I need you to remember as much as you can. I want every detail."

"But, Rekesh, I want to fish more than anything in the world. Why do we have to talk about dreams?"

"Yes, Maradh, I understand your feelings. A lad your age feels he'll explode if he don't have an opportunity to fish."

"Rekesh, we're here. Can I fish now?"

"Not yet. The dream. The dream comes first. First, you learn to fish for the wisdom within. Seeking the messages of dreams is like listening to God. Dreams can help you make right choices and do the right things. Things that lead to true freedom."

"But, Rekesh, how can I get wisdom from dreams? They don't make no sense to me."

"Maradh, sit here. Look into the water. Do you see fish?"

"No. The water is too dark, and the fishes are at the bottom."

"Tell me, how is it that you, who can't see the fish in lake, know they're there?"

"Because they live there. This is where we catch them. Right?"

"Maradh, look into my eyes and listen," Papa-horse said. "If you're sure the lake has fish in it that you can't see, then it's time you learn about the wisdom you don't know. The wisdom of your dreams."

"Okay," I said. "My dream was like this. I was lying on my back in the cotton field. I was looking up at the sky and watching the clouds. Then I saw a white fog in the middle of the field. It came and surrounded me. I was scared, so I jumped up. Then the fog turned into a white tree stump. It had something on top of it. So I went to look at it. There was a drop of blood on top of the stump. The blood started moving, and it spread. And then it turned into a book.

"Then I heard fighting and I was scared again. When I turned around, I saw Ol' Captain Sandridge laying face-down in the cotton field. On the side of him, I saw his wife, Mrs. Beulah. She was looking down at him. Then she looked up at me. Then she stepped over him and came at me. She stopped when she was close to me. She got down on her knees, and that made me scared. Her face was bloody. She looked back at Captain Sandridge. Then she took the book off the white stump and gave it to me. I was scared to touch it. It was a book. But she pushed it in my hands.

"It was the most beautiful book I had ever seen. A shiny red book that had snow-white pages. I was holding it like it was everything. Then the pages started moving. They flipped and flipped. Then I could hear them. They were talking to me, and I knew what they were saying. That's my dream. Now can I fish?"

"Do you understand what the dream is telling you, Maradh?"

"No. It was just a dream, that's all. Dreams don't make sense. They're not real. Can I fish now?"

"Maradh, this lake has fish in it, but you can't see them. And your dreams have messages from God in them, even though you don't know they're there. If you learn to catch the wisdom of your dreams, you'll gain freedom."

"Will you teach me to fish for wisdom, too, after we fish for fish?" I asked.

"Maradh, you just made an important step toward gaining

wisdom."

"I did? What?"

"You asked a question. When you ask questions you always get answers. Always"

"Do I ask you the questions? Or do I ask God?"

"Both. Just ask questions, son. Anytime you ask questions, you open your mind and heart for answers. You learn to receive the messages that lead to life's hidden treasures. The dream you had has several meanings. The first has to do with your inner life. You're gaining true freedom. The second has to do with the way God wants you to be in the world. The third has to do with your outer life, the world around you.

"So I have to listen to you tell me about my dream? Then we can fish? Deal?"

"Deal," he said. "Your dream is saying that, just as clouds always change their shape, your inner life will be in constant change."

"Change?"

"Yes, constant change. The dream is telling you that Captain Sandridge's wife is going to step over his authority, go behind his back, and teach you to read. This way, she'll avenge herself of the suffering he has caused her."

"What I need to read for?" I asked. "Slaves don't need reading. Slaves need freedom. How do you know my dream is saying all that? What if it's saying something else?"

"Freedom comes from within," he said. "Reading brings freedom out. And time will tell, my son, if what I say is true or not. Time will tell. Here, let me bait your hook. It's time you learned to fish." He gave me further instruction. "Lower the hook into the water and let this lake share its treasure of mud cats. And your dreams will share God's wisdom when you ask questions."

"You only gave two answers, Rekesh. You said there's three. What about the other one?"

"Later. You want to fish, right?"

"Yes!"

"So let's fish, my son."

———

I WAS DRAWN FROM MY DAYDREAMING when a growling voice came from the porch of the big house.

"Well, Mr. Nimrod, I guess you done finished that field over by Singers Ridge."

I looked up, and almost wet my pants. My sweet Miss Sadie's imitation of Master Sandridge was perfect. Her smile gave light to the night.

I burst into laughter. "Yes, suh!" I said. "I don', I don', don' finished dat dere field and mo', Mastah. Yes, suh, yes, suh. I done it tal'!"

Miss Sadie's smile became a hearty belly laugh. We laughed, and our bodies bounced. Then Miss Sadie jumped down from the porch, placed her hands on her hips, danced around a bit. "Nigga," she said, "yous best get a move on. Or I's gon' strap yous over the head."

We held hands and laughed. We spun each other around and around. The happy music from the slave quarters filled our hearts. We danced and laughed. We ran around in the grass and leaped towards the sky. I grabbed Sadie by the shoulders and said, "Yes, suh, yesss, suh, Mastah. Yesss, suh."

Our laughter made our legs weak and we collapsed on the ground. We sat face to face, still lost in uncontrollable laughter that made tears pour from our eyes. Sadie laughed and laid her hands on my chest. We moved closer. We held each other lightly. The laughter and tears flowed like thunder and rain. I fell back on the grass, and she fell on top of me. We held each other tighter. And tighter.

Our laughter became like a gentle rain passing over a field.

We were consumed by feelings, feelings that were filled with passion. We touched each other. Our faces gently touched at the cheeks, we rubbed noses, we moved our heads from side to side and up and down against each other. The passion grew. My hands moved up and down the crease of Sadie's back. Her hands moved from my shoulders, down my arms to my wrists and up again. Our actions were repeated. Desire pulled out of us the feelings we had kept hidden for years. Our feelings boiled up from the depths of silent longings and spilled over into tender acts. Our once unexpressed feelings bubbled up into new feelings, and we went beyond bodily sensations. Our feelings and desires needed to be satisfied through sexual pleasure, but then something different happened.

Love in its purest form seized us and led us into the space that lies between the past and future. We were fully in the moment. Her body was mine, and mine was hers. We had one thought. The same thought. Our feelings gave way to the sensation of invisibility. Our feelings became emotions, and our emotions turned into bliss.

My hand moved to Sadie's narrow waist, my other hand made its way over a protruding hipbone and down the front of her firm thigh. It stopped. I felt the warmth that radiated from the area where her thighs tenderly met.

Her hand moved over my chest, the other was firmly planted on my lower back, where it pressed me closer to her. I looked into her eyes and watched her face. It changed from pleasure to pain and back, an image that was repeated again and again. She was with me in heavenly bliss. She opened her eyes and looked into my eyes. We moved as one.

I shifted to the right and gently directed her body to the left, and she followed. I slid my arm from beneath her back and slowly made my way on top of her. She positioned herself. Slowly and gently, I began to rest the full weight of my body on her. She spread her legs, a little, but not enough. When I was fully resting my weight on her, she raised her head and I slid an arm underneath. She sighed. Her hips rocked and moved. Then I slid my right hand under her buttocks and she raised her hips. They were firm and smooth. I breathed deeply. She breathed deeper. Together we exhaled slowly.

There was a scream.

It came from the slave quarters. She grabbed my hand and pulled away, gently pushing me back. Teary eyes stared into my soul. Her mouth quivered. My eyes widened. I felt confused. Tears streamed down her face, and flooded her ears. I licked a salty tear from my own lips, and others came down my cheeks.

"Nimrod," she whispered, "you knows we best don't do this. I's the property of Master Sandridge ... and ... and you knows he been doing his business with me. He done told me, if I ever lets you grease the split, he'll kill us both. And I just loves you too much, Nimrod. For the sake of me, I can't never see you get hurt by the master. The Lord gots something special for you. And you gots to be here to do it."

I wanted to speak, but she placed her hand over my mouth.

"Listen," she said. "Listen, Nimrod, to what I's saying to you. Do it, not 'cause you wants to, but 'cause we needs you to. Do it for all of us. All the people, slaves and whites folks."

She slid from beneath me and stood up. I stood up. We stared at each other, then, without speaking another word, we headed for the big house. She walked up the steps, ahead of me, and I stared at her ass. Just as we stepped inside the door, Master Sandridge drove Nell and Jim through the gate. We stepped back outside and waited on the porch.

The wagon stopped. I went to help Mrs. Sandridge down from the seat. Master Sandridge looked at Miss Sadie, and his eyes were blazed with anger. He stepped from the wagon.

I said, "I hope you had a successful trip, Master Sandridge." He looked at me, then at Miss Sadie. His look was like green grapes in the hot sun.

"Productive!" he snapped.

Miss Sadie lowered her head and said in a dying voice, "I done got everything ready for you and the Missus, Mastah Sandridge."

He just stared at her, then walked up onto the porch, turned, and looked back again. He looked at Miss Sadie like a cat stalking a mouse. After he and Mrs. Sandridge had gone into the house Sadie glanced down at me, then walked in behind them.

Her eyes told me she was a hundred miles away. The awful gnawing in my stomach told me something bad was going to happen to my sweet, sweet, sweet Miss Sadie. I knew it and was helpless to do anything. I felt like a single bee defending a hive from a bear in winter coat.

I climbed onto the wagon and watched Miss Sadie walk down the hall. Like a widow in a funeral procession, she walked, then she stopped, turned slowly, and looked back at me. Then she disappeared into the dark kitchen. My heart dropped to my stomach and boiled. Thinking about what might come of my Sadie made me weak. I flapped the reins, and the horses headed for the barn. They knew their long trip would bring them extra feed and a good brushing.

The look in Master Sandridge's eyes haunted me. They spoke of his hatred. I knew a man of his temperament was capable of exploding, but nothing could have prepared me for the evil he would bring against Miss Sadie. That beautiful black lady, one who bubbled with the joy of life and had a love for all people, would not be protected, not even by God, from her master's rage. Her destiny was about to spring forth from a white man. Her fate was in his hands, and there would be no God to rescue her.

When at the barn, without coaxing, Nell and Jim stopped at the barn and went to their stalls. My mammoth friends willingly went inside, and halted in their own stall. They were eager to fill their bellies with hay, oats, and water. I had stepped off the wagon and was well along in my grooming when I caught sight of Papa-horse sitting in the hayloft, his short legs dangling in the air.

He clutched his pipe between his teeth and said, "You finish up that work and get on up here, son. Bring the dream, the one you've been wrestling with all day." How he knew about the dream I had no idea. He always just knew.

I hurried to complete my chores. I brushed and fed Nell and Jim until they were satisfied, then I climbed into the loft where Papa-horse waited. He was sitting on a bale of hay with his legs crossed and eyes closed. I sat down in front of him, closed my eyes, and waited. The flame in the lantern flicked wildly, and became as bright as the sun.

"You don't have time to continue your preparation," Papa-horse said in the old African tongue. "What's to be is already in motion. You have made changes in how you look at life. Your understanding of God has improved. You'll never see the former days again, as they've passed on ahead of you and are making way for the difficulties you're to experience in the future. Your dream this morning contains a message from God. You must listen and act on what it tells you. Son, Nimrod, if you're to gain freedom, you have no choice but to listen. God's will for your life is at hand. Your life is important for you and those who are ready for personal change. Close your eyes, Maradh."

Papa-horse placed his hand on my head and prayed. He prayed that God's mercy was with me, then and there. He told God I was still learning and was not prepared for the work that lay ahead. He told God I needed more preparation. At that time, I did not know what God's response was, but I found out later.

I told Papa-horse my dream, and his response, in the African tongue, was, "The house you were painting represents the old you, the person you were. The old you, it was disappearing faster than you can paint. Cover up. Falling away fast. The white paint is the many ways you've tried to whitewash, cover up, the old you, so you only appeared new. You were trying to change without changing. Even when you're careful at covering up those small areas of your life, the old you continues to vanish. When you looked around the left corner of the one remaining wall, that meant you must start looking at things from a spiritual view, the left side of life, the inner life. And not so much with that reason and logic you use. The man who lives from his insides is the man who can't hate others. Their hate does not engender his. The blacks you saw living a good life means you'll get the material things you want, the things you dream of having. Tree, the tall black man, came from the right side of the wall; the material things will come from standing tall and working hard in the outside world. Tree sat on a throne. A tree on a throne means you'll live a long life, and God will put his authority in you. God will do good things for others through you, both blacks and whites. God-given authority will open door after door as you make your journey to true freedom."

"What about the little girl I painted white?" I asked him.

"The girl represents your young spiritual nature, the part of you that's eager to live and learn. Live by spiritual laws and principles. Painting her white represents your effort to purify that part of you. All kinds of evil are going to come at you for the purpose of preventing God's work from being done in you and through you. Your own evilness will even try to prevent you from being what God created you to be. And personal evil, that's the worst kind of evil. You must be as clean and as white as snow, as innocent and pure as a virgin. You can't mix false teachings about God with God's purpose for your life. You must do things God's way.

"The question you asked about the girl's mother and father's concern with you painting her, well, that's not a matter you need to concern yourself with. God is mother and father. Certain things you're going to encounter are not in your hands. They're in God's hands. Listen to God, and you'll succeed. You'll gain the true freedom you seek."

Papa-horse's interpretation of my dream was both encouraging and fear-inspiring. I escaped from reality as his words led my mind into a trance. I went to the Nother World and stood before God. God spoke to me, and I listened to His instruction on how to live.

When I awoke, Papa-horse was gone. The answer to my dream and the presence of God inspired me with a greater excitement and fear for life. As usual, it was difficult for me to accept what had happened. I thought to myself, 'Who am I that God would choose me to do an important work that would help others?'

I was moved emotionally. I lost my desire to join the others enjoying the Saturday night feast. While they enjoyed their festival of food, drink, dance, and merriment, I sat in the hayloft. I filled the remainder of the evening with meditation and prayer.

PARTY AND PAIN

THE SMELL OF ROASTED FISH, CHICKEN, and corn on the cob drifted on the breath of the night. After I had meditated and prayed, I lay back and listened to the sounds of that summer night. In the darkness of my mind, I saw my slave brothers and sisters. They danced and ate. They all enjoyed themselves, each other, and a short-lived taste of white freedom.

Even though slave life was cruel for the children, who had been born to play, they were scurrying about, laughing and playing as if there was no tomorrow. I saw them as they held their favorite piece of chicken in one hand and played tag with the other. I saw Little Josh and the boys chase after Loddie, Tessie, and other girls. From time to time, the boys tried to trip the girls, hoping their dresses would fly up over their heads. The girls were aware of the boys' antics, and from time to time one would pretend to fall, but jump up before the boys could see anything.

Later that night, after I had returned to the slave quarters, Miss Emma told me what had happened. What she said seemed to have been connected to Papa-horse's interpretation of my dream. It was spooky. She said, "The night didn't have no order. It was a free-for-all. It weren't till the deep voice of Mr. Rabbit sang out that thangs changed."

She told me how Mr. Rabbit, the storyteller, leaped out of the shadows, ran into the center of the crowd, and jumped on top of the chopping block. His voice rang out.

———

"LISTEN UP, CHILLUNS," HE shouted. "He be a-comin'! Listen up, he be comin'! Y'all listen up!"

The music stopped. Dancers stood like statues. Dust fell like a silk blanket. Children, cooks, close friends, lovers who sat in dark places, and the drinking men all stared at Mr. Rabbit. Everyone made their way toward him.

Again, Mr. Rabbit sang out, "Listen up, chilluns, he be a-comin'. Listen up." He held a bony hand to his ear and repeated, "Listen … listen, he be a-comin'."

By ones and by twos the people sat on the ground, shoulder to shoulder in huddles of threes and fours, in a circle around Mr. Rabbit and the blazing fire. The dust settled. Everyone was in their place. They stared and waited.

When Mr. Rabbit was satisfied that he had their attention, he stomped with one bony foot atop the chopping block. He looked around and stared in the people's eyes. He stomped with the other foot. He stared. He stomped and stared. In a deep, low, and dragging voice, he said, "Listen up, chilluns . . . he be a-comin'. Listen up."

The people were like winter trees. A settled calm, silent stillness overtook them.

Suddenly, Mr. Rabbit yelled again, "He be a-cominnnnn'!" And he danced around the top of the chopping block. He twirled and whirled, and his head seemed to hang motionless while his legs, which looked like they had been borrowed from an old crow, moved without stopping. His dancing flat-footed movement carried him around and around as his long narrow toes gripped the edge of the block like eagle's talons. His bucked-eyed-stare, and white teeth shone in the dark. He yelped like a dog, he brayed like a mule, he hissed like a snake. He howled like a wolf and screamed like a mountain lion. Then he stopped. He looked like a dark mirror without a reflection.

The people leaned forward.

He hunched over and squatted to meet them. He pointed a twisted finger and laid his head to one side. He said in a calm, whispering voice, "Listen, chilluns, I say listen, he'sssss a-comin'. A long, long time ago, in the time before there was a white man, we the people, all the people, we all lived in the big house. That be's the time when all the people done been blessed by God," he moved and turned and rolled his head from side to side, "and there be's nobody who's sick and dying'. There be's no fightin'. No killin'. There be's peace." Then he jerked himself up, stood up, stretched his arms out, and twirled like a dog chasing its tail. He held his head back and yelled at the top of his voice, "Before there was whites, everybody be's happy! Happy and peace! Happy and peace! Happy and peace!"

The people came back to reality. They clapped their hands and laughed. There was movement among the children. Some pulled their legs up to their chests, others let their legs flop to their sides, and their mouths hung open.

The blazing fires' orange and blue flames of the cook fire stretched up into black sky. Like a panther Mr. Rabbit leaped from his perch with his legs tucked beneath his butt and flew high above the cracking cinders. He disappeared in the darkness. There was silence.

With a thud, Mr. Rabbit landed solidly on the ground, dust gushed up from beneath his broad feet, and the people reeled back and sighed. He gained his balance and wasted no time. He ran around the fire. He stomped and kicked. Dust flew everywhere. He pointed that crooked finger at the people and said, "Listen up, chilluns, he be a-comin'!" Then he stood still. There was silence.

Mr. Rabbit stared at the people, and they stared back. Like a child, he crawled up on the chopping block and squatted there. He pulled his legs together, up to his chest, wrapped them with his long arms around them, and stared. His head tilted to the side, and then his arms flopped to his sides. He shuffled to one foot, and the other leg hung off the chopping block.

"One day," he said, his voice sad and flat, "one day ... all the people's happiness be turned to sadness. The black people done soon forgit to thank God and praise God, their worship stopped. God was no more in the black people's happiness. The black people didn't remember God no more. They just wanted and wanted and wanted some more. One day, the blacks saw no reason why they shouldn't frat'nize with the blank people. The people with no color. The whites. One day they done give praise to them other gods. Them gods that was kicked out of heaven, them false gods of the blank people.

"The white people's god.

"Another day done came. The man with no color, the blank people, the whites, they come and take the black people's power. They brang them to a foreign land," he pointed at the crowd and continued, "and that be you. And that be's this land."

Mr. Rabbit jumped up and stood on the chopping block and yelled, "And he be a-comin'! The one that sets us free. Look! Come close! Y'all come close now, chilluns."

Everyone moved closer and leaned forward. Mr. Rabbit yelled, "That One, he be the one who gots the ancient wisdom that lets the people, all the people, go to the white house of white folk's freedom.

"God done give that one the powers of insights. That one gits the peoples together. That one pray, and a special kind of healing comes to the world of people. Blacks and whites. That one look the White Devil in the eyes. The White Devil come under the power of that one.

"He the one who gots love. He gots wisdom. He the one with God-love in his heart. And that be's the one that be's coming to give we'uns freedom. And that day be's sooner than it was. Sooner than the white folks thank."

The people sat like fence posts in red clay. The fire grew brighter, and shadows bobbed and danced a strange dance against the front of the shacks, a strange dance, indeed, and Mr. Rabbit was quiet. Again the people leaned forward and took shallow breaths.

"He be like that Mr. Lincoln. Tall and lanky. He be brave. His blood be's mixed. His skin be like pale dirt. His mother is this country and the country we's come from. His words be's the words of the man who can save the people. His wise thinkin' and pretty words put hope in the world.

"The table be's turned. The white folk's big white house be's . . . his house.

"Listen, chilluns, he be's comin'."

There was silence.

The silence was broken.

A blood-curdling scream came from behind one of the shacks.

The people turned and looked. They were shocked back into reality.

A man holding his side staggered from behind the shack. He yelled and screamed in terrible pain. There was a thud. He lay face down on the ground. He tried to crawl, but he could not. He stood up again and grabbed his side. His body lurched forward, one foot dragging behind. When he stopped, the flickering light of the fire showed the blood and dust on his face and in his hair.

It was Be Boy, Miss Mary's son. Miss Mary had been raped and killed a year earlier by the white slave driver, Mr. Jason, from the Johnson farm.

The long skinning knife protruded from Be Boy's rib cage. Be Boy fell again and sucked at the air like a baby sucking its mother's dry breast. Blood poured from his nose and mouth. He gurgled, and his body went limp.

Skinner, the best hog skinner in Franklin County, staggered out of the shadows. He clutched a bottle of moonshine to his chest. He walked over and stood next to the body, and looked down.

"I told 'im the last swallow was mine," he mumbled. "But he didn't listen." Skinner raised the bottle to his mouth, tilted his head back, and gulped the last swallow. He lowered the bottle to his side. It slipped from his hand, hit the ground, and rolled away. It stopped at Be Boy's head. Skinner turned away and staggered into the woods.

"That's one of them Saturday nights when our taste of white freedom was turned to sadness and confusion," Miss Emma said. "Pure hell. Slaves killing slaves. Our party of pain."

———

WHEN I HEARD THAT STORY, guilt rushed into my ears and my brain and filled my heart with pain, the kind of pain a whipping by a slave driver could never have given me. My savior mentality caused me to feel I should have been there, but reason and logic told me I could not have prevented Be Boy's death.

You may be wonder why I ramble as I do. Is it possible that my trying to help you understand the ways of whites and their thinking, and the effects slavery had on blacks and poor whites, is my attempt to release the pain and hurt they caused in my life? To show the further need for forgiveness? I am not sure. But what I do know is that I love you and want to make up for our lost time.

I ask you to be patient with what you are reading. There might be some good that you, and our future generations, can gain from what I relate. Who can tell?

Life's secrets are scattered across the years, and they cannot be found, except through time, dreams, and stories.

Please be patient and continue to read my story, our history, the history of a black man's life as a slave.

All whites do not have a passion to keep blacks in servitude. But from my experience, I know the white man to be the most formidable creature alive. I am telling you this: you need to understand his ways. If you do not, he will eat you up. He will destroy you from the soul.

NOT ONLY DID WE SLAVES FEAR the merciless beatings we received from our white masters, but we also had to deal with the murders that took place among us. After President Lincoln signed the Emancipation Proclamation, and the war between the North and South had come to an end, outwardly, my people seemed to have found more reasons to kill each other than before. As long as we killed each other, with no direct harm coming to the slave owners and their families, these murders were overlooked. We were in such a state that it was easy for us to explain the killings away. We simply used reason and logic such as we were frustrated because of the hopeless conditions we lived in. We said our murdering each other grew out of our desperation. When I was young, that was my logic. As I grew older, my reasoning became, 'It's better to kill whites and gain relief from slavery than kill another slave and continue to live as a slave with an oppressed conscience.'

I believe there was rhyme and reason for our killing each other. We were frustrated and desperate, and we had no way out of the deplorable conditions we lived under. No matter how much I tell you about slavery, no matter how many detailed accounts I give you, there is no way for you or any other person, black or white, to know slavery as it was or to see the white slave owners for who they truly were. The white man's burning hell and his red-suited devil would have been the choice of most slaves, had God asked their preference.

The reason for blacks killing blacks during slavery went beyond frustration. When the points I am about to bring up for your consideration are looked at from the slave's position, I believe you will have a clearer picture of what we had to endure. You will know the diabolical mind we had to deal with.

As I have related, President Lincoln did not free the slaves because he wanted them to live free. He felt like other slave owners, that the country could not prosper without them. The average slave owner could not live in comfort without slaves. What I am getting at is that the British were angry because the whites were not giving Britain the money she wanted. So they needed another war and created one.

At the beginning of the war, slaves were not directly involved, in that we were not fighting. But that crafty British governor of Virginia came up with the plan that would draw blacks into the war as British supporters. We became Britain's black war slaves, who would die for the white man's cause. The governor, through his barber, put the word out that he would free slaves who fought alongside the British. His snake-in-the-grass scheme worked.

What the blacks did not know was the governor only intended to use slaves to fight without giving them freedom, as the slave trade business was in full swing in Britain. On the other hand, what the slave-owning whites did not know was that the governors' intention was to weaken them by creating fear. If they feared their slaves, they would have two wars to fight at once. The governor's plan was crafty and brilliant. As I have said, it worked.

Within twenty-four hours more than a thousand slaves were at the governor's doorstep ready to join the British in their war. The white slave owners feared the British and the slaves who lived and worked on their farms and plantations. The whites could not sleep at night. Some slept with knives and guns, while others barricaded themselves in their bedrooms at night and took turns sleeping.

But things did not stop there. While slaves up north were fighting alongside the British, the slaves down south were being coaxed by the French to fight alongside them. The French also lied to the southern slaves as they promised them freedom.

What did we have? Well, we had blacks fighting for paper-freedom on opposing sides of the white man's war. They never gained any freedom.

After the war had ended, the British and French went back to Europe and the blacks remained slaves under cruel masters who were less than forgiving. Blacks paid dearly for their participation in the affairs of angry whites who had tried to annihilate each other over land and tax revenues. Those white slave owners beat and hanged slaves like never before.

Our reason for killing each other was that we had no way out of the hellhole white slave owners had locked us in. Slavery forced us to do whatever we could when an opportunity came to escape our captors. We were burned by their trickery at every turn.

If you are to be free, you must know these things.

That Saturday in the barn I prayed, meditated, and asked God to give me the things I wanted and the things I needed. My experiences and lessons had become increasingly more difficult. It was difficult to believe in God. Thought I was coming to understand what Papa-horse was trying to teach me about inner freedom, I did not want to accept his interpretation of my dream, which was too threatening to me. It put me under greater pressure to make changes I was not ready to make and do things I was not prepared to do.

After I had my prayed and meditated, I removed the lantern from the rafter and walked toward the ladder.

Papa-horse sat at the edge of the loft and puffed on his pipe. He patted the hay beside him with his gnarled fingers and said, "Come over here. Take your place next to me, son." I sat to his left. "It's time to raise your thinking and clear yourself of some of those outdated beliefs," he said. "You can't continue to look at life and its lessons from your present viewpoint. If you're to receive the wisdom and true freedom that's waiting for you, you must stretch your mind and open your heart. There's no time left for stubbornness.

"Let go.

"Surrender.

"You and the people must trust God. You," he leaned forward and looked into my eyes and continued, "you must learn to listen, my dear boy. The dream you're struggling with will not only bring you true freedom, but you'll help others, both blacks and whites. Anyone who listens to God within himself discovers the freedom that's within. You're going to experience hardships, mind you, and you'll suffer. But they won't kill you. Hardships and suffering can be paths to true freedom."

While Papa-horse spoke, my mind traveled back to 1832. I thought about the taste of freedom I had gained after MacHenry killed little Tom. Before that bit of freedom became mine, I was an emotional-cauldron that boiled with pain and anger. For years, Papa-horse had been trying to teach me to deal with my self-righteous attitude and unbridled anger, but I had not listened. Although my practice was to resist Papa-horse's lessons, he always drove them home in a way that overcame me and struck pay dirt in my heart and mind.

His hypnotic voice lured me back to the past. There we were. We were sitting on the damp bank of Tims Ford's Lake, fishing for mudcats and talking in the African language:

———

"REKESH," I SAID, "I HAVE a question. Why did you tell me killing insects, birds, and squirrels was the same as MacHenry killing Tom?"

"Maradh," Papa-horse said, "your question tells me you're ready to gain some freedom. That's good. Watch this. See how I'm gently moving my fishing line up and down in the water. Well, this action lures the big catfish from his hiding place. He will swim up from the bottom and grab the wiggling morsel and become hooked. And your question does the same. It lures wisdom from the deep places of your soul. Now, think, Maradh ... did I say it was the same, or did your inner knowing tell you that?"

"Sir, I don't remember."

"Listen, son. Listen to the water of the creek ... listen ... listen to the sound it's making as it pours over the rocks and spilling into the lake. The soothing sound of flowing water is a powerful medicine as it baits the mind and lures insight up from the sacred place of the heart. Sit still, son, and listen. Soon you'll hear the answer to your question as it swims from within."

"Rekesh, I know. No, you didn't say it the way I thought you had. After we talked about MacHenry killing Tom, I felt what I had been doing to insects and animals was murder. I killed them and didn't think about their pain. I killed them when they didn't need to die."

"That's true. Your heart corrected you, Maradh. I never said it was the same as what MacHenry did to Tom. Your love for life told you it was wrong to kill plants, insects, and animals needlessly. Son, please, lay your fishing stick aside and listen closely to my words. Listen, not with your ears only, but with your mind and heart. And answer this question clearly and honestly. The night MacHenry beat little Tom to death, did he do that because Tom did something wrong?"

"No."

"Well, if it wasn't because of wrong, why did he kill him?"

"Because he's white and whites hate blacks."

"Maradh, if what you say is true, then Billy Ray your white friend, he hated blacks, too. Right?"

"I don't think so." I thought about this for several minutes. "No. He was my friend"

"Then tell me, why do whites kill their own? Other whites?

"I don't know. But it's different when they kill each other."

"Different? How is it different?

"Killing is killing, isn't it?"

"Yes. I guess."

"You guess? Remember, the night MacHenry beat little Tom to death, he also beat his wife until she was unconscious. And, remember, he killed his eldest son, Billy Ray, when he tried to prevent him from beating his mother. Since whites do kill whites, it's obvious that they shouldn't have a problem when it comes to killing blacks. That's . . . logical. Right?"

"Yes, I guess."

"You guess? And remember, blacks kill each other, too. In fact, people everywhere kill other people. And their own. Listen, son, to your inner knowing, that part of you that isn't affected by emotionalism and untruth. You do want to live in peace and freedom, right?"

"Yes, sir."

"Then be led by God's love, the power that works in you and through you for the good of all people. Think about this. Your brain is at the top end of love and your heart is at the bottom end of love. At the center is a cavern. The mind. The mind stretches from one end of love to the other end. It rotates in a circle. It looks at all of your experiences, seeking from them the truth and wisdom of God. When you allow your brain and heart to stop at a truth, any truth, it brings love into focus. That way, God's love, that's in you, spills over into your logic and reasoning, and this gives you true freedom." Papa-horse paused, then went on. "I know what I'm telling you doesn't make sense yet, but, time and experience will lead you to the understanding of what I'm saying. You can have the peace and happiness and true freedom you want.

I didn't say anything.

"Son, wipe the tears from your eyes. Maradh, it's okay. When you come to know and accept truth that comes from the place that's deep within you, your true love for all people will clear your path to true freedom. Love is the greatest power. When you connect with love, true love, your thoughts and feelings about love, and freedom, will race faster than you are able to convey to others. Then you must slow down and not allow your life to be ruled by emotionalism.

"Lean closer, my son. Look into my eyes. Feel the joy and true freedom that's within you right now. Someday you'll learn it's not necessary to convey in words what love and true freedom are. Everyone will feel your love and freedom when they are with you. They'll feel their own love and freedom rise from within themselves. This is the way you're to share your love and true freedom with others. They taste and know that it really does exist within them. The time will come when you won't have to preach about love and true freedom. You'll live it. You'll demonstrate love for God, self, and others, your true freedom."

———

"NOW IT'S TIME TO COME back, son." Papa-horse said. "Where did you go?" he asked.

"Oh, I traveled back to my first experience of true freedom."

"Why did you choose that place?"

"It was a great lesson at that time. Papa-horse, I know I have to accept the fulfillment of my dreams, but in my logic and reasoning, the meaning isn't true. I know that God can speak through me. And I know what God says is true. I want to love all people. And I want this dream to come true." I paused. "But ... I'm not ready."

"Son, Maradh, listen. As long as you look for excuses not to do what God created you to do, you'll find them. Excuses are like weeds. They're everywhere, and you can't kill them all. But you can pluck them from your mind each time you put your trust in God and not your logic and reason. Time, she turns a deaf ear to excuses and life moves forward. Wake up and live, son."

I TELL YOU, THAT SATURDAY NIGHT was one of those times when everything was crazier than usual, out of the control of any man. It seemed as if everyone on the Sandridge farm as well as number of other slaves in Franklin County were affected by an evil spirit of suffering. It converged on us, and not one individual was spared from his mess of pain. Scarcely had one bad thing happened before a wrong thing had shown its ugly face somewhere else.

Down at the slave quarters, evil moved Skinner to kill Be Boy. Then the evil wrapped its wiry fingers around the necks of five slaves from different farms who had runaway and been recaptured. The whites punished them by hanging them, cutting off their sex organs and stuffing them in their mouths, then burning the bodies. But that was not all. That ill wind spirit even brought suffering against Master Sandridge and his wife. Things had been brewing at the big house, and they boiled to an overflow of shocking change. The change, which had been destined by Mother Time, was to affect the slaves on the Sandridge farm and all people of Franklin County.

At the big house Mrs. Carol Jane Sandridge was sitting in the parlor and knitting, and Master Sandridge was walking back and forth across the hardwood floor like a raging bull. His heels pounded against the floor in rhythm with the grandfather clock. He ranted and raved, he protested the good he had received, as that was one of his ways to stew in guilt. Dressed in one of those white suits he was known for and with his hands folded behind his back, he paced the floor. His flushed face looked like a cherry atop a pile of white cotton. His eyes beamed with hate. Like a child pitching a fit, he stomped his foot again and again.

"Wouldn't you know it," he yelled, "those damn niggers completed work at the Singers Ridge Field! And that's not all. They've done most of the work I had lined up for the next three weeks! That damn nigger is going to be the death of me! Why can't he be like the others? A dumb nigger?"

When Master Sandridge realized that I had walked into the parlor, he stopped in his tracks and jerked around. The force of his movement caused his pipe to fly from his hand. It soared over Mrs. Sandridge's head, where she sat as calm as a cat and continued to knit the corner of the blue baby blanket she had worked on for years. The pipe hit the window, ricocheted, and landed on at my feet. When it hit the floor it broke into halves, spun around, and spewed its contents of dark-brown tobacco and white ashes. As it spun and stopped at my feet, a deafening silence rang out, swept through the room, filled the house, and covered the Sandridge farm.

I stared at the dark tobacco and the white ashes. The silence clicked in my left ear. Whenever that happened, I knew God was speaking. I picked up the pieces of pipe and walked toward Master Sandridge. He stood speechless. I extended my hand, and the interpretation that Papa-horse had given to my dream rushed into my mind. The ghostly silence turned Master Sandridge's beet-red face and eyes into a snow-white gaze of fear.

Mrs. Sandridge was frozen stiff.

I looked at the blanket draped over her lap. She shifted her legs, and looked up at me. She almost smiled, but she lowered her head.

That bull of a man stomped toward me. His feet pounded the floor like hoofs digging into the earth. I swung around and met him full view.

We made eye contact.

He stopped.

I clenched my left hand into a hard fist. We stared at each other.

I extended my right hand, and exposed the broken pipe. The cold white ivory lay in my warm hand. It's luster became a winter's gray.

He looked at the broken pipe, then into my eyes, and down again. He said nothing.

That ivory pipe that had been in the Sandridge family for at least four generations, and had been handed down to each male who took charge of the Sandridge farm.

That full-lit moon Saturday night, my master had to look at the pipe, his family's symbol of male power and authority, lying broken in the hand of a black man, his slave. My hand.

Minutes that felt like hours passed, and Master Sandridge began to shake like a maple leaf in a stiff November breeze. His sadness turned into tics. He was a man trapped in quicksand with nowhere to go and nothing to grab hold of. His wide-eyed stare drew compassion from the depths of my heart; like water in a hand-pump, it rose from my heart. I wanted to rescue him. He was a child who had lost his way, but I had to let things take their course. Even if I had tried to rescue him, his pride would have blocked any attempt.

We stood face to face, locked in a stare. His bloodshot eyes told me his days were numbered. The glimmer of a faint smile that remained in Mrs. Sandridge's eyes told me she knew it too.

Master Sandridge stared at the pipe, and his tics and tremors were interrupted by a momentary calm that turned into violent jerks. His head jerked to the left. His face twitched. His emotions seemed to be radiating from his belly, and he was consumed. His presence reeked with the stench of hatred. Although a tempest of emotion raged between us, a swell of love also tugged at my heart. In a moment, I was overpowered as my love for him swept through me. I was connected to the man whose hate and contempt for me had become evident in his whole being. In some strange way, we had become connected by our strong emotions. I saw it in his eyes. I felt we both were being pulled, beckoned back to the fall of 1843, when he was forty and I was twenty.

That was the year he bought the last five hundred acres of the Sandridge farm from his alcoholic eldest brother, J. R. The day it happened, I stood behind him and watched as he craftily placed the fifty dollars in J. R.'s shaking hands, hands that were cupped like a beggar's hands receiving a handout.

J. R.'s drinking had finally led him into the same position, and condition, the middle boy, James Earl, and their father, Ol' Captain Sandridge, had both found themselves in: they drank themselves either penniless or into poor health, or both.

Other than Master Sandridge and Miss Sarah Ann, his spinster sister, they were the only children of Ol' Captain Sandridge and Mrs. Beulah who did not attempt to escape their personal demons by boiling their brains in alcohol. Miss Sarah's chosen method of escape was to walk, stark naked, in the dead of winter, into the rushing icy-waters of Tims Ford's lake. Her body was found the following spring.

Master Sandridge was the last son, and he naturally took possession of his great-great-grandfather's hand-carved ivory pipe, which was the Sandridge clan's symbol for manhood, authority, and power. The destruction of the pipe was the sign of their fall. The irony of it was I, his slave, was the one who picked the broken pipe up and placed it in his trembling hands, which looked like the cupped hands of J. R. when he received Master Sandridge's meager pay for the last acreage of the family's farm.

That significance, and memorable happening, of the broken pipe would affect every individual on the Sandridge farm.

The first Sandridge had taken the land from the Indians. The power the family held over the lives of the blacks that slaved on that land had come to an end with the broken pipe.

I, Nimrod, a black man, knew the events of that evening meant that I was destined to become involved in something I had never dreamed imaginable, the Sandridge family legacy.

Now I ask you, my dear reader, do you recall the dream I wrote about earlier, the one I had when I was six years old? The one I told to Papa-horse when he and I sat fishing on the bank of Tims Ford's lake? If you do recall, you will remember he told me the dream had three parts, but he only shared the meaning of two of those parts with me. As you may recall, the dream was about the stump, white fog, Mrs. Beulah Sandridge stepping over Ol' Captain Sandridge, and the Red Book. After he had interpreted the first and second parts, Papa-horse said, "And the third has to do with your outer life, the world around you."

Remember the part of the dream where I held the Red Book as if it were everything? And it was everything to me. The pages of the book moved. As they flipped and flipped, I heard them speak. They talked to me, and I understood them. That was the part Papa-horse had not told me during his interpretation.

Well, the third part of the dream was about my becoming a part of the Sandridge family legacy.

At this juncture I will return to my encounter with Master Sandridge at the big house. Master Sandridge and I continued to stare at each other. Eventually, our staring was broken by a single soft sniff. We turned and looked at Mrs. Sandridge, and at that very moment, the grandfather clock struck eight times and stopped. But its loud tick-tock seemed to pull at portions of my past, ripped them from the recesses of my mind, and presented them to me as if they were happening there and then. As strange as this all must sound to you, I felt Master Sandridge had the same thoughts brought up from his past. As he looked up at me, it seemed as if I saw the same memories flash across his eyes. He looked at the blue blanket Mrs. Sandridge held in her lap, then at me.

Mrs. Sandridge pulled the blanket up to her mouth, and her eyes met mine. Tears flowed down her cheeks. Not only did I see something new in her eyes, but I also felt a flutter of emotions at the pit of my stomach.

Master Sandridge jerked himself upright.

We stared into each other's souls.

The ticking of the clock seemed to grow louder. It carried our minds back into the past, and the noisy ticking became silent. We drifted into the past. It was the spring of 1832, he was twenty-nine and I was nine. He had come home from college and had decided to ride the fences on the east end of the farm. As usual, he wanted me to accompany him. He mounted his favorite Arabian horse, Smoky, and I trailed behind on foot. Master William, as I called him back then, took me with him whenever he inspected work that had been done by the slaves. Once I over heard him tell his mother, Mrs. Beulah, he saw something special in my eyes.

———

"MAMA," HE SAID TO HER, "that boy, Nimrod, he's as quick as a rattler. He has a good mind and a solid body. I believe he can learn 'most anything. He's dependable, trustworthy, and eager to please. I want him when I take over the farm."

"Yes, William," she said, "what you see is true. But you must always remember he can't serve your purpose by working in the hot sun like the others. He's not a field slave."

I tagged along and studied the fence while Master William rode with his head touching the clouds. After a short distance, he shifted to one side of the saddle, rested his weight on the horse's rear with one hand, turned, and said, "Nimrod."

I twirled around and flung the straw from my mouth and

answered, "Yes, suh, Master William."

"I have a question I'm going to put to you. Answer if you can."

"Yes, sir, I'll do my best."

"This question has been with me for a long time …"

"Yes, sir."

"… and it needs an answer. You people work in the hot sun all day and never complain. You tromp around on the frozen ground in winter. Not a mumbling word. You're beaten until your flesh pops like a ripe melon. Not a word. Now for my question, how does it feel to be a nigger and a slave?"

Although I was eager to answer Master William's question, he was not ready for the answer he received. Papa-horse had been teaching me the importance of questions, and my mind ran like a thoroughbred turned loose to pasture at the front end of spring. I was eager to answer my master's question. But before I answered, I thought about something Papa-horse had said: "One should ask questions when he wants doors to open, when he's seeking treasures, and when he's expecting to receive good."

With all the innocence and honesty of a child, I thought I was supposed to answer any and all questions that were directed to me. So I answered, "Well, Master William, sometimes I think you white folks is more a slave then we is. I learned from Papa-horse that …"

Master William jerked the reins as hard as he could and Smoky stomped his powerful hoofs hard against the ground. His sudden and violent reaction frightened and confused me. The anger I saw in his eyes, and the fear I felt in my heart, hurled me against the fence rails while he tugged at the reins and brought the horse under control.

Master William glared at me, pointed his finger, and shouted, "You dirty nigger! If you ever open your mouth like that again, I'll kill you!"

To say the least my answer angered Master William to point he was madder than a wet hen. My youth and my answer had given him more than his traditional way of thinking could relate to. I thought to myself, 'White slave owners don't see their slaves as humans who are intelligent.' I looked him straight in the eyes and said, "Yes, sir, Master William." And we stared at each other.

Then Master William pulled Smoky around and started off again. I was angry and lagged behind and did not pay much attention to the fence anymore. I was a child, and so I began to make a game of watching my feet as I walked, and I glanced at Smoky's hooves, too. I thought about what Papa-horse had taught me about sure-footed horses. He said, "The sure-footed horse is more intelligent and has greater awareness of his surroundings than other horses. He can walk the rocky paths of steep mountains and along narrow ridges with the ease of a mountain goat. Other horses, the clumsy ones, are unsafe in mountainous terrains."

As soon as I stopped watching Smoky's hooves, he stalled. He tensed every muscle in his body, jerked his head up and back, lowered his rump toward the ground, and then thirteen hundred pounds of muscle lurched toward the sky.

Master William flew from the horse's back like a rag doll tossed by a child. I braced myself and watched him as he flew over my head. He landed straddled-legged on a fence post, fell to the ground, and rolled. His head hit a rock, and he lay in the fetal position with his hands between his legs.

I climbed through the fence rails and ran to his side. I saw blood gushing from his temple and ran as fast as I could to the next field with the focus of a honeybee. I went from plant to plant. I pushed clumps of weeds aside and searched for certain healing plants. As I found the ones I needed. I plucked the leaves, stuffed them in my mouth, and chewed them until they were soggy. After I had filled my mouth I ran back to Master William. His fingertips and lips had turned blue. I grabbed his hand, and his fingers felt like icicles.

I took the soggy mess of leaves out of my mouth, pressed some into of it on the gash in his temple and the rest into his mouth. Then I closed my eyes and prayed.

———

THE SOUND OF A DISTANT VOICE called as if from a tunnel. It said, "William.... William, what's going on? Is something wrong, dear?"

I was disoriented.

Master Sandridge jerked and blinked. He stumbled forward. He looked at me, took two steps, and snatched the broken pipe from my hand.

Mrs. Sandridge jumped to her feet and flung the blanket and yarn to the floor. The ball of yarn rolled and stopped at my feet. She looked at me, then marched past Master Sandridge, crying, and rushed from the room. We both watched as she disappeared at the top of the stairs.

Master Sandridge gripped the broken pipe until his knuckles turned white. His clenched jaws stiffened his neck. He turned and marched to the fireplace and stood there like a slab of granite. "Why are you here?" he barked. "What do you want?"

"I brought the key, Master Sandridge. I came to tell you we're ready to start work on the new barn."

He took three steps toward me and yelled, "Do you think I'm stupid? You damn nigger! Who do you think is in charge of this farm? I am, damn-it!"

I looked him in his eyes and calmly said, "Yes, sir, Master Sandridge. I know."

Master Sandridge's anger boiled over. He moved a step closer to me and pointed his finger at me. Although he was madder than Lucifer when he came to understand that Jesus' death and resurrection would lead people to life, he said in a calm voice, "Nigger … you best leave this house. Leave now. Right now. And I do mean now!"

I slid my hand into my pocket and searched for the key, but I did not feel it. I searched all my pockets and did not find it. I searched the first pocket again. Finally, I found it and laid it on the table, then I slowly backed out of the parlor and into the hallway. I felt someone watching my every step, and I took a quick glance down the hall, towards the kitchen, and there she was, leaning against the doorframe with her face slightly touching the back of her hands. Miss Sadie peered at me from the dark, and her eyes were empty sinkholes.

With one eye on Master Sandridge, and the other on the love of my life, Sadie, I backed out of the house, and closed the door. I thought about how much I loved Miss Sadie's rainbow smile and honeysuckle voice. I loved her more than anything. In my mind I heard her say, "Nimrod, you's have a smile just like that of a child. And I's in love wit' it."

I loved the look I saw in her eyes when she served me those fluffy buttermilk biscuits that floated in raw honey. I loved the gleam in her eyes and the sparkle of her smile, which were the greatest treats a man could ever receive. I had never refused myself a moment of her time. She gave me reasons to live, a reason to try to be what God called me to be. Miss Sadie was God's gift to me and the people on the Sandridge farm, a gift the world never had a chance to enjoy.

That Saturday night was the last time I saw Miss Sadie alive. Later that night her cabin, a hundred feet or so behind the big house, burned to the ground. It was early the next morning before we were able to put the fire out and dig her charred body out of the smoldering ashes. I was sick for weeks. My soul left my body, and for five years I felt empty. The sunny days of spring and summer wore the gray mantle of winter, and the blank days of winter were filled with the agony of a slow death. Melancholy, my constant companion, slept in my bed with me at night and held my hand during the day. Laughter was frozen in my throat. Joy was as lumps of ice lodged in my chest. Tomorrow hid behind every bend. Fear licked at my face.

TABLES ARE TURNED

IT WAS AT 11:30, TUESDAY morning, April 16, 1867, one year and three days since Miss Sadie's death. Three days after her death, Master Sandridge came down with one of his sick spells, the one that made the difference.

He could no longer care for himself physically, and he had finally lost his cotton-picking mind. Not speaking a mumbling word he lay on his back and stared at the ceiling. His ice-cold stare seemed to make the room cooler than any other room in the house, and the house slaves complained about the spooky feelings they had when they were there, and they feared it. Mrs. Sandridge and Aunt Gussie had to attend to his every need. For years I had felt that kind of thing would happen to him, yet I had no idea it would lead to what happened later.

As I explained earlier, the Sandridge family's symbol of white male power and authority had been shattered when the pipe was broken. But the family's generational curse would be carried on and run its course through Mrs. Sandridge, as she was married to Master Sandridge, and through the slaves who bore the name Sandridge and any child or children born to them. We all had to bear the Sandridge family's curse.

If I do not make this important point on generational curses clear, it would be a disservice to you, my descendants, and to all who may read this journal.

It is like this. The generational curses that were on slave masters, such as Master Sandridge and his family, were passed on to their wives, children, and slaves, in addition to their own family curses. Papa-horse said a man cannot be a part of a group and not be affected by its good spirits and its bad spirits. He said, "If one man sees another man in a mud puddle crying for help, the first man can't get into the puddle without getting muddy himself."

The important point that I am stating here is this: not only did we slaves receive generational curses from our African ancestors, but we also received generational curses from the white families we were enslaved to. This is where you come in and are to be affected. I will explain what I mean later, but first I must continue to tell about other matters, as they support my reasons for writing my story.

Another point you must understand is that slaves lived under the rule of white masters and were forced to take on the slave master's surname, which meant slaves received all the family curses the name carried. Papa-horse told me, "From ancient times, people have placed high value on names, and rightly so. In the beginning, God told the first man to name the animals according to their nature, and he did so. He named them according to their ways and temperaments. But it did not stop there. The practice of naming according to nature was extended to humans as well. When a man shares his name, he shares his nature, his spirit. A family's spirit and name are conditioned by their beliefs. If one man goes into another man's environment and spends time there, he becomes affected by that man's nature and spirit. And if the second man is not careful, he retains the first man's nature and spirit when he leaves."

We, the slaves of America, received family beliefs, natures, and spirits from our masters. We were not allowed to think for ourselves. We were forced to think and act as our masters thought and acted. If a slave master had muddy beliefs and thinking, his family and slaves had muddy beliefs and thinking. We took on the beliefs and practices of our masters, beliefs that were not from Africa. Our people were so weary and desperate that many robed themselves in the beliefs whites had about their idle god. According to their church fables, he was a giant with a long white beard who lived in heaven, sat on a throne, and had made a deal with the devil. The god would get the good people, and the devil would get the bad people, while all people had good and bad in their heart and deeds.

Even today, some blacks continue to live under the power of the beliefs and practices that came from white slave owners, beliefs that do not come from the Motherland, Africa. The thing that ties people closer together than blood is what they believe.

Unlike the white man, the ancient Ishermans did not mix the blood of fathers and daughters. They knew that practice would increase family curses and create emotional weaknesses that would affect the mind and heart. They did not eat swine, nor drink whiskey, the two poisons that weaken the will and create emotionalism. They did not believe that man should own land. They did not kill animals for sport. They did not believe in war and murder. They did not believe in the bearded god who punishes people for being what they are. They did not believe in the god who loves whites and who hates blacks and all others. They believed in Yahweh, the god who loved all people.

A white man and his beliefs are like a dog and his fleas. If a dog lies in your bed, he is going to leave fleas. The white man has many beliefs that are based on curses, and those cursed beliefs affected us, the slaves. It was the white man's beliefs about slavery that caused whites who lived in the South to kill whites who lived in the North, and likewise.

After his collapse, Master Sandridge's poor health kept him from caring for the farm, and that meant Mrs. Sandridge had to take charge. Although she had the final say about what, when, and how things were to be done, she depended on me to keep the farm operational. That also meant she needed someone to travel with her when she went to the grits mills. I was her choice.

We would travel from Decherd to Winchester and back. On some trips to deliver corn meal, we went as far northeast as Sanders, Tracy City, White City, down to Mount Eagle, and as far south as Jasper. Other trips took us northwest to Franklin and Cowan, and back to Decherd. In the beginning, we worked together well and enjoyed the good it brought the farmers and their families. Not only did other farms benefit from our hard work, but the Sandridge farm also became more productive than it had ever been. Mrs. Sandridge became the most industrious and respected individual, man or woman, in southern Tennessee. Her reputation as a shrewd, calculating, honest, and hard working businesswoman even reached Texas, Iowa, New York and Washington DC.

And this is where you, my dear reader, personally come into the picture.

One morning in 1869, after Aunt Gussie had cooked one of her perfect southern breakfasts, I walked into the kitchen with a pail of fresh goat's milk. I said, "How're you this fine spring morning, Aunt Gussie? You're looking prettier than ever!"

"Awh, go on, Nimrod!" She blushed and straightened her head rag, then flipped another flitter and said, "Don't y'all try butterin' me up none with sweet talk, boy. I's old enough to be your mama's mama."

I laughed and set the milk pail on the table, then went over and gave Aunt Gussie a bear hug from behind and a kiss on the cheek. She pretended to move her head to the side, but I knew she enjoyed my antics as much as I did.

"Y'all go on now," she said. "I's got me some work to be done." We laughed again, and I poured the milk into the canister.

"Have you seen Mrs. Sandridge this morning, Aunt Gussie? She's never been this late before. Just to be sure things are all right, you might want to check on her."

Aunt Gussie cut her big brown cow eyes at me, and said in her loud children-calling voice, "Why y'all so hot and eager this morning to git workin', huh?"

"Well," I said, "this is the day Mrs. Sandridge and I are to make our trip to the mill. We have a long journey ahead of us, you know."

She laughed, and I poked around with the firewood. "You no never mind child," she said. "I'll go check on her … and the good doctor. Does y'all thank y'all can wait until I's gets back?"

"Oh, yes," I said. "Take your time. I can do some things here in the kitchen."

Aunt Gussie laughed again, waddled down the hall, and started up the stairs. She went up those stairs, cursing every step. "Damn house gots too many steps to climb. Damn white folks gonna work me to death. If the Lord 'spected we'uns to live up high, he woulda give us a tail like a monkey and wings like birds. That way, we could climb and fly. White-folks don't do nothing that make no sense." When she reached the top of the stairs, she sighed and wiped her brow with a swollen hand, and said under her breath, "Thank the Lord. I's done made it again. And that's no thanks to white folks."

Aunt Gussie walked into the bedroom and was surprised to see Mrs. Sandridge sitting on the edge of her bed, fists pressed into the mattress, her head bowed. Next to her lay Master Sandridge, whose frail body was swallowed up by the wide feather mattress and dwarfed by massive bedposts and wide headboard.

"Mrs. Sandridge, what's be ailing you, child?" Aunt Gussie asked. "You all right?"

Mrs. Sandridge looked up and rubbed her stomach. "Never mind me, Aunt Gussie, I'll be all right. I'm feeling a little peaked this morning."

Aunt Gussie's scowl turned into a smile and tears welled in her eyes.

Mrs. Sandridge was confused. She laid her long porcelain fingers on Aunt Gussie's dark hands and asked, "My dear Gussie, what's bothering you?"

Aunt Gussie shook her head and said, "Shucks, child, old Gussie don't be ailing none. She be's happy. Happy for you."

"Happy, for me? What in the world for, Gussie?"

"My, my, my, Missus. The Lord done answered your long years of praying. Just like I's knew he would."

"Gussie, what on earth are you carrying on about?"

"Ma'am, you be 'specting."

"'Specting? 'Specting what?"

"Yes, Ma'am! You's with child!"

Mrs. Sandridge looked up and grabbed Aunt Gussie by the arm and pulled herself to her feet.

It was later that day when Mrs. Sandridge told me that she remembered something I had told her that Papa-horse had said. It was something like this: "Time, life experiences, and wisdom teach the faithful and trusting that God answers all prayers."

Although she was both excited and frightened, her fears were calmed by Aunt Gussie's understanding, and loving support. Tears of joy streaked her face. Aunt Gussie said she saw the new life glowing from Mrs. Sandridge's insides when she entered the bedroom. For the first time in years, Mrs. Sandridge seemed to feel the excitement that had vanished from her life and had been long forgotten.

Mrs. Sandridge's newfound joy inspired the skeleton of a man, Master Sandridge, to move. He stiffly turned his head and looked at her, then raised his head. His sunken, bloodshot eyes glared from their deep sockets. He whimpered to Aunt Gussie, "Gussie … go … go fetch … that nigger, Nimrod. Fetch him here now."

Aunt Gussie bounded down the stairs with ease, a sight I had never seen. She told me what had happened and said the master was calling for me.

As I walked up the stairs, I felt change hanging in the air. I walked into the bedroom, and Mrs. Sandridge got up from the bed and walked out. When Master Sandridge caught sight of me, he reached behind the side of the headboard, pulled something out, and gripped it in his bony hand. His arm collapsed at his side, and he said, "Here. Come here. Stand close."

I stood next to the bed.

He raised his head and said in a faint voice, "Now it's time you hear this. About that night." He struggled to breathe. "The night of the fire." His chest rattled with each breath. "You need to know this ... know what happened that night."

I really did not need him to tell me what was on his mind. I sensed what he was about to say, for I had already lived the thoughts and feelings he needed to tell me, or tell someone. I knew anything that would come from his mouth would be filled with the guilt that created his need to talk about that night. His guilt created his need to try and strike out and hurt me and show himself as the superior one, even though he was flat on his back and dying. This secret he needed to share, like other secrets, had been buried deep in his mind and heart. It had been festering there, and now it rose to the surface of his black heart. He was the typical slave-owning white man who had an inbred need to be in control. This was his last attempt to control me. He wanted to beat me down one more time with his painful news. His story was like this:

———

"THAT NIGHT, AFTER YOU LEFT, I went to her cabin," he said. "I walked up to the door and saw her standing next to the bed. She was facing the wall, swaying from side to side, something she never did before.

"I watched her parade around in the dim light. She was possessed by sin.

"She opened her dress, one button at a time. She looked like a whore stripping for hire. She was stripping for somebody other than me. I knew it. I could tell. She let the dress fall from her shoulders. Her body was exposed to my view. The sweat on her dark skin sparkled like diamonds. She was making a spectacle of herself.

"She just kept swaying from side to side. She was out of her mind.

She raised a heel off the floor, and moved her knee up and down, rubbing her inner thighs together. Like a whore, she was. I knew in her mind she was with some one else, having strong thoughts about him, 'cause she smiled from time to time. It was not for me. My feelings went from disappointment to anger to rage. I continued to watch from the door, and she swaggered like a whore bragging over her body.

"She bent over to pick the dress up. Her full ass looked like an upside-down heart, sitting on a pedestal. Her long legs looked like they had been sculpted by a Greek god. Her near-perfect body was on display.

"I interrupted her performance when I opened the door. The squeaking startled her, and she turned and cupped her breasts with both hands. I pushed the door open and walked in. She looked at the floor. Her arms dropped to her side, and she pulled one leg in front of the other.

"'Who're you stripping for, Sadie?' I asked. 'I sure wish it was for me, but I know better. It wasn't for me.

"She said nothing.

"I took my coat, pants, and shirt off and draped them over the back of the chair. I put my boots and the other things on the table. We both were as naked as newborn children. God created man, and he created woman for man's pleasure.

"I stood next to her. I moved my hands up and down her body like I had done for years. She was cold like a statue. She didn't move. Her arms dangled at her sides.

"I palmed her left breast and gave it a firm squeeze. She tensed. I traced my fingertips over that dark skin, made a path down between the breasts, over the stomach, and stopped at her navel, and she tensed. I moved my finger around and around. My hand moved below the waist and stopped in that patch of coarse hair, and the edge of her protruding hipbone. She clenched her teeth. I licked her face.

"She despised me, and I knew it. But it didn't matter. I gripped her between the legs. She squirmed and tensed up.

"I jerked my hand back. She was puzzled, and so was I.

"For the first time, she was lubricated. She was never like that before, always dry as a bone. I thought back to the early part of the evening, when I saw the two of you coming out of the house. That's when my mind went blank. I lost control. I called her a black bitch and punched her in the stomach with all my might. She doubled over and fell to the floor. She coughed and gasped for air.

"She knew better. I had warned her plenty of times.

"I grabbed her hair and jerked her to her feet, then hit her again. She fell against the table and knocked the lantern to the floor. I called out to her. She didn't answer. She just lay there, whimpering like a wounded animal. She moved her head and looked up at me. She looked straight into my eyes. Something she'd never done before. She coughed, and muttered some faint words.

She said, 'You be's the only man I done ever been with, Master. But now, I's free.'

"She trembled and struggled. She got up on her feet. She spoke her last words. 'The Lord only knows … I wish I'd give my sacredness to the only man I done ever loved. That be Master, Nimrod!'

"I didn't want to be like my father. But she made me. God knows, I couldn't help myself. She should've never put me in that position. She knew better. Anger rushed into my fists. For the first time I beat her. I beat that bitch without mercy. She got what was coming to her.

"After she stopped moving, I stood over her and shouted for her to get up. She wouldn't move. She just lay there, defying my authority. I kicked her, and she continued to lie there. I reached down and grabbed her by the wrist and jerked her up. She fell back down to the floor.

"When I came to myself, I felt the heat from the fire. The lantern was burning out of control. There was nothing I could do. It was too hot. I looked down at Sadie. She lay there with her arms stretched out. The index finger of her left hand was stretched out into the moonlight that peeped through the crack in the door. She was trying to tell me something, something about the way to heaven, maybe. I don't know. My mind was too cloudy to understand. All she had to do was say it. Say what she meant just by telling me. That's what she should've done, but she just lay there. She didn't try. She stopped trying. She just stopped. That was it.

"I didn't want to be like my father. I've tried hard all my life not to be like him. I never wanted to be that way. But the Lord must have wanted something different for me. I had no control over my fate. No one does. God calls the shots."

———

MASTER SANDRIDGE FROWNED, TURNED his face towards the wall, and whispered, "You damn nigger . . . Nimrod . . . you've been the death of me."

THE KEY AND ITS SECRET

THE DAY OF MASTER SANDRIDGE'S funeral, a flock of crows flew overhead. Gray clouds showered mourners with a cold drizzle of rain. Master Sandridge was laid to rest at the north end of the farm, next to his mother and his father, with the rest of the Sandridge clan. Relatives, friends, and neighbors stood close to the pine casket and paid their last respects to the man who had tried to escape his father's demons.

The freed slaves on the Sandridge farm, who had supposedly been freed by the Emancipation Proclamation papers, stood a short distance back from the open grave, closer to the hill.

Everyone cried. Blacks and whites cried for Master Sandridge, the doctor who could not heal himself. Like any man, he did his best to do right, but that was just it: he was like any other man who lived and suffered with family curses. Papa-horse said, "All people have family curses and wrestle with them daily."

When I looked at Master Sandridge's evilness from the vantage of family curses, I did not judge him as harshly. As Papa-horse used to say, "There is at least one pound of evil stored in the heart of every man, woman, and child, and a lifetime of circumstances will reveal it."

Raindrops fell on my head and traced wet paths down my face. My mind wandered through my past, picking through the lessons Papa-horse had taught me about curses. My memory stopped at an early morning, when a steamy mist rose from Tims Ford's lake. We were waiting for the unsuspecting fish to bite the hooks that were concealed in the tempting, wiggling morsels.

———

PAPA-HORSE SAID, "MARADH, you're remembering your dreams. And you understand their messages quite well. You're progressing. Now I feel its time for you to learn about curses. I believe you're ready."

"What's curses, Papa-horse?"

"Speak in your tongue, Maradh. The African language, not the slave language."

"Yes, Rekesh."

"A curse is a spiritual affliction. It's like a disease or a plague, except it goes against the spirit, the body, and the soul."

"Where do curses come from?"

"They can come from three sources. The first two come from two kinds of people. First, from people who don't know they're cursing. Second, from people who know they are cursing. People who don't know they're cursing do it when they're angry and are being hateful. When they think, believe, say, and do evil things to others, they're cursing them. They're calling down evil."

"What do you mean, Rekesh?"

"When a man and his wife are angry with each other, they feel, think, believe, say, and do evil things to each other. That's cursing. When they think, believe, say, and do evil things to their children, that's cursing too, and the children learn to do the same thing. They curse others with their evil thoughts, words, and deeds. Curses are contagious evilness that's passed from one person to another, from one generation to the next."

"Why would people do that?" I asked.

"Some don't know they're doing it. It's human carelessness."

"Why do others do it?"

"For many reasons," he said. "Three common reasons are, one, these people have a need to control others. Two, they are stuck in evilness. And, three, they're cursed themselves. Do you understand?"

"I think so. But I don't understand how curses work."

"Do you understand prayer?"

"Yes. You taught me. It's when I talk to God, and God talks to me."

"That's right. Prayer is talking. So is cursing."

"Cursing is praying?"

"Yes, Maradh. But it's a different kind of praying."

"If God is good, why would God listen to curses?"

"The God of good doesn't listen to curses, but the god of evil does. That evil god is partly the reason why humans have problems and suffer."

"Is the evil god the reason why blacks suffer in this foreign country?"

"Yes."

"Is he the reason why Ol' Captain Sandridge, and other whites do bad things against blacks? Are whites cursed too?"

"Yes. But, Maradh, you must remember that not all whites are evil because they're white."

"So why do they do bad things to us?"

"The ones who do evil things to blacks also do evil to other whites. They do evil things to anybody. And blacks, like whites, do evil things to whites and other blacks. One man's evil is no better than another man's evil. Evil is evil. Whites are not the only ones who are cursed. Blacks are cursed too."

"But, Maradh, blacks don't make slaves out of whites. We don't beat them. We don't make them work until they fall dead. We're the slaves! Not them."

"That's true, Rekesh. Blacks are the slaves at this time. They suffer and die from beatings, murders, and hard work. But things haven't always been this way for blacks. Remember the stories I've told you about Africa and her people? Life was good then."

"Yes. I enjoy hearing about Africa and the Isherman people. I wish I could go there. That way, I could see the gardens, the temples, and the kings and queens with my own eyes."

"One day your eyes will see Africa, Maradh, but the kings and queens as they were known will be long gone."

"How can I do that? I'm a slave. I don't have freedom like Ol' Captain Sandridge."

"Remember there are two freedoms. Paper freedom, the first freedom, is the freedom that's given by man to man, on paper. The man who gives it can also take it back. The second freedom, true freedom, only comes from the inside. It's in you. God put it there, and it can't be given by man or taken by man.

"Oh, I tell you," Papa-horse said, "the time is coming when whites will be forced to set blacks free. And that'll be paper freedom. A tall man dressed in black, wearing a smokestack hat will sign important papers giving slaves paper freedom. But that won't give blacks what they really want. Their bodies will have some freedom, but their minds will still be enslaved. And that'll cause their bodies to go back into slavery, poverty, and hard work."

"All blacks?" I asked.

"No. Some blacks will make their way in the world by owning businesses and land. But that won't last, either. Slave owners are not going to let go of the easy life they've become accustomed to. They're stuck in their evilness, and they won't break free from their family curses. The blacks that become freed slaves only and still have slave thinking will continue to depend on the whites. The worst thing about a man being a freed slave is that he lived under slave conditions for so long that he passes his slave thinking on to his children. And the children will pass it on to the next generation. On and on it goes. If blacks only gain paper freedom, and don't gain true freedom, they'll never be free."

"Rekesh, how do you know these things? Who tells you this stuff?"

"God talks to those who ask questions and listen, and obey."

"Will God tell me things?"

"Yes. When you ask questions, God answers. But you must learn to listen to the answers and follow them."

"Will you help me learn to listen?"

"I can't help you, son. I can only assist you. I've told you before. You'll learn to listen through time and practice. Now it's time you understand why blacks are in this country as slaves to whites, and how and why they're cursed."

"Okay, Rekesh. I'm ready to listen."

"Long ago in time past, there was the time when your African ancestors worshiped the true God, Yahweh. He was their god until they began to mix with people who worshiped many gods. Those people had gods for the weather, seasons, insects, crops, animals, and everything. Yahweh warned the elders of the Isherman not to worship with those people. They didn't listen. They began to worship the many gods. They stopped looking to Yahweh. And Yahweh stopped blessing them. Their new ways of worshiping forced Yahweh out of their minds and hearts. When that happened, the many gods gained control over the Ishermans' thoughts and beliefs. They came under the curse of wrong thinking and wrong believing."

"But, Rekesh, why did the Ishermans become slaves to whites?"

"Well, Maradh, it happened like this. After many years of having a king, queen, and priests ruling them, some of the Ishermans who had lived among the people who worshiped many gods decided they wanted a different way of life and new rulers. They wanted a government like the other people had, and that divided the Isherman people. The division created new problems and the problems spread. The king and queen had to divide the land and set up governorships and smaller kingdoms. Soon the governors wanted more power and began to set up their own armies to enforce their laws. The different armies began to go to war with each other. In the beginning, they fought over land rights, but the fights were settled through contests and games. The army who won took the losing soldiers as prisoners, and they became indentured servants. No one was killed."

"What's an indentured servant?" I asked. "Is that a slave?"

"An indentured servant is a person who works for another for a period of time, and after that, they're set free."

"Set free? That sounds like a slave to me."

"Well, yes, it was."

"Did they work until they dropped dead, like blacks do in this country?"

"No. They only worked at what they were good at, what they were trained for and taught to do. And they worked only when their caretakers needed the work done.

"Oh."

"In the beginning, some of the people thought that kind of slavery would work. Things started out good, but they soon changed for the worse. The indentured servants became prisoners who were forced to do work they didn't want to do and weren't trained to do. They started complaining, then they rebelled and became angry and violent. The rebels began to kill their masters. So the governors decided to rid Africa of violence and murder by selling them as prisoners to whites, the Europeans, Portuguese, Dutch, and Spaniards.

"The whites took the prisoners to other lands and sold them as slaves. Once the whites knew they could prosper by selling Africans as slaves, they went back to Africa for more. Not only did they buy more slaves from the governors, but they also captured entire villages and took everybody as slaves.

"And that, my son, was how your parents, you, and the others ended up as slaves in this foreign country. When the black man left

Yahweh he became cursed. Without favor of God."

"But how could the governors sell their own black people to the whites? Why didn't they just keep them in Africa? Didn't they know the white man was going to hurt them and kill them?"

"The Ishermans who sold their brothers did not have God's love in their hearts. They couldn't act with wisdom. And it is true that in the beginning, the Ishermans didn't know that the whites were selling the prisoners as slaves. But they did learn later that they were."

"But they didn't know how bad that was. Right?"

"No, they knew it was a very bad thing to do. But they continued to sell their brothers as slaves."

"Why?" I asked. "How could they, if they knew it was bad?"

"Maradh, there are people who only seek paper freedom, money, and material things, and they want more than they need. So they'll do anything to feel powerful, even when it means harming others."

"That can't be true. The Ishermans wouldn't do that. I don't believe it."

"I understand how you feel, Maradh, but your feelings and emotions can't erase the truth. Some day you'll see things through different eyes, my son."

"Did they become wealthy? Was it gold, silver, or paper money they wanted?"

"Maradh, if you're to benefit from what I'm gong to say about wealth, you must listen closely."

"I can do that. We talk all the time about listening. I understand it now."

"You do?"

"I can listen, Rekesh. I can listen. I'm listening now."

"Alright.

"Back in the days of the kings and queens, African people didn't need gold, silver, or precious stones. They had no use for the white man's paper money."

"So what did they receive?"

"The whites gave them beads, cloth, and flour for fritters."

"Fritters? How could the Ishermans be that stupid? I would've never done that. That was dumb."

"You must understand," he said. "The Ishermans had all the gold, silver, and diamonds they wanted, and the white men's paper money had no value in their kingdoms. It meant nothing. The whites understood that the Africans had no need for paper money, but they also knew the Ishermans enjoyed eating fritters more than anything else. So they bought the prisoners with beads and cloth and fed them fritters. Then they also raped Africa of her gold, diamonds, other riches ... and her people."

"But, Rekesh, I thought you said the Ishermans were powerful and had great wisdom."

"They were, Maradh. But when they lost favor with Yahweh, they lost everything, including godly wisdom, insight, and love. Their separation from Yahweh was the beginning of their living hell. He could no longer bless them and protect them. And the many gods were free to curse them in any way they wanted to."

"So that means the black people are in this foreign country because of fritters? Because of food?"

"No, my son. We are here because our ancestors turned away from Yahweh and turned to the many gods. That's the curse."

———

THE RAIN FELL HARDER. My head and clothes were soaked. People shuffled from foot to foot as Reverend Smith bored us with half-truths from the Bible and his whole lies about Master Sandridge. I wondered if he really believed what he said. Most of all, I wondered if he thought his lies were convincing God. I looked around, then reached into my pocket and fished for the key. The other people paid no attention to me, as they were busy trying to keep from dozing off. I pulled the key from my pocket, rubbed it between my fingers, and asked, 'What could be so important that Master Sandridge had to keep it under lock and key?' I held the key to my chest and thought, 'Maybe you'll lead me to true freedom.'

Although Papa-horse had taught me well, I was not thoroughly convinced that true freedom was inside me. Besides, I was still angry with him for always being right and then abandoning me. From time to time I had continued to look for him. I still hoped that true freedom would pop up from some unknown place, or from some unseen force, or from someone else who would kiss me on the forehead and say, "Nimrod, from now on, everything is going to be all right. You're free."

After the funeral, the whites went to the big house to eat and drink and the freed slaves went back to work. When Mrs. Sandridge's company stopped coming and going, I told her I would take the things she wanted moved from the master bedroom and put them in the attic. I went up the stairs and stopped at the banister, where I listened to Mrs. Sandridge crying. Aunt Gussie and the other house slaves were bumping around in the kitchen. I was free to do what I had been waiting to do—use the key.

I went into the bedroom and closed the door. I stood at the foot of Master Sandridge's bed and prayed. Then I took the key from my pocket and rolled it between my fingers. Suddenly a voice called out.

"Nimrod, Nimrod."

The voice sounded like Master Sandridge. I looked around and saw no one, so I prayed again and asked God to protect me. I waited. The voice did not return. All was silent. Then it dawned on me that I did not know where the key was to reveal its secret. I thought, 'Its secret is locked in what and where?' I had no clue.

"What am I to do?" I said aloud. "All this time, I've only concerned myself with the secret, the key. Not with the lock. Where is the lock? If I don't find the lock, the key is useless. What am I to do?"

I looked around again, then thought, 'The bed. It must be under the bed.' I got down and looked under the bed. Nothing. I looked under the mattresses. Nothing. I looked under the other bed and mattresses, and still found nothing. I looked in the clothes safe. I pushed the clothes back and looked in boxes, and still found nothing.

Then I thought, 'Yes! I know where it is!' I remembered the time I walked into the parlor and seen Ol' Captain Sandridge facing the wall. When he realized I was in the room, he turned and came toward me, but I saw the trapdoor in the wall. He came over and slapped me to the floor. He grabbed me by the arm, shoved me out into the hall, and slammed the door shut, but that was too late. I had seen his private place for hiding special items. The opening in the wall was about twelve inches square, large enough to hold a small box with a lock.

But there was still a problem. The trapdoor was in the old house. And since I could not go downstairs right then to search the parlor walls of the new house we were in at that time, I became so desperate that I began to pat the walls in that bedroom. I had waited so long to discover Master Sandridge's secret that I was not about to wait any longer. I searched for a trapdoor in the bedroom walls. I patted and searched and found nothing.

Frustrated, I leaned against the attic door. The doorknob poked me in the butt. I began to laugh. Then I sighed, and my tempest of emotions calmed. I was elated. I turned and faced the door. Dread gripped me about the chest, and my shaking hand reached for the knob. As if holding a snake by the head, I held the key fast. I had no idea what I would find. The secret that had been hidden in the dark attic by Master Sandridge was about to be brought to the light. My heart raced faster than Ol' Blue's legs moved when he chased squirrels. My hands shook like leaves in a stiff breeze. I tried the key. It did not fit the keyhole! But I was not about to allow that key to keep me from what I was destined to know. I pressed it in harder and wiggled it from side to side. Suddenly that stubborn key leaped from my fingers and fell to the floor. I immediately scooped it up and shoved it at the doorknob again. This time it worked.

One more twist, the knob turned, the door opened, and I reeled backward as darkness and silence leaped out at me. My mind went blank. I paused and stared up into that black tunnel. I took two steps into the dark stairwell. The darkness grew blacker. The air was stale and musty. The silence grew louder. It rang in my ears.

"What secrets would a man like you hide?" I asked aloud. "What could be so important that you needed to lock it up? Is it a good secret, or bad secret?"

The dark and the silence had the answer, but said nothing. I started up the stairs with my palms pressed against the walls. It was so dark that my feet had to feel for each step. The silence echoed in my ears.

Winded, I reached the top of the stairs. The mystery of what I would find in the attic swirled about my head and painted my every thought black. That total silence sang in my ears like a chorus of crickets. I took deep breaths to clear my mind. My heartbeat slowed down.

I looked to my left, and saw the thin ray of sunlight that had pushed its way through a single, dirty windowpane. I came to rest on a pedestal. A lone brown box sat on the pedestal. Master Sandridge's secret had been kept safe in paper walls.

The lone brown box sat on the pedestal, and had been protected from the dark by that sliver of light.

That brown box had waited on top of that whitewashed Bible pedestal, in that stream of sunlight that had entered the attic, everyday at the same time, for who knows how many years.

Although I had known that Master Sandridge had a secret, I did not know it had been connected to the outside world by God's sunlight. As Papa-horse would say, "What's done in the dark someday comes to the light."

Today was that day. And that was the day. My day.

I stood next to the pedestal, bent over, and blew the dust off the box. Shiny specks of dust flew up the stream of light to the window. They were like tiny angels abandoning a secret that no longer needed their protection.

"Time to let go of your secrets, Mr. Box," I said aloud. "I'm going to know in a minute what you've known for years. Who knows? You just might be what I need to lead me to freedom. And even if you're not, well, you still have something important to share with me. Something that Master Sandridge kept hidden from the world. I feel your power now. I feel it stronger than ever."

I took a straight-backed chair off the wall, dusted it off, too, and sat down before the pedestal. I stared at the box for another minute. Then I pulled the top off. The paper crumbled. The dusty smell of long and lonely years filled my nose, and I sneezed. I next pulled at the sides of the box. They fell apart, their pieces crumbling and turning to dust before they reached the floor.

The only thing that remained on the pedestal was a bundle wrapped in brown paper and tied with a faded red ribbon. I picked the bundle up, and the wrappings crumbled in my hands and poured through my fingers like fine flour. The secret's protection had turned into a mound of brown dust.

Still fearful of what I might discover, I closed my eyes and blew as hard as I could.

I opened my eyes.

And there they were, as white as clouds. Two folded sheets of paper resting in my palms.

I set the pages back on the pedestal and sat back in the chair, wondering why the two sheets of paper had remained intact, although the box and the wrappings around them had turned to dust. I thought, 'Must be an act of God.'

I moved my chair closer to the window and wiped the glass until more sunlight shone through. I thought about a comment that Papa-horse had made concerning freedom. He said, "A man can have a secret today, but he can't hide it forever. Tomorrow, life will take it from his bosom and share it with the world."

I unfolded the first sheet of paper, a letter, and held it in the light. It glowed:

May 21, 1831
To Whom It May Concern:

I, Vincent B. Sandridge, being of sound mind, body, and health on this twenty-first day of May, of the year 1831, declare that all my slaves, young and old, male and female to be free from this day forth and forever. Such slaves are free to come and go as any man will without being caught and detained as run-away chattel. I decree that each be given one acre of land for work that has been rendered and performed on said farm, the Sandridge farm. All heirs who come after me, sons, daughter, or their heirs, shall know this decree and abide by its proclivities of law, my sworn words, and follow these my instructions as they are set forth in writing herewith by my hand.

Except that a slave choose to leave this farm, and keep his acre as stated above, he shall remain a part of this farm as a freed slave, working as he always has for the rest of his natural days.

Honoring this deed entitles each eldest male child of the Sandridge family to own and oversee all Sandridge lands, properties, and belongings as inheritance for as long as these words are honored and abided by in good faith and intention.

Be it known to all men that my slaves are free.

The Twenty-First of May,
Eighteen Hundred and Thirty-One

—Captain V. L. Sandridge

Ol' Captain Sandridge's hand written letter all but knocked me off my chair. I broke out into a cold sweat.

We, the slaves on the Sandridge farm, had been freed years before President Lincoln signed the Emancipation Proclamation, but we did not know that. As Papa-horse told me, "Nimrod, paper-freedom is an idea that comes from the outside, from men, from someone other than yourself. It's an idea about freedom that is expressed but can't be experienced. True freedom, when you have gained it, you know it on the inside because you feel happiness and peace. That constant river of happiness and peace will flow from you to others. You seek it, and it will find you."

I thought back to one of the few times I experienced a taste of freedom. This happened many years earlier, when I was fourteen.

It was late one night. Papa-horse and I were at Lonesome Bend with our feet resting in the waters of Dancing Pond. That night the water seemed to have bubbled stronger than any time before. I told him about an article I had read in The Liberator. It reported how Nat Turner and other slaves up North had killed a great number of whites. I told him I was tired of being treated less than a man, and I was ready to do what Nat Turner had done, ready to take the matter of freedom into my own hands. Papa-horse slowly looked up from the water and, with a stern look that sent chills dancing up and down my spine, replied in African.

———

"MARADH, MY SON, MY DEAR son ... now listen closely. You can do what Nat Turner and the others did, all right. You can kill white men, women, and children alike. That's true. Then you can run and hide for a time. That can work, too. But the whites you don't kill? They will search and find you. They'll hunt you down no matter where you go. There's no place that will keep them from you. And even if you could find a safe place, there's something that you can never hide from. Conscience. That inner voice, conscience, its relentless chatter will make you pay. It won't turn you loose, even if you get down on your knees day and night and beg for mercy. It will beat you longer and harder than any slave master ever could. That voice will beat you for the rest of your life. Son, the man who takes the lives of others, even when he does it in the name of God, finds no escape from the inner voice of conscience. The lawful punishment of the inner voice does not know the word 'mercy.'"

"But, Papa-horse," I said, "what about the murdering whites who kill our people for nothing? Are they to keep beating and killing blacks as they please? Don't they have to pay? They must be stopped! It's not right! They must pay!"

"The senseless murders that some whites, not all whites, commit against blacks and their own don't go unpunished, son. Those who are guilty, they pay. They all pay in full. They're paying this very moment. Right now!"

"How? How are they paying? By living in luxury? By having all their needs met? To hell with conscience! Tell me how they're paying and—"

"I will. Now listen—"

"Don't tell me that again. No, not to listen! I've heard that word enough! Tell me how they're paying!"

"Yes, son. I will. They're paying by giving away their true freedom."

"True freedom! Sometimes I think that's just a word you made up to scare me with!"

"I love you, Nimrod. You have the right to be angry. And you're right to demand an answer. I love you, son."

"Papa-horse, I just want to understand, that's all. Sometimes this life's too hard to live."

"You're right, son."

"I just need to understand...."

"Let me try to help. Okay?"

"Okay."

"Nimrod, no man can commit murder. Those white men cannot take the life of another human being and be free. When one murders another, he becomes a slave to both fear and guilt. The murderer is awakened every night by the acid of pain and the emotional sickness that invades his sleep. He sleeps, but finds no rest. His dreams are nightmares. Evil spirits are the constant companions who sit on his shoulders and rub salt and pepper in his eyes. Guilt urinates in his stomach. Pain rises up to his heart and mind and clouds his thinking with hatred for others. That kind of pain burns deeper and longer than the flames of hell. There's no escape."

"What you're saying may be true, but that don't stop the suffering they cause my people."

"But son, doing what Nat Turner did won't cause the suffering and murderers to stop, either. Maradh, there'll always be other whites to take the place of the ones you kill. And, son, they'll kill you and God's purpose for your life."

"So you think it's all right for us to suffer and die? And for them to live?"

"Son, the lives they're living, that isn't living. It's a walking death. Those who are guilty, and that includes blacks, have become men without souls. Each breath they draw into their lungs sustain the daggers that stab them repeatedly. And that's not living, son. It's existing.

"They're paying, all right, paying with their lives and the lives of their families. Even their family members, though they may be innocent, will suffer with the perpetrator. Although you don't see their suffering, believe me, they're suffering. They try to escape their guilt by drowning their pain in whiskey. But the whiskey adds additional problems and more pain. They suffer from a lack of self-control and try to soothe their whiskey problems with sex. This additional pain causes some of them to commit atrocities against their wives, daughters, and sometimes their sons. Their sex pain forces them into another pain, the pain that comes from greed. Then greed causes them to rob others of land and money, taking more than they can use in their lifetime. Pain added to pain only creates more pain. There's no escape for taking the life of another.

"Maradh, because of your attitude and what you've said, I'm forced to ask you a question. Of all people, how is it that you, the one who cries when the life of an animal is taken, can even think about taking the lives of men, women, and children? Think again, my son. Know the source of this evil thinking and death-inspired emotional desire. Such evil thoughts can only come from evil, not from good. You need help. Talk to God. Pray, Maradh. Pray for deliverance from this evilness."

———

I MUST ADMIT THAT MY YOUTHFUL feelings and thoughts about killing whites were appalling. My memories of times I did not listen to Papa-horse's sound advice rushed into my mind and filled it with the murky waters of shame. My desire to kill whites cut me to the heart and coated my soul with the guilt of unrealized sins. Tears gathered and puddle at the corner of my mouth. I bowed my head and talked to God. I prayed for hours, and then listened for a response. Peace arrived and filled my mind and heart with calm. God answered me. I was still loved. I turned to thank Papa-horse, but he had gone.

Later that night, still angry with him, I tossed and turned. Sleep did not come to hold me gently and cradle my head in its loving arms. I was never angry at Papa-horse because he was wrong. It was because he was always right and I was wrong and wanted to be right.

That day, when I felt the need to kill whites, I did not know what it was, but knew something was different in the way Papa-horse dealt with me. It was not how he dealt with me as much as how I felt about what I had said and thought.

The next day I went to the bottomland at the foot of Singers Ridge, where Papa-horse's little cabin was. I went to ask for his forgiveness, as I had done many times before. When I arrived, I was shocked speechless for the second time in my life. A heavy emptiness filled my chest. Fear crawled out of my eye sockets and rolled down my face.

There was no cabin.

There was not a trace that anyone had ever lived in that area. I searched the whole valley and found nothing. I even climbed the ridge that overlooked the valley. I saw nothing. I searched the valley a second, a third time, and a fourth time. I found nothing. Nothing. I went back to the slave quarters and wept like a hungry baby whose mother's breast had gone dry.

I never saw Papa-horse again.

FEAR AND DOUBT

⟫⟪

WHEN I FOLDED THE LETTER AND started to put it away, I heard a voice call out, "Nimrod! Nimrod!"

The words vibrated the boards beneath my feet. I looked around and saw no one. Then I heard it again. "Nimrod! Nimrod, where is you!" I was relieved. It was Aunt Gussie yelling up the stairwell.

"Yeah, Aunt Gussie!" I shouted back. "I can hear you and feel you!"

"Never mind what you's feeling, boy! Come on down here now! There be's white folk business to take care of!"

"Be right down, Aunt Gussie."

I knelt and prayed out loud. "Dear God of Heaven, Creator of Life, I humble myself in thy presence and ask that my request be answered. Lord, I need a miracle. The people on this farm need a miracle. Lord, the world needs a miracle. Have mercy on our souls. What must I do?"

I ceremonially replaced the letter on the pedestal and picked up the other folded sheet of paper. I was just beginning to unfold it when I heard noise at the stairs. I thought it might be Aunt Gussie, so I grabbed the letter and stuffed both papers into my pocket. I turned. I could not believe what I saw. He stood between me and the stairs. There was no escape. In all my life, I had never seen anyone so big, so tall. His head nearly touched the under side of the roof, his shoulders were as broad as a wagon, his hands were wider than a horse's face, his face glowed like new steel in the morning sun. His gown was like snow, and a bright light seemed to have radiated from inside of him. The light made the darkness of the attic roll back like clouds before a wind. The smell of roses and the sounds of music and singing filled the air. I felt like I had drunk a bottle of wine and was ten miles inside a dream. The walls, the floors, everything in the attic glowed like new silver. I closed my eyes and tried to rub him from my sight. When I opened them again, he stood closer than before. I got down on my knees, but he took my arm and pulled me up.

"Nimrod," he said, "your prayer was heard by The Creator Of Life, that which you call God.

"The Creator Of Life has favored you, and is pleased to call you a dear son. You are chosen. And not many days from now The Helper will come to you. He will live in you, and remain as long you are obedient to the voice within.

"Have faith, and trust The Creator Of Life.

"The Creator Of Life is faithful. Do not lean on what you only think, but be guided by your thinking and understanding. Follow wisdom and trust your yes feeling and your no feeling.

"Listen.

"Listen to the voice within.

"Let all your deeds come from a clear mind and open heart. Let your actions be in faith and trust.

"Listen. Follow.

"Whatever you bind in words and trust on earth will be bound in heaven by spirit and manifested on earth. Whatever you speak in words on earth in faith will be done in heaven in faith and manifested on earth.

"Be careful with your thoughts and your speaking.

"Thinking and speaking are the tools, or the weapons, that bring good or bad. In time, what you think and speak comes true."

I was nearly speechless. Finally, I was able to ask, "Who ... who are you? Are you, Jesus? Are you my Lord?"

"No. I am a humble messenger of the one you call God. The one you call Jesus has been in the bosom of The Creator Of Life for more than two thousand years."

"You said the helper would come," I said. "Will he help me? Who is he? Is he like Jesus? Or like you?"

"There is but one Jesus. As there is but one you, Nimrod. But there are others like me, and we are as countless as the stars of heaven. In your counting of time, since 1784, we are the ministers who have served Great Mother Time's Evolutionary Phase of Life and earth's human avatars. The Helper is the Whole Spirit of The Creator Of Life. He is what men call the Holy Spirit."

"Who is he?" I asked.

"All who talk to The Creator Of Life are heard. All who have conversation with The Creator Of Life are responded to. And all who ask questions of The Creator Of Life are answered. Jesus lived on earth like all men, but before he lived here, he was with God, as you were."

"With God? Jesus . . . and me? We were in heaven with God?"

"No, not the heaven pious men preach about. And, no, not the man-created god you and other men have idolized. But, yes, with The Creator Of Life. And, yes, Jesus, you, and countless others were with The Creator Of Life before you were born on earth to live for a season in bodies that are formed of flesh and blood. Dust of the ground."

"Why would Jesus, or I, or anyone leave God and come here?"

"For Love. As humans are born helpless, they need lots of love. And Jesus, you, and others came to assist weaker brothers and sister to know real love, to help those who do not understand love for what it is, a way of life, how one should live.

"Jesus came to show human beings not only how to give and receive love, but how to be Love. By being Love, it is what it is, itself. And he, Jesus, your elder brother, was to assist others to successfully deal with their unavoidable fate of accepting unnecessary suffering as a way of life. He, like other great avatars, taught truth. He was a truth teacher. To know the truth about life is to live in what you are now calling true freedom. Until the end of his earthly life, that great avatar, Jesus, taught people how to worship through gratitude. Though his life and work on earth were short, Jesus did more good for humankind than most of the great men and women who lived before him. Before he left, he promised his friends, those like you, that he would send The Helper, the Whole Spirit.

"The Helper came to empower individuals as you to continue the work of teaching and spreading the truths that Jesus taught, the Greater Truths. Jesus told his friends to go throughout the world and make students of others. He taught them to do what he did. He wanted all people to be free by knowing the Greater Truths. Today, he wants the same for you. For that to happen, you must be taught what Jesus did, why he did it, and how he did it.

"And then you are to teach the same to others."

I could hardly speak. "Me, teach? Who am I to teach? Others? I don't know what to teach, nor do I know how to teach. That won't work."

"The Whole Spirit of God will help you."

"Help me do what? Where do I find this Whole Spirit of God?

Surely he's not on this farm. If he were, I would have found him by now. And I doubt I'll find him in the white man's churches. I won't find him where we blacks are forced to worship God. I've never met him in the woods."

"No, he is not there. For centuries, men have built temples and churches for The Creator Of Life. But The Creator Of Life's majesty is greater than all human understanding. The Creator Of Life cannot dwell in buildings made by men. Yet there is a temple that The Creator Of Life can live in, and does live in. It is the one temple that The Creator Of Life built."

"Where is that temple?" I asked. "In Africa? Will I have to go there to find him?"

"You need not go anywhere, Nimrod."

"Then how am I expected to find God's temple?"

"Through faith, trust, and love. You will find The Creator Of Life when you look within.

"A man will travel the earth and spend his entire life looking for The Creator Of Life in church buildings and temples, but never find The Creator Of Life. On his deathbed, when he is no longer capable of running and hiding, man turns within and sees The Creator Of Life, which is his own face. The last place that man thinks to look is within himself.

"The Creator Of Life lives in all humans and can be seen by all who will but open their minds and hearts, in endless acts of love."

"God? In me?"

"No, not God. Yes, The Creator Of Life is in you. And he who really loves himself, as he is the Love, loves all his brothers."

"God lives in my people?"

"Yes. The Creator Of Life."

"If that's true, then why are we slaves to whites? Why are we enslaved by the people who hate blacks for no real reason? Why doesn't God save us from the senseless deaths we suffer? Why doesn't God lead blacks to the promised land of freedom? Didn't God do that for Moses and the Israelites?"

"The Creator Of Life lives in you and in your people. And in all people who love. Color and race are not concerns of The Creator Of Life. Those things are human matters. All people are children of The

Creator Of Life, no matter what they believe or do. You must become one with Jesus, with all people, with the Whole Spirit of God, with The Creator Of Life.

"Nimrod, The Helper has been leading you to freedom all your life. You are not on earth for yourself only. When a man is young, he thinks he was created for himself, but when he is at the midpoint of his life, he discovers that he was created for a purpose. He must seek that purpose.

"You have been chosen you for a work. A purpose. Your purpose.

"You must learn to listen to when you are spoken to. When the Whole Spirit of God is active in you, a spiritual work can be done in you and through you for the good of all people. The Whole Spirit will lead you and guide you in those things. He wants to lead you, your people, and all people to a freedom that is greater than the freedom the Israelites received. Their freedom was leaving their slavery under the Pharaoh of ancient Egypt. That was not the freedom The Creator Of Life wanted them to have. There was more. There was true freedom. The people who left Egypt, including Moses, never made it to the Promised Land—true freedom. They were not ready for that freedom."

"Those were his words. Papa-horse told me the same thing."

"The Creator Of Life wants you, your people, and all people to have true freedom. But people, individually, must turn to The Creator Of Life with his heart, mind, soul, and love. Each person must trust and surrender through deeds of loving neighbors and strangers without stipulations."

"You're asking for the impossible. What man can love like that?"

"All things are possible when the Whole Spirit is invited to participate."

"But why me?" I asked. "Why would God pick someone like me? I'm not a good man. I'm not a man free from blame."

"No man is blameless. The Creator Of Life chose you because of your sincere honesty and your genuine love for others."

"Do I have to die for others like Jesus did?"

"We find your arrogance amusing. Neither you nor anyone else has to die for others. There is no reason that any man should die for the human race. Jesus volunteered. He did that because he wanted to. He gave his life as an example that all human beings need to die to selfishness and live for the love of self, others, and The Creator Of Life. That example has been filled forever."

"What I meant was . . . I sin."

"That is understood. You are human, and all humans sin. The Creator Of Life does not recognize what you refer to as sin. Human sin is to The Creator Of Life as a baby's cry is to a mother, the infant's plea for breast milk. Your sins, your cries for help, are met with eternal patience. Your need to be forgiven, after you have sinned, is your need to love yourself and the offense that was committed."

"Love ....the offense?"

"Yes, Nimrod, love the offense. By loving it, you awaken yourself from your desperate plea of begging the man-created god for help it has not given, cannot give, and will not give, as that god is only an idol created by you and other men who lived millions of years before you. As for your need of repentance, once you have sinned, it is your attempt to awaken from the dream that you are a lesser creation than The Creator Of Life created."

"Are you saying I do not have to repent?" I asked.

"Yes."

"I can't believe that."

"And that is why you continue to sin and repent, Nimrod. Sin and repent. Sin and repent."

"What? I have to stop sinning?"

"You will continue in your notion of sinning as long as your true being is wrapped in flesh and you believe in your invented god that gets angry, hates, kills, and promotes wars. The Creator Of Life cannot participate in your belief of sin, repentance, and forgiveness. That is the way it is. These are the Greater Truths your brother Jesus wants you and others to teach to this world of God-fearing lost sheep that are tossed about and skinned by manmade untruths."

"You mean I don't have to be obedient to the Ten Commandments?"

"Be obedient to the spirit of those Commandments. You are to be obedient by loving The Creator Of Life with all your heart, mind, and soul and loving your brothers, sisters, and neighbors as you love yourself. Be the Love you are. You are it. The Love.

"The greatest test of human obedience, the one that gives men their greatest difficulty, is loving and forgiving others.

"Listen, Nimrod, and gain the freedom of The Creator Of Life."

The light that emanated from the man grew brighter, and my mind and thoughts became clear. "That means I have to forgive everybody?" I asked. "Even the whites who enslaved me and my brothers?"

"Yes. Think. You and your brothers do ungodly things. Yet The Creator Of Life allows the clouds to rain on you and the sun to shine on you and those who are loved by you. And what you refer to as forgiving others has to be not a choice, but your way of living. You must do so."

"I don't know if it's possible for me to do. But I do trust God."

"Your trust, faith, and repentance are not magical concoctions that can make The Creator Of Life do good things for you or anyone else. If a man is less than loving, does not love all people, and continues to pray that mercy to be shown in his life, that man toys with The Creator Of Life. But The Creator Of Life is not one to be mocked. A man reaps as he sows. Your trust, faith, and repentance can only be demonstrated through acts of love for all people. A man's love is true when he listens to The Creator Of Life all day and does what he is told to do. The acts of men who are less than loving separate them from the Whole Spirit and The Creator Of Life. A man's love unites him with The Creator Of Life, and he is empowered to love with The Greater Love."

"What is the greater love?"

"For you, or any human, to understand the Greater Love, you must know that it does not resemble your human notion of love in any of its many facets or expressions. Love is the human word that describes an individual's personal beliefs, thoughts, emotions, and feelings. It is the one word that allows all humans to discriminate as to what person or race is to receive love, when and how and at what time of year or occasion love is to be given, and how and when it is to be parceled out, based on mood, situation, and circumstances. The same practice holds true for your manmade god that waits for you in his heaven.

"The Greater Love is only brought into existence on the plane of human life when a certain knowingness is experienced by one who knows, speaks, and listens to The Creator Of Life and is thereby moved and acts on it. It is ... connectedness."

I looked around the room. "How do I know all of this is real?" I asked.

"Know? Know if all of … if all of what? … if all of what is real? Do you doubt The Creator Of Life, Nimrod?"

"What I'm saying is, what if I'm dreaming? What if … what if this is my mind playing tricks on me?"

"Nimrod, never doubt The Creator Of Life."

"Oh, no, I know God, the Creator, I mean I know The Creator Of Life is real. I would never do that. I could never doubt God. What I'm … what I'm saying is … is I'm afraid that what's happening may not … be real."

"Being afraid of something and doubting The Creator Of Life are different matters. To fear the unknown is natural. That is good. To doubt The Creator Of Life is seriously dangerous to your freeing your body and mind from earthly suffering. When your body is free, you have what you call paper freedom, the material things of this world. When your mind is free, you have what you call true freedom. It is well that you have sought both freedoms for the better part of your life, for both are gifts, or, as you say, blessings. These are your birthright, the entitlement all people are granted by The Creator Of Life when they are born on earth.

"As for the true freedom you seek, the opposite of paper freedom, it is and always has been inside your soul. Unlock the soul, and true freedom pours forth."

"What is the soul? And how do I unlock it?"

"The answers to these questions are to be understood only by you. What I tell you now will be heard by you only if you have developed your spiritual sense, which is known as listening.

"Now listen, Nimrod. The human mind and heart that are filled with the thinking of thoughts and the feeling of feelings that are based on love are the connectedness that link humans to humans, humans to The Creator Of Life, humans to The Creator Of Life to the earth, humans to The Creator Of Life to the earth to all life on earth, humans to The Creator Of Life to the earth to all life on earth to the seen and unseen universes to function as all creation. This is oneness. Oneness is experienced by humans only when their selfishness and fear are laid aside."

"Well," I said, "I'm dealing with a fear, the fear I've lived with all my life, the fear of God. And I'm not sure I understand what you said about the soul, nor what it is supposed to mean."

"You are not to be sure, yet you must know. Nimrod, of all human fears, the fear of God is a just fear. For a human being to fear The Creator Of Life, it is denying that The Creator Of Life's existence is beyond their invented re-creation of themselves through the notion of the existence of god. The god worshiped by man is a mere replica of man himself, and man's fear of that image should be his protection, yet it is not a protection. He who lives in fear and doubt of The Creator Of Life has become the agent that has made himself equal with the god that was invented by his ancestors who lived thousands of years past. Nimrod, if what you are experiencing at this time is not real, you could not be conversing with me. Think."

"I know. It's not that…. It's just hard to believe all of this. That's all I mean."

"First you spoke from doubt. Then you feared. Now you disbelieve. Be careful, Nimrod. Doubt, fear, and disbelief in The Creator Of Life separate man from the Whole Spirit of God."

"I just have questions, that's all. Papa-horse taught me the importance of questions. It's normal for me."

"Listen. Do you believe what you read in the Bible?"

"Yes, of course I believe. Well … most of it."

"Do you believe The Creator Of Life dealt with men and women of the Bible?"

"Well, yes. But what's happening to me doesn't make sense. It's not reasonable, it's not logical. Why should this happen to me? Why should I believe that God, The Creator Of Life, talks to people today through angels?"

Before I could blink, he stood just inches from me.

"Nimrod," he said, "whatever you do, remember this: never, never, never doubt The Creator Of Life. You cannot have an intimate relationship with and understand of The Creator Of Life's ways through reason and logic. Those human qualities have a place in human affairs, but not in The Creator Of Life's affairs. The way you think is not the way The Creator Of Life thinks. The way you do things is not the way The Creator Of Life does things. The Creator Of Life's ways are far superior. When you use reason and logic to define your relationship with The Creator Of Life, you cannot see The

Creator Of Life's works, nor hear the inner voice that is The Creator Of Life's voice. The Creator Of Life is not limited by human communication. The Creator Of Life uses the wind, other people, whatever is needed at the time. Your task is not to question The Creator Of Life's means of communication. It is to open yourself to the ways of The Creator Of Life."

"I don't doubt The Creator Of Life," I protested. "I just want to be sure about what's happening to me, to be sure this is from God, I mean The Creator Of Life. But what if it's me and not The Creator Of Life? What if it's the enemy who's trying to confuse me? I have traditions. I have to consider them before I make decisions."

"Fidelity to human traditions enslaves men. Connectedness to The Creator Of Life frees them."

"But what if ...?"

And "what if" were the last words I spoke. The man left, and the darkness returned. Desire filled my chest and directed my eyes to the filthy window. I looked up at it, and a voice just beyond the glass said, "Be watchful. Excuses become self-fulfilling curses."

I tried to pray him back. But, to my disappointment, he did not return.

A PRICE FOR NOT LISTENING

I AM NIMROD.

The words you have read in this book are my words, my life, and my story. From my encounter with an angel until now, I have spent my life traveling, preaching, and teaching about true freedom, life, and The Creator Of Life. And I must admit, I say that The Creator Of Life has worked miracles in me and through me. The assistance I have given to other people (black and white) in their healing and so forth has been The Creator Of Life's purpose for my life. In the beginning, I tried to live my life as I pleased. Being led by youth, I did the things of youth. Later I began to discover that life was not what I thought it was supposed to be, nor how I wanted it to be. Much later I became the follower, a follower of life's flow, a seeker who desired to follow The Creator Of Life's directives.

There were years when I spent time with anybody, no matter what they practiced or believed, but then I soon discovered that I was putting myself in harm's way. The Creator Of Life did not require that of me. Most of the suffering I have experienced has come from my self-centered, know-it-all attitude. I did not listen to the good advice that came my way, and that caused me, and others, much unnecessary pain. In spite of my not listening to all that The Creator Of Life has had to say to me, The Creator Of Life has been true to the promise to be with me and protect me.

By now, these tired eyes must have witnessed as many miracles as there are recorded in the Bible. I am well along in the evening of my life, and up to now, The Creator Of Life has answered all my prayers. I am blessed with the important things of life, things I have wanted and needed. As Papa-horse told me, "You'll have material things." As usual, he was right. Like Master Sandridge, I have had more material stuff than I have needed. I have discovered the three important things human beings need most. These are (1) physical health, (2) at least one close friend, or preferably a soul mate, and (3) an intimate relationship with The Creator Of Life. When these needs are met, we can feel the true worth of living.

Reader, I ask that you continue to be patient, for I assure you that I am going somewhere with this memorandum.

Today I have no regrets except for one. I have missed Miss Sadie. I have missed seeing her smiling face. But I cannot cry about that. If I did, life would run out of my body like water pouring from a broken faucet. I would dry up like an empty creek and leave no trail.

I hope my life experiences will benefit you and help you avoid the unnecessary suffering that many of us experience during the course of our lives. I want to help you in small ways discover the joy and beauty of living and survive the pain and suffering that cannot be avoided. It is never too early or too late to learn two important things we humans need to gain true freedom: the power of prayer and the art of listening. If you find these priceless treasures early in your life, you will save time and live a better life than I have.

My son, I beseech you, do not be foolish. Learn from the mistakes of others, especially from mine. Over the years, I have heard people say, "All you have to do is believe and have faith." I have come to see that this is true. I have also come to know from my many years of living that one must work hard at changing bad habits. These are changes that can only be made inside. We must turn them into personal freedom. We must busy ourselves doing what we believe and have faith in. If we want to live in freedom, we must discover and express the true freedom that dwells in the soul.

While it is true that others can force us into slavery, as history has shown, they cannot keep paper freedom from us indefinitely. We can surrender our true freedom to others when we live in slavery and are pressured beyond our capacity to endure, as blacks in America have done. As a case in point, I lived most of my life as a slave on the Sandridge farm, but my desire to taste the sweet nectar of paper freedom bloomed in my heart and was nourished by the stories Papahorse told me, even though he meant the opposite, true freedom. During that time, I had little interest in true freedom. I was tempted by what my eyes saw in my master's all to obvious paper freedom. I saw his luxurious lifestyle, and my heart desired it. In the end, not only did I experience paper freedom, I also became master on the Sandridge farm. I take no pride in some of the things I have done, and if I could change them today, I would. But I have worked hard all my life to experience freedom in any of its designs, and I took it any way I could get it. Now I know that true freedom comes with a price tag and can only be gained through connectedness with The Creator Of Life and all creation.

Although most of the narrative recorded on these pages comes from my personal experience, some stories were told to me by people I trusted and loved. Besides, all you need to know is that what I have written is true and valuable. That is, if your desire is to experience true freedom.

It does not matter that one is black or white, red or yellow, young or old, or rich or poor. We all gain true freedom when we come to know what The Creator Of Life has called us to do with purpose, and we do it. We must learn to listen to the many messengers The Creator Of Life places in our path each day. These messages come in all forms and fashions.

True freedom is within all men. We have to work hard at living a life of love and obedience to experience that freedom. When we do, we are sure to reach that state of being that The Creator Of Life created and placed inside the human mind and heart, the soul.

What I have to say at this point of my narrative is that I am now at a juncture where I can share two other important reasons why I am contacting you.

James, my son, the reader of my history (his story), I now must turn my attention to you.

At this point I am sure you are well aware of the fact that I am the father you have never known. And love moves me to tell you at this time of my life that I feel that circumstances have yielded their fierce grip and now permit me to contact you. What I have written is especially for you and our descendants, those who will come through you. I lovingly share this with all who may read my story. I plead that you please try to understand what I write.

I do not hate all whites. Your mother was white.

Mrs. Carol Jane Sandridge was your mother. I had the utmost respect for her, and she respected me. I am moved by that respect to say that I do not know if God has ever created another soul like Mrs. Carol Jane Sandridge.

Son, the blood that courses through your veins and your heart is black blood and white blood. In my humble opinion, that makes you more a member of the human race than your mother and I could ever be. I pray that you, my dear son, marry a woman who can be half the woman your mother was. Or maybe you have.

You were born seven months after Master Sandridge died. People in Decherd, Tennessee, both black and white, did not think it was proper for a black man and a white woman to have a child and work side by side. The pressure that came from that racist belief became so great that we had no choice but to send you away to live with your mother's two brothers, who lived in Langston, Alabama. You were too black to live with your white mother and too white to travel with your black father.

After we sent you away, our lives changed. Your mother and I ceased our intimacy, as it no longer seemed proper. For a short while, we continued to work together, but even though you were gone, the hatred for us continued. After a series of fires broke out and cattle and horses were poisoned when we traveled to the grits mills, we knew it was time to make a complete change in our relationship.

We resisted the hatred of blacks and whites for a year, but soon I had no choice but to leave your mother on the farm, in Decherd. We agreed to keep in touch through letters, but the postmaster always lost our letters somewhere between our sending and his delivering. We never saw each other again, nor did we communicate.

James, my dear son, living under slavery was not as painful as what I must share with you at this time. Your mother, Mrs. Carol Jane Sandridge, died in 1906 at the age of eighty. I do not know the circumstances of her death. The death certificate at the courthouse in Decherd was vague. It simply stated "found dead."

Son, I know that your reading what I have written is painful to you at this stage of your life, but I want you to try to understand that your mother, who loved you with all her heart, and I did what we thought was best at that time. Given the circumstances of the time in history, we had to endure and survive by making decisions and doing things we did not want to do.

You may be thinking we could have done things differently. We tried. God knows we tried, but nothing worked, and we had to send you away. If you were to live, sending you away was our only choice.

I can only imagine the painful thoughts of abandonment that you must have held in your mind, the pain it caused in your heart. Yes, I am saying it was abandonment. There is no other way for it to be said. Your mother and I believed we were demonstrating love for you and future generations by sending you to Langston.

Please, son, search for a place, that small spot in your heart that can allow you to forgive the hurt and pain we caused you. If there is any consolation in me saying this, I understand that sort of pain, for I do not remember ever seeing my own parents. I have no record of who my parents were or what they looked like. I never felt their touch. Nothing. I know telling you this will not heal your pain, but it does soothe my aching heart.

I also feel it is imperative that I tell you that your mother's pregnancy was not planned. But this does not mean that you were an unwanted accident of lust. It just means that we were not prepared to have a family together, nor was this country, America.

As I said earlier, your mother and I began to travel to the grits mills together after doctor Sandridge became ill. This meant we were gone from the farm for days at a time. During the day we traveled and worked in the grits mills. At night we had to bed down in the safest place we could find. In the beginning we worked hard and avoided all contact with each other, even to the point of having no conversation except when it was absolutely necessary. In time, the grits mills became money producers. I convinced Mrs. Sandridge to put the profits from the mills into other financially sound business ventures like thoroughbred horse breeding and sales, tobacco growing, and other ventures. It was during that time that we began to talk more. We discussed business plans and strategies for dealing with the whites that bought from us. Naturally, the whites could not know that I was involved in the business end of matters, so I played the role of the black servant. It was not an easy role, but that was what I had to do. There were times when I felt she went too far in her role as the owner, but that was the natural role for her to play.

Soon we began to argue over who was wrong and who was right. She looked at things from a white person's and a woman's point of view. I saw things from a black person's and a man's point of view. Many times, she threatened to put me off the farm. She said I was "too bullheaded." I can hear her now. She screamed, "Nimrod, you're the most impossible, stubbornest, bullheadedest person I know! I don't know why I tolerate you!" Other times, I threatened to take my share of the money and leave the farm and the business. I yelled back, "Carol Jane, you're the most confused person I know, and I don't know why I bother with you!"

We were as opposite to each other as day and night. She would say, "Let's go left," and I would say, "Let's go right." But somehow we managed to work together and prosper.

Then one full moon night, it happened. I will reveal all the details as things occurred. As I feel you must know them.

We were in Jasper. We had worked hard and fought all day at the mill, and we were exhausted. As we were too tired to travel back to Decherd, we decided to find a safe place to sleep. We planned to get up at daybreak and head home. Well, we found that perfect place.

The moonlight made it easy to drive the horses down a narrow trail that led from the main road and meandered through the woods to the backwaters of Nickajack Lake. I stopped the wagon in a clearing. We could see the water a short distance off. The view was beautiful.

Like tufts of white feathers on a velvet spread, the sparkles of light sat on the surface of the lake's dark gray water. The trees were trimmed with a faint tint of green and highlighted by moonlight. The dark blue sky was patterned with puffs of clouds that caught moonlight on their edges and blended it with shades of light blue and gray blue. The scenery reminded me of a painting that hung in the big house.

We climbed down from the wagon and made a small cooking fire. Our custom was that if one of us had to relieve himself of bodily waste or went to wash-up, the other stayed at the wagon and waited their turn. But that night things went contrary to custom.

While Carol Jane prepared our meal, I went to relieve myself of the piss I had held all day. I went off a short distance, found a large oak tree, and stood next to it and began to relieve myself. The warm stream seemed as if it would never end. I heard the sound of twigs being crushed. Someone was coming up from behind me. I could not stop the piss. I turned and saw Carol Jane walk up to a bush and lift her dress to the waist. I froze. The sight of a white woman doing such a thing was alarming.

"What's she doing?" I whispered. "Doesn't she see me?" Frozen, I stared. The dark strip of hair at the crease of her legs stood out like a streak of coal on cotton. She squatted. I watched. Pee poured from her like a pregnant bunny. When it hit the ground covering, it sounded like a soothing spring rain. I watched it as it formed a puddle between her legs. It smelled of sweat and urine.

I held my breath. I dared not move or make a sound. I knew if she screamed, every redneck within a hundred miles would come running with large ropes tied in nooses.

As I held my breath, the piss flowed harder. When she was done, she passed a fart. I took a deep breath. She wagged and bounced her bottom and stood up. She looked over at me, smiled, turned and walked off. I was so hard the piss was cut off. I felt my heart throb in my curled fingers and sweaty palm. I watched her walk away.

When I stepped from around the rear of the wagon, Carol Jane was at the fire cooking our supper. She said nothing. I said nothing. We hardly looked at each other. After we had eaten I asked her if she wanted to go to the lake and wash up first. "No," she said. "Why don't you go first this time? I'll wait."

"Well, all right," I said. "I'll make it quick so you don't have to wait long."

"Don't rush it. It's better when you take your time. Don't you think?"

"Ahhh ... yes." I stood and turned to walk away, and she said,

"The moon is bright tonight. It should be easy to find that right spot ... for bathing."

"Yes." My voice quivered.

I had walked just beyond the firelight when she said, "It should be good tonight. You should take your time. Don't rush."

I could not believe what I had heard, so, I tried to chase it out of my mind. But my efforts were futile, and my desires became fertile. I knew I should not let my thoughts and emotions meet in agreement, but my desires had taken charge. I was no longer in control. Any black man in his right mind knew what the consequences would be just for looking a white woman in the eyes. Let alone watch her pee and enjoy her overt flirting.

My pants began to bulge again. I turned quickly and walked off. I made my way through the woods, headed for the lake. The day had been long and difficult, and the thought of bathing my tired body pleasured my weary mind. I was ready to feel the water rise to my chin as I sank below the surface. When I reached the water, I stretched my hands towards the heavens and thanked God for another day. I looked out upon the black water of the lake. It lay before me like a sheet of untouched stained glass.

I undressed and walked into the cool water until it rose slightly above my knees. I splashed my face, arms, and chest until I was chilled. When I sat down, the water rose up to my chest. I shivered.

When my trembling had stopped, my mind went back to Carol Jane's squatting and pissing. Desire filled my chest, and made my heart to beat louder. I took a deep breath. I knew I was treading on dangerous ground that had been known to open up and swallow black men for doing less than what I had already done and thought.

I was reminded of the time a white woman accused David Johnson of looking her in the eyes. The whites that believed her rallied around what she had told, and set out to catch David and bring him to white justice. Five days later, a group of eight white men caught him crossing the Center Hill Lake up in Keltonbury. One of the men shot David in the right buttock with a musket, then they pulled him out of the lake and stripped him and tied him to a tree. As he screamed for mercy, they cut off his private parts and stuffed them in his mouth. Then they took turns shooting at his head.

I ducked my head beneath the water and thrashed a little, hoping to remove these thoughts and desires from my mind. I repeated this several times. At last, when I had completed my task of mind cleansing, I sat up and wiped my face with both hands.

I turned and faced the direction where the water entered the cove. I heard rustling in the bushes. I turned back around. The rustling noise came towards the water. I held my breath and sank below the water. Expecting a band of white men to emerge from the bushes with ropes and howling dogs, I backed into deeper water. I waited, only my eyes above the water. A hand poked from the bushes and slowly pushed them aside, and Carol Jane stepped forth. She stood a short distance from where I had entered the water. She said nothing. She didn't even look in my directions.

She began to strip as if she were alone. She removed her blouse and undergarment. Her breasts sat high on her chest. She held her skirt and slip at the waist, leaned forward, moved her hips from side to side, and wiggled out of them. When she stood up again her snow-white skin caught the moonlight and held it. It almost seemed to glow. It did not look real. There was something transparent about it. I had never looked upon skin like that before. It appeared to be delicate, fragile to the touch.

She turned her broad, flat butt in my direction and bent over and gathered her clothes from the ground and laid them on top of a bush. She turned again and removed the hairpins from her hair, and it fell about her neck and shoulders. Her hands rose to her head, and she ruffled her hair with her fingertips. Then she held her head back and shook it, and her hair floated from side to side like a silk shirt in a breeze. Her breasts made a slapping sound as they flopped against one another. Without hesitating, she stepped into the cool water and dove. I had heard that whites could take more cold than blacks, and she did not surface until she was a good twenty-feet out. She rose and shook her head. The water flew in all directions, sparkling in the moonlight.

I was in a compromised position, one that spelled death if I were caught by white men. I decided to quietly gather my clothes and take my leave. In an attempt not to be noticed, I slowly treaded water and headed for the woods. As my butt came out of the water, she called out and I hesitated.

———

SHE CALLED, "NIMROD, I need you ... to wash my back ... please."

She swam toward me. I waited. She stopped in front of me. The water rested at her nipples—they looked firm. She said, "Well, I need your help. It's okay, I don't bite."

"Are you sure?" I asked.

"Not hard, anyway."

"No. I meant washing your back. Are you sure?"

"Nimrod, it's my back, isn't it? Or at least it was the last time I checked."

"But ... what if—?"

"Nimrod we're all alone in the middle of nowhere. We did not see one house or one person all day during our drive. There's no one to see us. Look around. It'll be all right. Besides, I only want you to wash my back, that's all. Or are you thinking of something else?"

"No. Just your ass. I mean your back."

"Okay, Nimrod, then wash it."

She backed toward me, and I pulled my hips backward, I did not want to poke her. I cupped my hands, and poured water on her shoulders without touching her snow-white skin. I watched it wash over her shoulder blade and down her back. After three or four handfuls she said in her gentle voice, "Nimrod," she had never called my name so much, "I would like to have my back washed . . . please. And that means you have to . . . touch it . . . with your hands."

Her white skin looked as if it would tear if I touched it, or peel off. So I slid my fingertips gently down her spine. She quivered and sighed. A shock of excitement ran through my body. She must have felt it too. She whirled around with her arms crossed over her chest and fell against me. Her head was resting on my chest. She looked up into my eyes, something she had always avoided, and began to purr. She surrounded me with her unbridled passion. Like a fly caught in a web, I was trapped. Any movement at all meant my fate would be decided in that moment. My arms moved. They embraced her.

I raked my fingers through her hair, which was as straight and soft as corn silk. It had the faint scent of Narcissus. I was intoxicated. There was no turning back. For I had crossed that fine line that keeps men and women from following their impulse. I was consumed by her soft white skin. She would no longer lie awake at night and think about her dead husband; from that time forward, her emptiness would be filled with me. Her tears would no longer be caught by a pillow, but by my firm shoulder. My fingers would dry her eyes. She would no longer pace the floor in loneliness, as my entire self would be wrapped around her forever.

It happened. I was no longer the master of my ship, which had drifted out to sea, or captain of my soul, which had become a part of something greater than my will. I had met my fate. I held in my arms the one person Master Sandridge had prized more than he did life itself. Carol Jane. The man would have trampled over the gates of hell, had he known I held his dear wife's head next to my throbbing heart.

Our mouths came together. My broad and thick lips covered her narrow, thin lips. Our tongues caressed each other ever so gently in a wet pool of saliva. She grabbed my manly organ and commenced to stroke it passionately. I held back. My hands did not know what to do. She cuffed my balls and squeezed them ever so gently. I tensed. She looked in my eyes and squeezed again. I tensed again. One of my hands rose and cupped her right breast. The other grabbed her firmly between the legs. The index and middle fingers slid, unhindered, inside of her. I moved my hand from side to side with vigor, and she moaned. She stared in my eyes and spread her legs. She pulled me closer, then placed her hands on my shoulders and whispered, "Nimrod, it's okay, alright? Relax and enjoy it."

I thrust my throbbing self into her orifice. She flung her head back and screamed. Her mouth and eyes opened wide. We thrashed about in the water like two large fish caught in a strong net. She moaned and screamed and I groaned, thrusting and wiggling.

At that perfect moment, the moment when a man and woman leave their bodies in a split second of ecstatic bliss, we were interrupted by the sound of rustling bushes. Still holding each other we sank in the water to our eyeballs. The rustling stopped. We held each other. Left over passion caused us to squeeze each other. The rustling came closer. We squeezed tighter. The rustling came even closer and stopped. We pushed away from each other. Shadowy figures, a buck followed by two does, stepped from the bushes. They looked at us and drank, then disappeared back in the brush.

Carol Jane and I began again.

———

Son, as you can see, I am not a man who makes excuses for his actions. I never was and never will be. I want you to know everything about your mother and me.

My story is about my life, the full range of my experiences that reveal who I was and who I am and my quest for freedom, both paper freedom and true freedom. I have found that honesty is the single most valuable key to open the door to freedom, which comes in many guises.

Although white history (his story) is not quick to state the facts about what some white women felt for, and did, with some black men, what happened between your mother and me was a common occurrence. If white slave owners and the white men who wrote the white history thought they were the only ones who illicitly drank the blackberry juice of their slaves, they were greater fools than anyone else. While he was down at the slave quarters doing his business, there was likely a slave up at the big house taking care of his wife's business. White women drank their share of the blackberry juice as regularly as the white men did. Those white women were human beings and they had human desires and needs that had to be met with satisfaction. And their desires and needs were satisfied by whatever means that were available.

Who knows how many children of mixed blood grew up in the homes of those white slave owners? No one knows. And that is just as the SSSPBHCB wanted it to be.

Son, I feel that you need to know and understand that the world is filled with individuals who are like you, of mixed blood. Maybe you are the men and women who will eventually bring the races together. If so, that is what the SSSPBHCB wanted. It is what all races need. Oneness.

James, my son, if you are reading this paragraph, there is a chance that you can forgive your mother and me for what we did and did not do. I hope you have a desire to look into my eyes and see my love for you.

Before I die, and my days are numbered now, I want to look into those green eyes of yours. I want to hold you to my chest as I did when you were born. On that wonderful occasion, the morning of your birth, I sat on the edge of my chair and waited for you to exit the darkness of your mother's womb and enter into this world of light and dark and blacks and whites. Although this world is anything but perfect, it is nonetheless good.

I continue to delight when I think back on the morning you were born. Aunt Gussie had tried to convince me it was a woman's job to catch babies, but I would not hear it. You were my son, and I was proud. I had to be the one to catch you, my son. My hands had to be the first hands you felt. You were the son who would know his father and mother from their brief, but everlasting loving touches. I sat there and watched your mother push the crown of your head, a small patch of black hair, into view. After more pushing, your entire head came into view. Aunt Gussie screamed with delight. Crouched and waiting, I was on pins and needles. Your mother pushed again, and without warning a slick nine pounds of pure love was popped into my hands.

At that moment the room became a sea of The Creator Of Life's Whole Spirit and luminous light. While Aunt Gussie jumped around like a church lady, your mother and I kissed your tiny feet and legs, your hands and arms, and your head and face until we cried.

As I will share the intimate details of your life with you when you were with Carol Jane and me in Decherd, Tennessee, I desire to do this when we are face to face. At this time, I do not want to tell you such details, as your mother would have you and me sit at an open window and talk over a cup of coffee. That was her single most important thing to do when discussing matters of the heart.

The last time your mother, Mrs. Carol Jane Sandridge, and I saw each other was at three o'clock in the morning on a Wednesday. We sat at the bay window in the library and drank three cups of coffee. It was difficult to find a stopping place for our conversation, as it was all about you. There was no way for us to know what would come of us, and if we would see each other or you again. I watched the tears roll down her cheeks and fall from her chin to sweeten her coffee. I saw that her mind was a hundred miles away as she cried and talked about how much she loved you. She missed you from the very first day we sent you to live with her brothers in Langston, Alabama.

Thus far, all my prayers have been answered, and as I have attempted to make this point clear, I believe all prayers are answered for everyone. If The Creator Of Life answers the one remaining prayer I have, I will see you as soon as you decide to see me.

Though I will die soon and leave this earth, I will live on through you and my grandchildren for generations to come, and that makes me proud. God has given me a long and productive life. I do not fear death. As the day dies and becomes night, so the night turns into the morning of a new day, and so shall I. The messages of eternity are everywhere, all around us, in everything. Life, death, and rebirth are truths that set a man free.

In the beginning, time appears to be our friend. Then one day we discover it to be as elusive as the wind. And only love can break the generational curses I have written about. Love can make a difference in how you feel, and it can create a new beginning for you and me, for our family. I pray that you, James, my son and the son of Carol Jane Sandridge, are willing to be that brand-new beginning.

James, my son, for reasons unknown, life did not permit me to have an opportunity to love you as a father should. But I promise that the life that I have experienced has taught me how to be the perfect friend.

Given the chance, I will be that best friend you have never had.

With the everlasting Love of a father,
your best friend,

—Nimrod

www.ingramcontent.com/pod-product-compliance
Lightning Source LLC
Chambersburg PA
CBHW062209270326
41930CB00009B/1690